Online Advertising and Promotion:

Modern Technologies for Marketing

Payam Hanafizadeh
Allameh Tabataba'i University, Iran

Mehdi Behboudi
Qazvin Islamic Azad University, Iran

Managing Director:	Lindsay Johnston
Senior Editorial Director:	Heather A. Probst
Book Production Manager:	Sean Woznicki
Development Manager:	Joel Gamon
Development Editor:	Myla Harty
Acquisitions Editor:	Erika Gallagher
Typesetter:	Nicole Sparano
Cover Design:	Nick Newcomer, Lisandro Gonzalez

Published in the United States of America by
Business Science Reference (an imprint of IGI Global)
701 E. Chocolate Avenue
Hershey PA 17033
Tel: 717-533-8845
Fax: 717-533-8661
E-mail: cust@igi-global.com
Web site: http://www.igi-global.com

Library of Congress Cataloging-in-Publication Data

Hanafizadeh, Payam, 1974-
  Online advertising and promotion: modern technologies for marketing / by Payam Hanafizadeh and Mehdi Behboudi.
       p. cm.
  Includes bibliographical references and index.
  ISBN 978-1-4666-0885-6 (hardcover) -- ISBN 978-1-4666-0886-3 (ebook) -- ISBN 978-1-4666-0887-0 (print & perpetual access)
  1. Internet advertising. 2. Internet marketing. I. Behboudi, Mehdi, 1983- II. Title.
  HF6146.I58H36 2012
  659.14'4--dc23
                        2011048427

British Cataloguing in Publication Data
A Cataloguing in Publication record for this book is available from the British Library.

All work contributed to this book is new, previously-unpublished material. The views expressed in this book are those of the authors, but not necessarily of the publisher.

This book is dedicated to my late father who taught me to be an independent and determined person, to my doting mother without whom I would never be able to achieve my objectives and succeed in life, and to all my diligent students whose feedback has always helped me to be a better teacher.

Payam Hanafizadeh

This book is dedicated to my father for his continuous support, to my mother for her enduring encouragement during the writing of this book, and to all those in the advertising business who have a passion to satisfy customer needs and thus make our world better.

Mehdi Behboudi

Table of Contents

Chapter 4

Chapter 5

Chapter 6

Preface

Those of us who work with or study online advertising are often asked by other marketers, "What makes online advertising special?" After all, it seems reasonable to expect that advertising online should be like advertising in any other medium. For decades, marketers and advertisers have amassed an array of strategies, tactics and principles that, it is claimed, can be applied to any particular advertising campaign. In today's technological world, the challenge is to apply that knowledge to the discipline of online advertising, the assumption being that there is no need to claim any special status for a specific marketing effort such as sports, electronics or clothing.

During the past decade, two journals were created that focus explicitly on online advertising: the *Journal of Interactive Advertising* and the *International Journal of Internet Marketing and Advertising*. Graduate and undergraduate courses in online advertising have also appeared in university curriculum, and giant institutes such as the Interactive Advertising Bureau, *IAB.net* and *Emarketer.com* have been established to support leads. Plus, the American Academy of Advertising has a special-interest group on online advertising. With the weight of all this activity, we believe online advertising is not a subset of traditional advertising; it is its own definitive discipline of study.

There is a special place where customers gather each day, seeking services and products: the Internet. They want cars. They want plumbers. They want music downloads. They want vacation rentals, lawn care products, tax advice and more. You name the product or service, someone is looking for it online.

Advertising, just like medicine and engineering, is a universal discipline of study, providing insight into understanding the business process anywhere in the world. Ideally, due to its universal nature, that is how advertising should be taught.

Unfortunately, because of the dominance of American textbooks (and European textbooks to a lesser extent), advertising has always been taught from either the US or European perspective. In response, futuristic business schools are trying to incorporate an online advertising discipline into their curriculums in order to position themselves better in both the scholar's and businessperson's minds.

The conventional approach has been to offer just a few online advertising and marketing courses; this may result from a lack of appropriate sources. Keeping this in mind, this book is designed to fill the gap between offline and online advertising.

PURPOSE

Advertising, as a discipline of study as well as in practice, is dynamic, exciting, rigorous and challenging, and our approach in this text reflects this belief. *Online Advertising and Promotion: New Marketing*

Strategies has been written to educate executives and students on how to meet online advertising and internet marketing challenges – both now and in the future.

Designed for marketing majors and MBA students, this book provides solid foundations that are useful for explanation, prediction and control of electronic business activities. Due to its depth and breadth, the text is suitable for any advertising, marketing, IT or business management courses at both undergraduate and graduate levels. We believe that you will find this textbook to be one of the most, if not *the* most, authoritative source for online advertising, offering a futurist perspective, a comprehensive base of strategies and clear substance.

OVERVIEW

This book outlines the changes and challenges that have impacted how online advertising decisions are being made, and how decision-makers are getting their information in an online world. The fact is, marketing, advertising and IT departments have been lax in keeping up with those changes. They have been too busy creating new concepts, or moving to online tactics such as web optimizing and data mining to look deeper into the content and technologies that websites must incorporate to be popular and fast.

This book provides some preliminary theoretical rather than technical insight into online advertising.

Online Advertising and Promotion: New Marketing Strategies" is a new approach to advertising, and an important one because it not only defines online advertising concepts, it also directly addresses the most common advertising barriers on websites -- search engines, blogs, communities and social networks -- and focuses attention on explaining consumer behavior when confronted with different formats of advertising.

Technical issues are far from the scope of this book; we believe there are more than enough books on these subjects. Instead we focus on understanding who is a user, what they do with advertisements, and the relationships that exist between advertisers and consumers. Moreover, we reveal the managerial implications that will help advertisers manage their online marketing activities.

CONTENT

This book consists of 12 Chapters, delving into the subject of online advertising by considering 12 questions:

Chapter 1: What is online advertising and what is integrated internet marketing communication?
Chapter 2: How does online advertising works?
Chapter 3: What factors form the differences between online advertising, traditional advertising and social network advertising?
Chapter 4: What are the different formats of online advertisements and what are their functions?
Chapter 5: In an online world, how does the role of advertising agencies change and how can they execute the right strategies?
Chapter 6: How do advertisers pay online advertising fees?
Chapter 7: What are the key behavioral variables on the Web and how do consumers react to online advertising?

Chapter 8: What is the right online advertising strategy?
Chapter 9: Is there any significance relationship between an e-business model and that of online advertising?
Chapter 10: What is online advertising effectiveness and how can online advertising be effective?
Chapter 11: What is the right format for online advertising?
Chapter 12: What are Lead Generations and how do they provide leads?

AUDIENCE

We have written this book with two audiences in mind. The first is the *marketing profession*, which is always under pressure to deliver better results with reduced resources. Though we point out the deficiencies in advertising, we support advertising as a discipline. Advertising is a major expense for businesses; if advertising is not performing, then it undermines the entire company. Our second audience is the *graduate and undergraduate students* who study marketing, advertising, business management, IT and computer science. This book directly addresses their concerns about online advertising and is a good source for their information needs in regards to advertising.

In today's market, a website is a business' biggest advertisement format, shop-front or storefront. Students of the aforementioned disciplines must have enough knowledge to manage a virtual storefront, much like the front window display at a traditional store. Websites need to attract customers and keep them coming back for more; this book will give these students the necessary abilities to be successful with these issues.

Finally, in order to perform well in our online world, students need to redefine their value proposition as the possibility of these types of businesses in an online world was never before imagined. As Josh Peterson, CEO of Adteractive, states: "... *Performance is a way of life. 'Performance' is not just how we are measured by our clients and consumers, but it is also how we measure ourselves. Performance goals and accountability are embedded into the very fabric of our company culture; after all, if we aren't performance driven internally, how can we claim to be performance driven externally? Win the war, not the battle.'* Let us win the war.

Acknowledgment

While we took the lead in creating this book, many other people must be given credit for their significant contributions in bringing our vision to reality. We thank all of those who provided us with a workable environment for undertaking this endeavor.

We are also indebted to a number of companies and organizations who gave us permission to use their advertisements and materials. In particular, we would like to thank the Interactive Advertising Bureau, Air Canada, Hadef, and Zenithoptimedia.com for their cooperation. We would also like to thank the scholars who let us use their models and materials in this book, in particular, Dr. Kazienko, Dr. Cacioppo, Dr. Petty, Dr. Rossiter, and Dr. Bellman. Finally, we would like to thank the editors and advisors at the IGI-Global publishing house: Jan Travers, Vice President of IGI-Global, and Myla Harty, IGI editorial assistant. We are also grateful to the excellent professional production team: Anna Emily Golesh, former editorial assistant. Last, but by no means least, our thanks to Dr. Mehdi Khosrow-Pour, the President of IGI-Global.

Writing a textbook is a major undertaking. The reward is not monetary; the true reward comes in the form of kind comments received from the students and others who find the book a valuable resource. We sincerely hope that this textbook plays a significant role in advancing this important discipline of study.

Payam Hanafizadeh
Allameh Tabataba'i University, Iran

Mehdi Behboudi
Qazvin Islamic Azad University, Iran

Chapter 1
Integrated Internet Marketing Communication (IIMC)

ABSTRACT

The main goal of this book is to improve the reader's knowledge of Internet advertising and to explore novel marketing channels of communication. The information herein applies to a medium that has been playing a role in business for less than 20 years and yet has made incredible changes in this domain. Integrated Internet Marketing Communication (IIMC) is addressed in the first chapter of this book because, on one hand, it discusses the specific marketing issues related to Internet marketing, and on the other hand, it investigates the ways through which the concept of Internet communication can be expanded. IIMC is introduced as a theoretical comprehensive framework and a vanguard for Internet advertising approach. Explaining new marketing issues using core marketing concepts not only demonstrates the important role played by these concepts, but also illustrates the innovative tasks as applied to these concepts in a modern marketing arena. Hence, this chapter first examines the core marketing concepts and then explains the novel roles played by such concepts in Internet advertising. In this way, the reader is introduced to the IIMC model. Further in this chapter, some creative concepts of marketing, integrated communication and Internet advertising methods such as Self-Pulling and Need for Check, are explained.

MARKETING

In today's business world, some terms are used that either directly or indirectly relate to marketing, including: search engine marketing, viral marketing, direct marketing, affiliated marketing, permission marketing, email marketing, international marketing, Internet marketing, marketing mix, e-marketing, and one-to-one marketing. With all these terms, we must ask: what is the common concept implied by these terms? What is the integrated meaning of marketing through different methods? To answer these questions, first we must define marketing itself and the integrated concept. Marketing is a process that has different meanings for different people. Some may consider

DOI: 10.4018/978-1-4666-0885-6.ch001

marketing as merely a tool to improve sales, because their goal is to deplete product surplus. For others, marketing may be viewed as nothing more than pleasant words designed to attract audiences. It may also be defined as a means to identifying latent demands. For example, what marketers can create by using sunshine energy? Others see an opportunity for a new approach and believe marketing to be a market creator. Thinking a bit more about the concept, other questions come to the mind: Is marketing a device for suppliers to attract customers for their products? Does marketing result in customers purchasing a good product? Can marketing be a method through which buyers may find the right? Can buyers use marketing to identify producers' latent supply? For example, motivating suppliers to explore to design a new product, which heretofore did not exist. Comprehensive answers to these questions may be implied in the word "process." Marketing is in fact not a concept. It is a *process* that embodies various concepts such as need, demand, market, product, idea, service, exchange and transaction. However, all perceptions seek the same goal: the development of an overall accepted concept. In today's marketing arena, this same goal is labeled solution, offer, suggestion, product, service and satisfier. According to Kotler's definition, "Marketing is a societal process by which individuals and groups obtain what they need and want through creating, offering and exchanging products and services of value freely with others" (Kotler, 2001a, p. 4). From a macro point of view, marketing is the art of exchanging values with others. Surrounding us are products or services, and we are constantly looking for the best options by searching, scrutinizing the messages, negotiating, ignoring and rejecting. Hence, marketing is an integrated part of a person's routine life; some embrace the process consciously and some without conscious thought.

MARKETING AND DEVELOPMENT

Can marketing contribute to the economic development of a society? According to Klein and Nason (2001), the term "development" can be defined as "expanded economic opportunities and improved outcomes in domestic and /or export markets, employment, standard of living, and social conditions commonly included under the concept of quality of life (access to and quality of health care, education, cultural opportunities and civic freedom and harmony)" (Klein & Nason, 2001, p. 263). Governmental and non-governmental organizations and NGOs measure economic progress through indices such as Gross Domestic Product (GDP) per capita, growth rate of GDP, the number of people living below the poverty line and the level of exports. However, attention is also given to non-economic goals such as gender equality, preservation of local culture and strengthening the family (Aguirre, 2001; Mullen, et al., 2001).

According to a general principle, development of new businesses may increase the government's income due to the increase in the amount of taxes (Wood, 2004). An increase in revenue allows the government both to help entrepreneurs and to invest more in general goods. Hence, this may lead to economic prosperity while also improving public welfare and cultural status. The main question then becomes: how can marketing, and especially online marketing, contribute to this goal?

Through identification of potential demands, marketing allows a product or service to be presented concordant with a segment's demands. The fully customized product/service is delivered to the customer by implementing strategies developed from the combination of 4P (product, price, place, and promotion). Currently, marketing plays a promotional role, motivating the customer to buy based on its advertising support. The efficiency of the role played by marketing is undisputed. As stated above, marketing, in the sense of a process, has many concepts and key tasks, and each concept contains other tasks. By fulfilling these tasks, marketing takes an important step towards actualization of economic development. These concepts are introduced below:

Latent Demand

The major skill of a marketer may be the ability to recognize the demands hidden in the target market. A latent demand refers to a part of the market with a need not yet satisfied by a physical product or solution. In other words, most of the time, people are not aware of their own demands and do not know the explicit term of their demand. The explicit term of a demand is its satisfier. Technological improvements create new demands each day; gas engines, electric engines and solar energy have created intensive demands to satisfy a demand which heretofore did not exist. By recognizing these demands, marketers persuade customers to accept their products, and these vague desires which stem from a latent demand are converted to active demands. Thus, marketers do not create demands; they identify the demand, give it a name and provide the customer with a satisfier. Identification of latent demands and creation of new products is the main source for entrepreneurial progression. Through converting latent demands to active ones, marketing plays a significant role in increasing the variety of national products and creating new competitive potential.

Product: A New Role

The term "product" is anyone or anything that contributes to world development. For example, a product may be a student introduced to the labor market. The word "anyone" has not been duly considered in the definitions presented in marketing literature. For instance, according to Kotler and Armstrong (2001): "a product is anything that can be offered to a market to satisfy a demand" (Kotler & Armstrong, 2001, p. 7). Another defi-

nition is also presented by Hiebing and Cooper (2003) who believe that: "The product is a tangible object that is marketed to customers" (Hiebing & Cooper, 2003, p. 214). A well-educated person can contribute to market profitability and economic development by solving problems and creating innovations. A criticism as to this definition may be that an educator is not a product; the product is the service offered. At first glance, this may seem true, but on closer examination, you may ask how is an educated person produced? Is the service provided processed in a university or in the educator? Is the educator the physical product of the service? Why are some educators able to offer a service while others cannot? Even when both are products of the same production line (university) and are developed under the same system and production process (field of study)? On the other hand, as a university "product" progresses through a career, other products (educators) are generated from a marketing point of view.

Through developing the concept of product, marketing presents a new viewpoint for manufacturers. The principle of aligning services/products with target customers' demands has incentivized companies to develop new production lines. Producers may apply various methods to develop a product. For instance, they may develop their products in various sizes based on usage, or they may develop different product features to attract different target markets (Hiebing & Cooper, 2003, p. 215). However, marketing also incorporates strategies for companies that cannot afford to develop a variety of production lines. The proper strategy for these brands is to increase the demand for their products' appeal. Since different segments of a market respond to different stimuli, it is the main task of marketers to identify consumers' sensitivity in each segment. This allows marketers to develop their products' appeal according to the sensitivity of the audiences. In this way, marketing allows SMEs and companies that cannot afford to develop various production lines to provide their customers with a more desirable product.

Segmentation and the Online Environment

Markets are full of buyers with different tastes and demands. No company is able to offer one product to all potential buyers because different tastes demand products with different attributes. It is not possible to offer one product that will satisfy all potential buyers' demands or to motivate all customers to buy one product. By introducing the concept of segmentation, marketing can identify each segment and determine the right segment for each company. The right segment of the market includes that part of the market to which a company should offer its services using all its capacities. This concept of marketing stress incorporates the philosophy of centralization to concentrate all marketing efforts into one specific market segment (or niche market), satisfying the needs and wants of that segment more effectively.

With market segmentation, buyers can be classified into various groups based on their similarities and their differences. Anthropological characteristics are tools by which marketers differentiate among various segments of a market. Some elements of market segmentation include: geographic (region, density, and climate), demographic (age, family size, gender, income, occupation, education, race, social class), psychological (lifestyle and personality), and behavioral (occasions, benefits, user status, usage rate, loyalty status, readiness stage, and attitude toward product) (Kotler, 2001, p. 149) (see Figure 1).

The existence of such differentiating criteria proves that developing one product for all market segments will not be a successful strategy because the increasing use of communications and distribution channels provides customers with access to new information and resources faster and easier than in the past. Thus, mass marketing is no longer efficient, because the great number of marketing messages sent through various channels have created new wants in customers and redirected their tastes toward a higher level of diver-

sification and uncertainty in their decision-making process. Therefore, companies should find the right segment of the market to serve, and customize their services and products for that segment.

Tendency towards diversification is a valuable service of marketers that contributes to the economic development of a society. By raising society's tendency towards diversification, the customer can compare various products and then make an educated purchase. In this way, the customer obtains a higher level of satisfaction, which itself is one of the main goals of marketing, while new competitive opportunities are created as markets become more customized. As more customized production and distribution systems are required, manufacturers will become more competitive. By becoming fully aware of their business plans based on segmentation, these new producers know what should be produced for whom. The deep understanding of this approach allows society to utilize its resources and production agents in the most advantageous way. As explained above, by introducing thoughtful and influential concepts, marketing plays an obvious role in a nation's development, and this role has become more evident with the application of modern technologies. The next section addresses the influence of new technologies on markets, marketing and businesses, and provides readers with some marketing innovations (see Figure 2).

ELECTRONIC MARKETPLACE AND ONLINE MARKETING

Markets play a key role in economic development through exchanging of data, goods, services, and payments (Bakos, 1999). Markets include potential and actual buyers who share a certain demand and satisfy those demands through exchanges. Moreover, according to the definition of Kotler *et al.* (2005), a market is the set of actual and potential buyers of a product. These buyers share

Figure 1. Advanced online segmentation that is offered by Google analytics

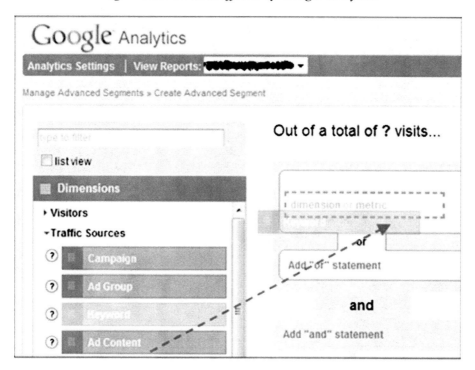

a particular need or want that can be satisfied through exchanges and relationships. Thus the size of a market depends on the number of people who exhibit the need, have resources to engage in the exchange and are willing to offer these resources in exchange for what they want (Kotler, et al., 2005, p. 11). Generally, marketplaces have three tasks to fulfill: 1) coordinating buyers and introducing them; 2) providing the facilities required for exchanging data, goods, services and payments based on the common transactions; 3) providing the legal frameworks and infrastructures required for individuals and organizations to attend the market more effectively (Zwass, 2003).

According to the United Nations Development Program (UNDP), "Information and Communication Technology (ICT) has become an indispensable tool in the fight against poverty" (United Nations Development Program, 2000). In different fields of activity, commercialization of new technologies removes existing limitations; this also applies to marketing. When the Internet

entered into the world of transactions, it brought with it a unique competitive advantage: foreign direct buying. Through foreign direct buying, online marketing provides domestic businesses with an economic development boost with benefits such as:

- **Changes in goods and elimination of physical product:** Every product includes three aspects: physical product, service and idea. The physical product plays a protective and covering role. Most packaging strategies are based on this aspect, and a major part of the end price of a product is a result of the expense of packaging. The digitalization of markets has changed the physical product into a digital one, thus reducing that expense.
- **Global access**: The development of computer technologies has changed store's shelves into global display windows, and customers from every corner of the world

Figure 2. International Revolution Co.'s customer segmentation (in-rev.com, 2009)

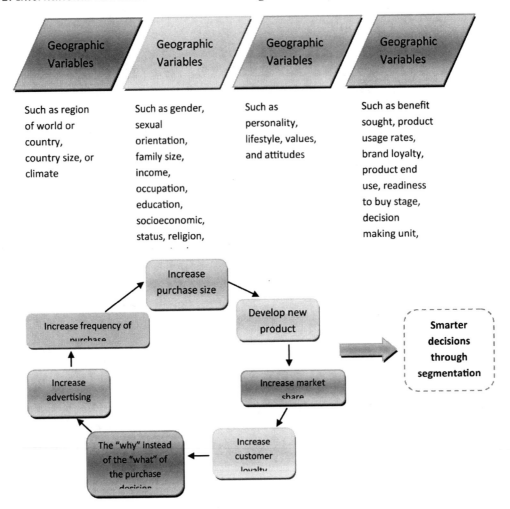

can view the online display windows to search for and purchase their favorite products.

- **Decreasing the size of the space for production:** Due to the elimination of the physical aspect of a product, the space required for raw materials warehouses, production halls and end product warehouses become stored in a digital database.

- **Online delivering and elimination of transportation costs:** Within the production and sales processes, transportation is a non-recoverable expense that could be decreased by applying transportation

methods that are more cost-effective. As a free transporter, the Internet provides companies that opportunity.

- **Improvement of buying power:** With easy global access and a large number of service providers offering the same service, customers have many alternatives from which to choose.

Foreign direct buying has eliminated the political and transactional obstacles that previously impeded international marketing activities. At the same time, marketers still do not ignore the first marketing principle of "demand-based production." Marketers should consider demand conditions, distribution channels, logistics, and after-sales services prior to production. It would be against marketing principles to ignore the characteristics of a marketing channel that has the potential to advertise and establish contact with a target audiences yet still allow customers to order and receive their products and also provide after-sales services.

Electronic markets have changed many processes common to the supply chain. Studies reveal some tangible changes, such as decreasing the expenses imposed from searching for information, decreasing the level of asymmetry in the information received by both buyers and sellers, decreasing the time it takes for a purchased product to be delivered to the end user, and allowing businesses to transact with customers around the world (Varadarajan & Yadav, 2001; Norris & West, 2002). Current businesses have also been changed by entering into electronic markets, adopting new earning methods. In this section, some electronic market issues are discussed.

Business to Business (B2B): B2B is the most common E-commerce method in online markets (Cunninggham, 2001). B2B includes interorganizational information systems, IOS exchanges, and exchanges made within the electronic markets (goods, services, and information). B2Bs known as public markets are generally administrated by a group of companies which could be either buyer or seller (See *nte.net* for an example of B2B).

Business to Customer (B2C): companies such as *Nokia, Ikea, Apple,* and *Coca Cola* are the best examples of this electronic form of business. The business-to-customer market includes all transactions made between retailers and individual buyers. The fundamental difference of these two online markets is the decision-making process. In a B2B market, the customer follows an *organizational decision-making model,* while in a B2C market, the customer follows a *personal decision-making model.* Various information sources are used for

each of these models which determine the buyer's behavior.

Intermediaries: Retailers, wholesalers, distributors, and suppliers are the main marketing intermediates in a traditional market. However, due to the nature of the virtual world and its specific requirements, other intermediaries have also emerged. Making use of the unique business models, these intermediaries play a major role in the virtual marketing world. Among these new mediators are networks and lead generations which will be discussed in detail in following chapters. Roles played by these electronic mediators are far different from their roles in the real world. According to Yarom, Goldman, and Rosenschein (2003) and Turban *et al.* (2006), electronic intermediaries eliminate the five following limitations that exist in virtual markets:

1. **Information-seeking expenses:** It is as important for a producer to find a customer as it is for a customer to find a producer. When designing a database, intermediaries save the information pertinent to their users' tendencies and measure demand based on that information.

2. **Security:** Trust is the main principle for a successful transaction (Jan & Zizi, 2009). Privacy of users shall be secured (Prabhaker, 2000). Most users like to remain anonymous or at least reveal only a small part of their personal information. Intermediaries transfer messages, adjust prices and ultimately make decisions without revealing the identities of either the supplier or the customer.

3. **Completion of incomplete information:** Buyers needing additional information about the quality of the product, products manufactured by other competitors or the opinions of previous consumers may refer to intermediaries. Some intermediaries, like *consumerguide.com*, receive the users' requests and gather information by asking the opinion of previous buyers.

4. **Transaction risk:** A buyer may refuse to pay the price or a seller may fail to deliver a product. By publishing the past transaction behavior of both parties, mediators ensure proper behavior and thus reduce the transaction risk. Entities such as *escrow* agencies are intermediates that finance transactions using own special mechanisms.

5. **Customer's inability to find the right price**: Customers may lose the chance of buying due to an inability to find the "right price." By applying established pricing methods, mediators can be a great help for customers in an electronic market.

"Informational intermediate" is the correct interpretation of relationship marketing. Establishing relationships and creating marketing networks are the two principles required for a successful marketing effort, and these principles are strictly observed by the intermediates that link the databases of the parties involved in the transaction. Extranet is a mediator's joint product. Historically, due to a growing tendency toward direct marketing, the number of mediators involved in electronic markets was reduced (Turban, et al., 2006, p. 49). However, by redefining their methods, intermediates have evolved into a profitable Internet business. This is interpreted as a reintermediation in online marketing *(For more information on this subject, refer to Chapter 12)*.

Multi-Channel Strategy

It is imperative to find the right marketing mix for various possible outcomes. Devising a strategy than can target specific users, applying all potentials of a multi-channel medium like the Internet, and convincing customers to buy requires an intelligently conceived plan. In this regard, a marketer's mind may ask following question: Should we centralize all marketing forces in the Internet channel or should we allocate some to traditional channels?

Multi-channel marketing is divided into three parts (Duffy, 2004):

- Search term marketing
- Shopping portals
- Affiliated marketing

Each of these Internet channels has its unique requirements explained in detail in subsequent chapters. Search engine marketing, however, is the basis of all online marketing and advertising efforts because users enter into the digital world through such search engines. Consequently, this type of marketing cannot be underestimated. The important question is whether an organization can achieve its predetermined goals through only one of or a combination of the above channels.

According to a study conducted by Teltzrow and Kobsa (2004), customers tend to rely on websites that have a number of actual brick-and-mortar stores. Previous studies revealed that this behavior is due to three factors: information intermediate, guarantee and reputation (Chellappa, 2000). The customer will acquiesce to buy if it is confirmed that 1) the website in question is well known, 2) an information intermediate is involved in the transaction that will be responsible if the customer's demand is not satisfied, and 3) there is a guarantee for the transaction. From a guaranty-oriented point of view, the website's reputation determines the level of customers' trust in online shopping. This allows marketing strategists to revert from traditional channels and focus on online channels, the main point being to develop a positive reputation for the website. How then can a good reputation be developed? Reputation is the result of previous desirable behavior of an individual or organization, and it plays an important role in the users' tendency to enter into a transaction with a website (Andrade, Kaltcheva, & Weitz, 2002). Previous good references and the subsequent positive reputation are concepts that are not easily attained. Reputation forms through years of having a successful presence in the marketplace with proven operational capabilities. The main challenge for all electronic businesses is that they do not have such a history. Many websites are active in different commercial fields, and all claim to be the best. The problem has been worsened due to the increase in the users' access because users cannot immediately identify which online store is trustworthy and which is not. At the same time, most electronic stores present new unprecedented business models strange to consumers, so they often turn to their past attitudes and positive memories and do not trust businesses that are purely online. Studies have revealed that American multi-channel retailers have increased their market share in the online market from 52% in 1999 to 75% in 2003. An inverse ratio was observed as to purely online retailers (shop.org, 2004; Forrester Research, 2004).

Taking all above anxieties into account, it is advisable to develop an artificial reputation on a website; this electronic guarantor can be any mechanism, process or construct that gains customers' trust and motivates them to the transaction point. Three other fundamental questions in this regard require a comprehensive study:

1. What organization should verify this artificial reputation?
2. Where on the web should it be placed?
3. How should users be informed of its reliability?

Competition in a Digital Economy

In spite of all for the benefits of online marketing, a business is confronted with many challenges when it enters into electronic market competition. In the past, companies used to develop their marketing networks using relationship marketing by integrating suppliers and distributors into their marketing system. These exclusive marketing networks mean little today when online data-based systems allow each supplier and distributor to transact with numerous companies. In addition,

applying the concept of segmentation, each supplier and distributor can have a customized offer so that the issue of providing service to a few well-known companies is no longer important. Taking the above statements into account, how can we explain Internet competition when all competitors have equal access to raw materials and distribution channels? Businesses must select their competition strategy taking the four following strategies into account:

1. **Developing new business models:** The new cyber-environment requires a new business model. Creation of an affiliating role is one of these models. For instance, *priceline.com* has learned how to be profitable in this new environment despite many other competitors by executing a business model which is as relevant in today's web-focused market.

2. **Offering differentiated products:** When suppliers, distributors and customers are not inclined to cooperate with a company, it is evident that the company has not acquired a valuable competency that is motivating enough to link and lock suppliers and distributors to the system. For instance, presenting a product named "Windows," *Microsoft Co.* required all software producers to design their products based on the Windows platform while also requiring all hardware manufacturers to design their products accordingly.

3. **Customer-oriented:** Providers of similar services or products should adopt a well-defined, customer-oriented strategy. Such a strategy is considered well-defined when it decreases a customer's expenses (monetary expenses, time, and energy) and as time goes by, the strategy becomes more vital due to the steadily increasing number of similar services offered on the Internet.

4. **Retrenchment:** The emergence of databases and the feasibility of establishing relationships among the databases that are

members of a marketing network have made clear the real meaning of "Just in Time" and "Elimination of Finished Parts Inventory." That is why the retrenchment strategy is a practical one. Companies should redefine their mission statement and focus more on their main mission, delegating other activities which are not specifically related to that mission.

Online Negotiations

Previously, communication systems operated on analog information; however, most systems today operate within digital systems. Digital systems are based on bytes or streams of zeros and ones which allow the new medium to display image, data and videos. A connection is required to allow these digital systems to exchange data. Therefore, Internet, intranet, extranet and networks have been developed to redefine communication. Due to the progress made in this domain, "negotiation" as a buying approach has taken a new form. The important point is that the negotiation will take a shorter time if the company prepares the customer's mind beforehand by enhancing customers' attitudes about the company, ensuring them about the after-sale services and improving the overall public image of the brand. These anxieties should be lessened after negotiation. Chapter 8 introduces methods by which the web can practically eliminate such anxieties.

INTEGRATED MARKETING COMMUNICATION (IMC)

Consumers' migration from standard media like TV, radio, and newspapers to the Internet has made advertisers and information disseminators seek new solutions for enhancing communication, because creating preferences and reserving the organizational image is the central goal of marketing communications.

Integrated marketing communication is such a challenge that many studies and tools have been used to increase its efficiency, some of which include advertising, promotion, personal selling, public relations and direct marketing (Kotler, 2001, p. 272) *(Chapter 2 discusses these elements in greater detail)*. The importance of IMC planning is emphasized by dynamic streams of various marketing areas including market segmentation, relationship marketing and direct marketing (Durking & Lawlor, 2001). Based on this, the Internet is expected to have a decided impact on IMC because the marketing domains specified above have stepped into the electronic world, and it is clear that they cannot achieve success if they follow standard historical patterns. Therefore, a redefined paradigm of IMC is required for the online world.

Integrated marketing communication was introduced late in the 1990s to reduce mass advertising budgets and focus on segmented and personalized communication as well as the ultimate buyer (Eagle & Kitchen, 2000). Integrated marketing communication is recognized as a logical answer to the problems occurring in different businesses by increasing the efficiency of innovative ideas, allowing constant communications and increasing the number of customers with regard to the investments made (Novak, Delorme, & Cameraon, 1996; Kitchen, et al., 2004). According to some researchers, the integration of marketing communication methods resulted from centralized budgeting and management requiring that the same message be distributed in all communication channels (Smith, et al., 1997; Shimp, 2000).

According to other IMC definitions, integrated marketing communication is not the uniformity of messages in various channels, but the complex management of transmitting information through various data distribution channels to present an integrated image of the organization to its audiences (Kitchen, et al., 2004). The procedure followed in IMC is the development of synergy, where the company's image and its brands are promoted simultaneously. The simultaneous promotion of the image and brands is considered important because once the company's brand is established via promotion; the company's new brands will then stand out among other newly introduced products. In addition, the simultaneous promotion of the company's images and brands develops added value for the company, because when customers assume that the company has several accepted strategic business units or brands in the market, they move through the stages of decision-making faster.

Marketing communications decisions should be focused on channels that provide the highest level of profits for all stakeholders (Gurau, 2008). According to Duncan's definition (Duncan, 2002), integrated marketing communication is a multi-functional process to establish profitable relations (Duncan, 2002, p. 8). All parts interacting with customers and stakeholders must cooperate with one another to develop a common concept for the customers and stakeholders. The outcome of this joint cooperation is the establishment of a long-term relationship. This is important because today's competitive environment is not that of the rivals, rather it is a competition among the marketing networks to which these rivals are linked. In spite of the emphasis on the importance of IMC, the organizational structure of most companies impedes its proper implementation. Therefore, one of the important points is the identification of the host's organizational structure. This helps make the required changes in existing limitations to convert them to leading levers for and tools of IMC implementation. Quite often, such structural limitations are classified under two general categories: specific limitations and general limitations. Specific limitations are more related to the organization's specific requirements, such as the creative units linked to the main communication message because of a specific task. However, general limitations include those obstacles with which almost all organizations are involved. To identify general obstacles, Percy conducted a

study in 1997 and introduced these organizational limitations:

- Lack of horizontal communication
- Functional specialization
- Decentralization
- Lack of IMC planning and expertise
- Lack of budget
- Lack of database technology
- Corporate culture
- Fear of change

The key questions still remain: what is the most suitable IMC model and what is the best method through which marketing communication operations can be consolidated according to the specific conditions of each company?

INTEGRATED INTERNET MARKETING COMMUNICATION (IIMC)

Finding the right integrated Internet marketing communication model is one of the most important goals for a company that applies proven marketing methods. Matching a comprehensive IMC model to Internet marketing requires proper knowledge of the tools and formats developed in this field. Through applying a homogenous approach and complex management, a harmony is established to navigate users toward the website. In this section, different methods of establishing relationships with online audiences are introduced, and then an Internet marketing communication model is presented.

Integrated marketing communication incorporates numerous methods to stay in touch with customers. In traditional media, advertising, sales promotion, public relations, personal selling, and direct marketing are the major methods connecting a customer and a company. Now that the Internet has been added to the mix, the scenario has changed. Traditional media are considered fundamental routes in integrated marketing communications, but these methods must be redefined to be compatible with the new digital medium. The methods for integrated Internet marketing communication are as follows:

Advertising

Expenses spent on advertising demonstrate of its importance for today's businesses. According to statistics, advertising in the United States amounted to 5.7 billion dollars in 1950, 27.9 billion dollars in 1975 and 279 billion dollars in 2007 (Globithin, 2008). The goal of commercial advertising is no longer to introduce products and producers to the consumers, and there is no more effort to create motivation for mass sales. Nowadays, it focuses on interacting with consumers, and satisfying their demands sooner and better than their competitors.

Internet advertising and the pertinent various publishing methods are the first influential activities considered in IIMC. As it will be further explained in Chapters 4 and 11, more than 18 Internet advertising formats exist, each of which is considered more efficient in a specific target market. Generally, various classifications have been presented for Internet advertising. For example, IAB classifies advertisements within seven categories: display ads, lead generations, search, sponsorship, classified, email ads and rich media (IAB, 2009). This differentiates among various Internet advertising methods and formats, not in terms of a segmented and targeted market. Hence, another classification may be presented based on three general approaches where a proper channel can be established for distributing data and a proper navigation system can be designed to push the user towards the web.

1. **Display advertising:** Most online advertising formats (publishing and broadcasting) are of a display type according to a classification presented by the Interactive Advertising Bureau. Expanding on common display ads like buttons, skyscraper and banners, other formats in the category include rich media and digital video.

2. **Networking and affiliation advertising:** Advertising formats, such as hypertexts placed inside the contents of a host website to direct the users toward the advertising website, form the second category. In networking and affiliation advertising, a central site of a networking business model gathers a group of websites similar in content and links them together through its exclusive network. The central website receives the ad from a promoter and sends it to the central server. These ads are then redirected to users according to the documented behavior of the users on the sites which are members of this network.

3. **Search-Based Advertising**: A search for a word on the Internet is one of the most obvious examples for advertising in this media. Following up and adoption of information within the same context as the searched word is a unique feature that can yield excellent results. Reports (IAB, 2006, 2007, 2008) indicate that advertising in search engines represents more than 40% of Internet advertising income. Organic SEO and Paid SEO are two different kinds of advertising in search engines. In Organic SEO, the use of its specific algorithms assign a rank to any website which has registered in a search engine. At each search, the websites search for those registered keywords that are either in concordance with the entered keyword by the user or within the content website. Paid SEO operates under a different mechanism *(see Chapter 8).*

Online Direct Marketing

Our second category of IIMC unified Internet marketing communications is sending a persuasive message to potential customers in their E-mailbox. Email Marketing is a method in which the marketers send advertising messages composed of promotional elements from a website to the user's mailbox to persuade the user to visit the website. Compared with offline direct marketing, online direct marketing allows customization, personalization and niche targeting in a much more flexible, easier, quicker and cheaper way (Kitchen & Pelsmacker, 2004).

Personalization and customization are approaches that work best when online direct marketing has been well-defined since a user's traffic to different websites has left signals of interest. Tracking of these signals, called Click-Stream Information (CSI) (Ansari & Mela, 2003), creates a specific profile for each user. Creating and sending a message according to the registered information in this profile reveals a defined pathway to satisfy a user's needs. In that way, the main problem of marketing communications, being rejected by the audience, is removed. Several studies verify this conclusion. For example, Taylor and Neoborne (2002) suggested that emails with several personalization elements have a 10% greater response rate than common emails.

Online direct marketing is not simply sending messages to a user's mailbox. Wireless technology allows users to send and receive promotional messages without respect to location. Receiving advertising messages from a favorite supplier is one method; however, the essential condition of these methods is the user's permission and acceptance (Barnes & Scornavacca, 2004; Kavassalis, et al., 2003). Placing systems such as NFC (Near Field Communication) in mobile devices such as cell phones creates a new orientation for online transactions or LBA (Location Based Advertising), undertaken in two forms not requested or indirectly requested (Steiniger, Neun, & Edwards, 2005, p. 5). In "requested" advertising, the user must enroll in the main database and enter some favorites so that ads are received that reflect those favorites. In "not requested" ads, advertising may be determined based on a device's location based on the presence of the user in places where this system has been set up. For example, a user who is near a boutique may receive a message on the new fashion trends.

The selection of new tools for marketing communication has created an opportunity for IIMC because past communications tools have updated for today's shopping environments. The time spent gathering information by users has become decidedly shorter. Traditionally, costumers used different tools to research information sources, but now a mobile device is available, and with a monitor, a keyboard, and access to the Internet, they can receive an advertising message and complementary information about the message via one device.

The remarkable point and the book's main purpose is to introduce a new model that takes into account the incredible decrease in the time required to make a buying decision. Since a cell phone is always with the users, Location-Based Advertising (LBA) has provided a unique situation for marketers; in other words, it is a marketer's dream come true!

There are four other main issues in unified Internet marketing communications: public relations, personal selling, sales promotion and websites discussed in the second chapter in complete detail. However, solutions for staying in touch with customers on the Internet are slightly different from the real world. Integrating all Internet messaging methods and the leadership of IMC's new members must be considered by the marketers. In this book, we will determine the tasks of all 5+1 main players of advertising campaigns (promotion mix) as shown in Figure 1.

As Figure 3 shows, five peripheral elements are designed to generate a route toward an advertiser website for an experimental visit. The core elements in IIMC must be designed to sustain, support and do anything to entice the user to visit the website again. The main task of the peripheral elements of IIMC's funnel-shaped model is to push the customer into the website. Marketers should consider three key tasks and tactics in the development of the peripheral campaign:

1. To persuade the customer to visit the website;
2. To establish a way for users to enter the website; and
3. Advertising activities must be well-planned and placed in locations with heavy traffic so that they will be noticeable among other brands. This will highly motivate users who lack the necessary motivation to pay frequent visits to the website.

The key orientation is the experimental visit. By navigating users to the website, the peripheral elements have successfully performed their task.

However, that is not their only task. They also function to improve the image of the company, change consumer preferences and support the buyers' decision to ignore competitors' strategies. The website itself is tasked with motivating the customer to return to the website; we have termed this effort "self-pulling." Self-pulling is a motivational mechanism by which the audience's involvement with the website is increased, and they recognize a new need that we call "need for recheck." Need for recheck is an emotional deprivation that has emerged with the use of Internet-based advanced technologies (the need for search and purchase to be easy fast cost-saving and without any location limitations). By rechecking registered favorites on the website, the consumer achieves a kind of temporary satisfaction. This temporary satisfaction is

Figure 3. The Funnel Model of IIMC

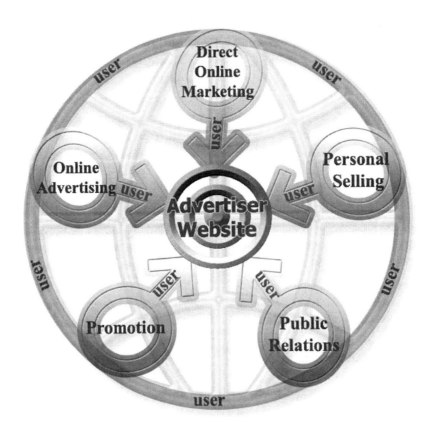

a tentative feeling strengthened by observation, receiving information and services, and/or being offered a new premium. However, this sense of satisfaction is not permanent, because the nature of this need creates a permanent anxiety where the user is afraid of missing something on the website such as a new product or message; this persuades the user to check the website often.

The customer who visits the web for the first time does not have this need or, is not aware of it. The art of marketers is to familiarize the user with this need which fulfills the user's requirements. However, with so many websites and experienced marketers, marketing in general has become more difficult. In such a competitive environment, marketers must recognize customers' new needs and develop the right solutions to satisfy their requirements. This will create customer loyalty.

As we will discuss in the next chapters, these motivations can involve: presenting updated data and statistics on issues which are of interest to users; involving the user in surveys resulting in compensation or other perks; employing initiative strategies such as highlighting on the website a value-added message like "A gift for you!" The website is also tasked with motivating the user to remain on the site and increasing the amount of time spent at the website *(This is discussed in Chapter 7)*.

In order to gather users' information and provide customized service, many website's marketers require users to register. This method may give customers the idea that their information may have tangible value for the website (some customers with little technical knowledge are not familiar with intangible value), thinking that in return for the data, they will receive free services. This approach makes the users wary about the website and may cause them to input incorrect data, resulting in inaccurate customized service. Such a situation may also cause the user to respond negatively to follow-up messages and to ignore them.

CONCLUSION

This chapter discussed marketing from both the approach market-oriented and online market-oriented perspectives. At the beginning of the chapter, it was suggested that marketing is not a concept, but rather a process which has been developed from different concepts like need, want, demand, exchange and transaction. The chapter also discussed each marketing field and the relationship between marketing and development, a topic which is rarely discussed in other literature. Latent demand was defined as a constituting element of development capacity, and it is suggested that identifying latent demands is one of the marketer's' tasks.

This chapter presented a new definition of product with a human-based approach where products produce other products. It also identified the segmentation concept and emphasized its role in the market. Based on this background, the chapter described the online marketing approach and introduced foreign direct buying as an economic development tool and discussed its benefits. This chapter also suggested various types of business and marketing approaches in the online environment. Then it challenged the current strategies of online marketing and competing concepts and provided useful strategies for both. In addition, online negotiations and better-developed strategies were discussed that would lead to less time being spent on buying negotiations.

This chapter introduced integrated marketing communications and after a comprehensive description, suggested the concept of integrated Internet marking communication, illustrated via the funnel-shaped model. The model has five peripheral elements: advertising, sales promotion, public relations, direct marketing and personal selling, and has a central element which is called "website." We have learned which parts are successful in what areas, and which approaches must be taken into account for peripheral and central elements. Finally, a new need that is related to the web and new technologies was introduced.

REFERENCES

Aguirre, M. S. (2001). Family, economics and the information society - How are they affecting each other? *International Journal of Social Economics*, *28*(3), 225–247. doi:10.1108/03068290110357645

American Marketing Association. (2006). *Marketing terms dictionary*. Retrieved from http://www.marketingpower.com /index.

Andrade, E. B., Kaltcheva, V., & Weitz, B. (2002). Self-disclosure on the web: The impact of privacy policy, reward, and company reputation. *Advances in Consumer Research. Association for Consumer Research (U. S.)*, *29*, 350–353.

Ansari, A., & Mela, C. F. (2003). E-customization. *JMR, Journal of Marketing Research*, *40*(2), 131–145. doi:10.1509/jmkr.40.2.131.19224

Bakos, Y. (1998). The merging role of electronic marketplace on the internet. *Communications of the ACM*, *41*(8). Retrieved from http://portal.acm.org /ft_gateway.cfm?id=280330&type=pdf&CFID=18384839&CFTOKEN=72033081 doi:10.1145/280324.280330

Barnes, S. J., & Scornavacca, E. (2004). Mobile marketing: The role of permission and acceptance. *International Journal of Mobile Communications*, *2*(2), 128–139. doi:10.1504/IJMC.2004.004663

Bennett, D. P. (1995). *Dictionary of marketing terms* (2nd ed.). Chicago, IL: American Marketing Association.

Chellappa, R. K. (2001). *Consumers' trust in electronic commerce transactions: The role of perceived privacy and perceived security*. Retrieved from http://asura.usc.edu /~ram/rcf-papers/sec-priv.pdf.

Cunningham, M. S. (2001). *B2B: How to build a profitable E-commerce strategy*. Cambridge, UK: Perseus.

Duffy, D. (2004). Case study: Multi-channel marketing in the retail environment. *The Journal of Consumer Research*, *21*(4), 356–363.

Duncan, T. (2002). *IMC: Using advertising and promotion to build brands*. New York, NY: McGraw-Hill.

Durkin, M., & Lawlor, M. A. (2001). The implications of the internet on the advertising agency-client relationship. *The Services Industries Journal*, *21*(2), 175–190. doi:10.1080/714005026

Eagle, L., & Kitchen, P. J. (2000). IMC: Brand communications, and corporate cultures. *European Journal of Marketing*, *34*(5), 667–686. doi:10.1108/03090560010321983

Globithink. (2008). *Annual U.S. advertising expenditure report*. Retrieved from http://www.galbithink.org /ad-spending.htm.

Gurau, C. (2008). Integrated online marketing communication: Implementation and management. *Journal of Communication Management*, *12*(2), 169–184. doi:10.1108/13632540810881974

Hiebing, G. R., & Cooper, W. S. (2003). *The successful marketing plan: A disciplined and comprehensive approach*. New York, NY: McGraw-Hill Professional.

IAB. (2006). *Internet advertising revenue report, October 2006*. Retrieved from http://www.iab.net.

IAB. (2007). *Internet advertising revenue report, October 2007*. Retrieved from http://www.iab.net.

IAB. (2008). *Internet advertising revenue report, October 2008*. Retrieved from http://www.iab.net.

IAB. (2009). *Internet advertising revenue report, October 2009*. Retrieved from http://www.iab.net.

Ibid labs. (2010). *Ibid Labs announces IBID release*. Retrieved from http://blog.ibidlabs.com /?page_id=48.

Jan, F., & Zizi, P. (2009). *Online privacy as legal safeguard: The relationship among consumer, and privacy policies*. Retrieved from http://nms.sagepub.com.

Kavassalis, P., Spyropoulou, N., Drossos, D., Mitrokostas, E., Gikas, G., & Hatzistamatiou, A. (2003). Mobile permission marketing: Framing the market inquiry. *International Journal of Electronic Commerce, 8*(1), 55–79.

Kitchen, P. J., Brignell, J., Li, T., & Jones, G. S. (2004). The emergence of IMC: A theoretical perspective. *Journal of Advertising Research, 44*(1), 19–30. doi:10.1017/S0021849904040048

Kitchen, P. J., & Pelsmacker, P. (2004). *Integrated marketing communication: A primer*. London, UK: Taylor & Francis.

Klein, T. A., & Nason, R. W. (2001). Marketing and development: Macro marketing perspectives. In Bloom, P. N., & Gundlach, G. T. (Eds.), *Handbook of Marketing and Society*. Thousand Oaks, CA: Sage.

Kotler, P. (2001). *Marketing management millenium edition* (10th ed.). Upper Saddle River, NJ: Prentice Hall, Inc.

Kotler, P., & Armstrong, G. (2001). *Principles of marketing* (9th ed.). Upper Saddle River, NJ: Prentice Hall.

Kotler, P., Wong, V., Saunders, J., & Armstrong, G. (2005). *Principles of marketing* (4th ed.). London, UK: Prentice Hall Europe.

Libai, B., Biyalogorsky, E., & Gerstner, E. (2003). Setting referral fees in affiliate marketing. *Journal of Service Research, 5*(4), 303–315. doi:10.1177/1094670503005004003

McDaniel, C., Lamb, C. W., & Hair, J. F. (2006). *Introduction to marketing* (8th ed.). Cincinnati, OH: South Western Publishers.

Mullen, M. R., Beller, E., Remsa, J., & Cooper, D. (2001). The effects of international trade on economic growth and meeting basic human needs. *Journal of Global Marketing, 15*(1), 31–55. doi:10.1300/J042v15n01_03

Norris, M., & West. (2001). *E-business essentials* (2nd ed.). Chichester, UK: John Wiley and Sons, Ltd.

Novak, G. J., Cameron, G. T., & Delorme, D. (1996). Beyond the world of packaged goods: Assessing the relevance of integrated marketing communications for retail and consumer service marketing. *Journal of Marketing Communications, 2*(1), 173–190.

Papatla, P., & Bhatnagar, A. (2002). Choosing the right mix of on-line affiliates: How do you select the best? *Journal of Advertising, 31*(3), 69–81.

Percy, L. (1997). *Strategies for implementing integrated marketing communication*. Chicago, IL: NTC Business Books.

Prabhaker, R. P. (2000). Who owns the online consumer? *Journal of Consumer Marketing, 17*(2), 158–171. doi:10.1108/07363760010317213

Shimp, T. A. (2000). *Advertising promotion: Supplemental aspects of integrated marketing communications* (5th ed.). Fort Worth, TX: The Dryden Press.

Shop.org & Forrester Research. (2004). *The state of retailing online 7.0*. Retrieved from http://www.shop.org /research/SRO7/SRO7main.asp.

Smith, P. R., Berry, C., & Pulford, A. (1997). *Strategic marketing communications: New ways to build and integrate communication*. London, UK: Kogan Page.

Steiniger, S., Neun, M., & Edwardes, A. (2006). *Foundations of location based service*. Retrieved August 5, 2007, from http://www.geo.unizh.ch /publications/cartouche/ lbs_lecturenotes_steinigeretal2006.pdf.

Taylor, C. P., & Neuborne, E. (2002). Getting personal. *Adweek, 39*(44), IQ1.

Teltzrow, M., & Kobsa, A. (2004). *Impacts of user privacy preferences on personalized systems: A comparative study.* Retrieved from http://www.ics.uci.edu/~kobsa/papers/2003-CHI-kobsa.pdf.

Turban, E., King, D., Viehland, D., & Lee, J. (2006). *Electronic commerce: A managerial perspective.* Upper Saddle River, NJ: Prentice Hall.

United Nations Development Program. (2000). *Driving information and communications technology for development.* Retrieved from http://www.undp.org.

Varadarajan, P. R., & Yadav. (2002). Marketing strategy and the internet: An organizing framework. *Academy of Marketing Science, 30*(4), 87–99. doi:10.1177/009207002236907

Wood, M. C. (2004). Marketing and e-commerce as tools of development in the Asia-Pacific region: A dual path. *International Marketing Review, 21*(3), 301–316. doi:10.1108/02651330410539639

Yarom, I., Goldman, C. V., & Rosenschein, J. S. (2003). The role of middle-agents in electronic commerce. *IEEE Intelligent Systems, 18*(6), 15–21. doi:10.1109/MIS.2003.1249165

Zwass, V. (2003). Electronic commerce and organization innovations: Aspects and opportunities. *International Journal of Electronic Commerce, 7*(3), 35–47.

Chapter 2
Internet Advertising

ABSTRACT

The ideal advertisement is one that has the best possible reach within a well-organized range of customers (selectivity) with proper possibilities of feedback and low cost. Conversely, mass communication often forces the marketer to accept high reach with relatively low selectivity and no feedback opportunities while achieving reasonable cost-effectiveness (Steptrup, 1991; Thomsen, 1996). The marketer's challenge is to decide which medium, or combination of media, can best achieve the advertising goal for the company. This chapter provides an integrated definition of Internet advertising, describing its features and advantages. Additional discussion involves the emergence of Internet advertising, statistics of incomes, and costs. Finally, the chapter explains how marketers should select the right website for their advertising placement.

FROM BILLBOARD TO BANNER

Because of the accessibility of the Internet, this electronic medium is rapidly becoming a dynamic and user-friendly place for advertising. Considering the diminishing life-cycle of a product in the current market, presently at less than six months, there is a concern that traditional advertising channels and strategies may not be capable of achieving a company's business and sales goals. Companies who are motivated by entrepreneurship are well aware of how effective this new medium is in a challenging environment. Today, we are faced with global customers, producers, consumers, suppliers and markets, all in need of global advertising. Standard broadcasting channels are no longer enough for companies' long-term advertising objectives. Instead, they need a flexible channel based on in-house broadcasting as many customers now work at home. When compared to outdoor billboards, for example, banners on websites take up little space while still being able to advertise a variety of brands. As Randall Rothenberg, president and CEO of IAB, says: *"We are seeing an ongoing secular shift from traditional to online media as marketers recognize*

DOI: 10.4018/978-1-4666-0885-6.ch002

that ad dollars invested in interactive media are effective at influencing consumers and delivering measurable results. In this uncertain economy, where marketers know they need to do more with less, interactive advertising provides the tools for them to build deep and engaging relationships with consumers—the experience marketers gain from this will deliver dividends especially after the economy turns around" (IAB, 2009.

THE INTERNET

The Internet is the most important medium for the 21st century. The Internet consists of scattered computer networks which are linked internationally, working on global communications protocols. In 1968, the United States Defense Department established a new system called the Advanced Research Projects Agency NETwork (ARPANET). This new invention was a communications system developed to link governmental and military sites to one another. For security purposes, the Internet was designed in a way that no organization or country could have control over it.

The next step for the Internet was in academic organizations. It served the science and education fields as an electronic library for information exchange through online discussions. At first, the structure of this new medium was quite basic, utilizing mostly text. Moreover, the lack of a well-designed software system meant that the communication process was extremely slow.

In 1990, after the development of the World Wide Web by Berners-Lee, the Internet entered a new arena. This new innovation allowed users to view pictures, photos and artifacts, and also send them to each other. Using pages, websites developed rapidly, and by 1994, nearly three million web-pages had been created with informational, entertainment and advertising purposes. Due to this rapid growth, the Internet evolved from an individual environment to a commercial communications environment. By 1996, 89% of the websites belonged to commercial companies.

The Internet is innately a flexible medium; furthermore, it appears to be a powerful tool for the transfer of information. The advantage of flexibility allows the Internet to provide marketing communications tools such as e-mail, chat rooms, communities, forums and news groups.

The popularity and growth of the World Wide Web grew much faster than other media; five years was enough time for the new medium to attract 50 million users (Meeker, 1997). Compared with radio (30 years) and TV (15 years), this statistic reveals the incredibly fast development of Internet diffusion (Sterne, 1997). As Berthon, Pitt, and Watson highlight, "The Web is not a transient phenomenon. It warrants serious attention by advertising academics and practitioners. Statistics support this, although one astute observer recommends strongly that all estimates be made in pencil only, as the growth is so rapid. No communication medium or electronic technology, not even fax or personal computers, has ever grown as quickly" (Berthon, Pitt, & Watson, 1996, p. 44).

Nowadays, the Internet is a part of everyone's life, and for many customers, the Web has become the major medium for consumption (Morris, Woo, & Cho, 2003). The Web is not only being realized by consumers, it is increasingly being accepted by marketers as well (Prasad, Ramamurthy, & Naidu, 2001) (see Figure 1).

ADVERTISING ORIGINS

From a historical point of view, advertising can be seen as far back as the public criers in town markets (Dyer, 1982) in ancient cities such as Sumer, Babylon, and Jerusalem. The public crier served the function of providing timely, and sometimes persuasive, information about goods and services available in the market. In a similar vein, today's modern advertising communicates with customers about available offers. The crier's behavior and

Figure 1. Examples of the first types of advertisements

the advertisements of today's world are different in many aspects but share the same principle. Advertising is not only a new phenomenon, it has also been a crucial element in human society from the day of creation up to now (Nilsson, 2006). As a scientific field in academic studies, advertising is similar to marketing and sometimes is considered as one of marketing's remarkable sub-categories. Advertising approach and knowledge is mainly an interrelated course that takes advantage of other subjects and their theories, including linguistics, psychology, sociology, anthropology and economic to achieve its goal. Methods like anthropology, quantitative modeling and survey research are used to make sure that advertising is understood as a whole. According to a beautiful analogy by Mr. MacInnis of blind people discussing an elephant, people acquire knowledge from multi-dimensional ideas and multi-method approaches (Maclinns, 2005).

ADVERTISING

Advertising is an entity of concepts, which marketers are, be able to use to introduce products to the market, mostly based on formerly created communication. Advertising is based on two premises: the first is marketing, which attempts to communicate and establish a relationship with customers by transferring value (Darroch, 2004); the second is communication, which serves as a process to create a unified idea between a sender and a receiver (Schramm, 1995). In other words, advertising is the process of sharing concepts among people (Dibb & Simken, 1991). However, some scholars like Richards and Curran (2002) are not agreed with this argument and stated, those processes must be termed as "advertising" that embrace "persuasion." They believe that promotional activities without persuasive cues cannot be named as advertising.

Marketing and communication theories have the same origins and thus reinforce each other. The combination of marketing and communication created the emergence of the new subject of marketing communication.

Advertising has been defined in many different ways. Since the definitions are based on researchers' observational approaches, finding the best one is impossible. In order to find a definition upon which many researchers agree, a content analysis was undertaken, and the following definitions seem to be compatible with Internet advertising. Richards and Curran (2002) states: "advertising is a paid non-personal communication from an identified sponsor, using mass media to persuade or influence an audience" (p. 63). It is believed that the purpose of advertising is to create an image of the product and persuade the customer to buy it. Therefore, advertising is a part of an organization's communications policy in its marketing mix. Decisions on types of advertising formats should be made with respect to introducing a product. Therefore, we define online advertising as follows:

Online advertising is an Internet-based process by which advertisers communicate, interact with, and persuade online users in order to position a brand, which allows a company to promote both consumer awareness and preference in a customized and personalized way, and decrease the time needed to make a buying decision.

As customers in an online communication channel are able to click on ads and obtain information rapidly compared to traditional advertising.

From an economic point of view, advertising serves two major functions: persuasion and information. Persuading deals with the correct design of the ads. A successful ad is one with a high economical-encouraging function. However, an informational function is also important.

Information-providing companies have to create a sense of loyalty in their customers by integrating and completing the customers' knowledge (Thomson, 1996).

To better understand the relationship among different advertising events, it is necessary to understand the comprehensive and integrated perspective of advertising.

Advertising has considerably expanded on the WWW during the last decade. In the beginning, ads on the Internet appeared in the form of simple rectangles which were called Banners. The first website that showed an illustrated ad was *hotwired.com,* an electronic magazine in 1994 which advertised banners of companies such as *zima.com, volo.com,* and *AT&T.com* (Nilsson, 2006) (see Figure 2).

Early banners were hindered by bandwidth and infrastructure limitations which limited the use of animated banners for pioneers in Internet advertising. Since animated banners could not transfer a large amount of information due to the amount of space taken up by animation and graphical shapes, there was little opportunity for message exposure and typeface flexibility. Larger banners resulted in two major problems: increasing both a website's occupied space and broadcasting costs. Moreover, using animated technologies and designing larger banners tended to increase loading time; therefore, banners usually failed to perform their mission (Zufryden, 1997). With improvements in the infrastructures, Internet technologies and user facilities to attain higher bandwidth, advertisers utilized more graphics in ads (*discussed in detail in Chapter 4*).

Figure 2. Sample of early banners

In early advertising and especially with the first banners, advertisers used simple and short massages such as *Click Here, Click Now.* That was appropriate because the advertisers had just one target that was "pulling the customer to the Web." Unlike those initial banners, today's Internet ads feature pictures, descriptions of products, brand identity, message text, and an enticing title that together puts everything into a framework for consumers. Today's banners work completely differently from those original ones. Modern advertising is focused on images, and the objectives are also different from the past. In the old sense of banner broadcasting, there was just one target—persuading users and pulling them to the Web. In the new sense of banner broadcasting, there are integrated communication messages for which the banner content changes continually, providing a unique situation in which banners are able to attract niche audiences to other websites.

Advertising and Its Environment

There is no doubt that marketing activities such as advertising occupy an important position in today's technical environment. You cannot imagine a place in which there is no advertising. For instance, when an individual reads the morning paper, he is exposed to a number of advertisements placed in a certain setting. Every day, consumers are constantly exposed to brand names, company names and window displays affecting them in various ways (Nilsson, 2006). It is nearly impossible to count the number of ads that exist in one working day, and that would be even more difficult within an electronic business workday.

As more users encounter advertising, the need exists for a new place to display those ads. According to Kakkar and Lutz (1981), consumer behavior is greatly influenced by environmental aspects. They believe that this fact can substantially affect the way people receive and understand the communication process.

For a better identification of the variables which affect a consumer's situation, Belk (1975, p.159) introduced five categories of situational characteristics:

- **Physical Surroundings:** These are the most apparent features of a situation. The physical surrounding includes geographical and institutional location, décor, sounds, aromas, lighting, visible configurations of merchandise or "other materials surrounding the stimulus object.
- **Social Surroundings:** These provide additional depth to the situation, including other persons present, their properties and roles and interpersonal interactions.
- **Temporal Perspective:** This is a dimension of a situation specified in time units and related to some other entity.
- **Task Definition:** "The features of a situation include an intent or requirement to select, shop for, or obtain information about a general or specific purchase. In addition, a task may reflect different buyer and user roles anticipated by the individual" (Belk, 1975, p. 159).
- **Antecedent States:** These are moods or short-term conditions immediately antecedent to a situation. They are states that the individual brings into the situation, not the result of being in a certain situation.

Recognizing the advertising environment is important, as that environment consists of different elements which are important in processing information and advertising messages. The webpage that is exposed to a user is a critical environmental factor. It should be designed in a way that can entice the users and motivate them to revisit the website. The other factors such as surrounding area, focal area of user interest, external areas and other factors such as infrastructure are elements necessary for appropriate illustration—a broadcasting environment.

Advertising Consequence

Advertising campaigns are usually launched in order to achieve a distinctive set of goals. These goals are developed by the organization or a third party tasked with that duty. The organization undertakes an advertising campaign with different goals, but all of those goals are aimed at trying to effect basic responses. Organizations' reasons for designing and publishing vary and usually are designated to reach the following goals:

- The advertising should inform the whole or part of the target market about the organizations' products (Keller, 2001).
- Advertising is sometimes geared toward changing the customer's attitude toward the organization (Petty & Caccioppo, 1984).
- Advertising can cause people to avoid things which are harmful to their health.
- Finally, advertising can be used to encourage and persuade the customer to buy the products (Richards & Curran, 2002).

For profit-motivated companies, increasing sales and revenue is the primary goal. However, these companies should be reminded that there is a crucial objective for any transaction—attracting and captivating the audiences' attention. From a communication point of view, a company must first persuade its target customers in order to be able to create a new attitude in their minds. After that, the company should expand their communications and deliver the right message to the potential customer. Essentially, developing a long-term relationship with the customer is the first stage of any promotional campaign.

Core Concepts and Function of Advertising

Like any other phenomenon, advertising has a core set of concepts. Scientific research on advertising was initiated in the late 1900s and was mostly focused on personal selling. The first advertising model is AIDA (Attention, Interest, Desire, Action), which mainly concentrated on personal selling. E. St. Elmo Lewis was the first author who published a book about advertising in 1908. In his book, Lewis states that "Advertising should attract the attention, activate the interests, and create desire in the users" (Coolsen, 1947). To identify and understand advertising concepts and their functions better than in the past, Vakratsas and Ambler (1999) introduced a model, the major concepts of which begin with advertising input including message content, media scheduling and frequency of exposure. In the next step, the customer filters the message by using different tools. In this step, there are three elements that reveal the consumer's previous attitude toward a company's ads in comparison to other advertising. The final step is consumer behavior, which is one of the critical concepts in advertising and will be discussed in detail in Chapter 7. The concepts mentioned in this model are part of the most important advertising construct and are scrutinized by scholars in various ways (see Figure 3).

In comparison to conventional advertising, the online advertising mechanism is somewhat different. As Figure 4 illustrates, advertising input consists of ad format and online media. In this step, in order for a message to grab a customer's attention, it needs to have a unique format and an appropriate host. Advertising, as we will discuss in Chapter 4, consists of 18 formats, each of which has its own requirements. However, online media involves different kinds of sub-media, which resulted from and are available on the Web. Filters clarify the features that shape a viewpoint. When a user enters the Web with the motive of "entertainment" (Ko, et al., 2005), that indicates a behavior different from those who are online in a "searching mode" (Rogers & Thorson, 2000). The product appeal, consumer involvement and arousal are the other factors that delay or accelerate the consumer's processing of information. If

Figure 3. How online advertising works

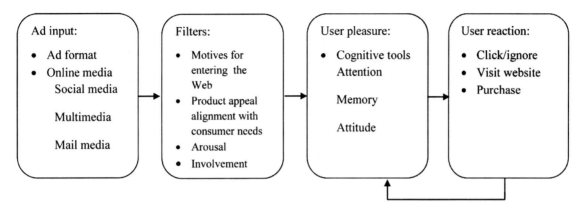

advertising can successfully navigate the filtering step, the consumer will form an opinion, usually through the use of cognitive tools. As the first tool, Attention is the degree to which an advertisement's appeal is unusual for a consumer, and will provoke a deeper reaction. As to Memory, consumers more often remember things that are aligned with their previous stereotypes or clichés. The more advertisement content is aligned with a consumer stereotype, the more reaction is expected. Attitude is the critical antecedent of user reaction, specifically in making a purchase on the Web; consumers will not trust a website (Heidarzadeh, Behboudi, & Sadr, 2011) or buy (Ko, et al., 2005) from a website until they develop an appropriate attitude toward the brand and the website itself. In the online world, the answer as to how advertising works involves clear and sensitive tracing and targeting which we will discuss in detail.

Internet Advertising and Its Position in Marketing

Marketing communication is the fourth P of the marketing mix, with the purpose of establishing a relationship between a company and its target markets. Marketing communication can be described as representing "the voice of a brand and the means by which companies can establish a dialogue with consumers concerning their product offerings" (Keller, 2001, p. 823). Although the reasons why firms communicate to their markets differ, the purpose is often to bring to customers' attention information regarding new goods and services, to change attitudes toward a product or to remind consumers about products (Keller, 2001). The companies' communication actions can moreover be part of an information exchange between firm and buyer with the intention to preserve and develop customer relationships (Reid, Luxton, & Mavondo, 2005). Regardless of the purpose, communication can be defined as a crucial and integral part of the marketing function and is carried out by employees and functions within the organization or together with external organizations specialized in the area of communication.

INTERNET AND PROMOTION MIX

Promotion mix is a determinant tool, which identifies core promotion strategies in order to communicate with and deliver messages to a target market. Promotion is responsible for matching product performance with customer expectations. It must announce, protect and publicize a brand's attributes in the marketplace. The promotion mix

Figure 4. Web advertising as a sub-function of marketing communication and advertising

is traditionally perceived as consisting of five elements: *advertising, sales promotion, public relations, direct marketing and personal selling.* When it comes to the Web, however, the elements of the promotion mix have changed a little.

Advertising Mix

Promoting and keeping a company's brand image with the purpose of increasing market share is the first goal of advertising. Different market segments present a variety of desired results for the advertisement. For example, when a company introduces an unfamiliar brand into a market where there are several familiar brands, it is difficult for the new brand to be heard. Giving that new brand a voice is the function of advertising.

Advertising, as the first element of the promotion mix, calls for stating an existence announcement. In the case of a new product, repetitive broadcasting of a brand name in the market encourages the customer to make an experimental purchase. Advertising also plays a new role of confirming and protecting the market leader and so must constantly remind customers why its products have a larger share of the market. Advertising should also be able to show the perceived

value of the previous customers from the use of familiar product.

How will advertising be able to perform this function on the Web? And what kind of efforts can advertising make to increase the impact factor of an unfamiliar brand?

The online environment has some requirements which cannot be ignored: a two-way communication channel, increasing reach for accurate information, price filtering, new shopping technologies, frequency of selling channels, increasing number of intangible products and customer's price-sensitivity. If we are to understand these requirements, we must acknowledge that virtually every environment, product and process causes these differences. In this case, the thing that should be considered more than anything else is advertising's new role.

Various advertising strategies should be employed to maintain the target audiences in an online, sensitive environment. A lowest-price strategy can best be applied for products which aim at the segment of sensitive users. For this strategy, advertisers should put their banners or pop-ups in high traffic online gateways in order to attract users. Also, they should provide intelligent agent and search facilities in order to ensure that their users are able to buy at the lowest price.

When the customer is more sensitive to quality than price, existing brands can utilize a confidence-making strategy. Advertising has to create a positive attitude toward the unknown brands in the user's mind. Since decision-making for Internet shopping is beyond a zero-one pattern, Internet advertising should be directed mostly to a personalizing or customizing orientation. This means that the ads should constantly link to the company's server and recognize previous customers, and align with former leads to provide favorite subjects. In other words, the ads should be customized and published to each individual customer.

In the case of known brands, the ad function is far easier, because the customer can distinguish these ads easily among other brands and quickly understand the message. However, the Internet can also be an appropriate channel for these types of ads *(see Chapter 4)*. Designing and administrating advertising and relevant strategies, and choosing the best form of ad for each strategy represent the most important chapters in this book.

Sales Promotion

Sales promotion is defined as short-term incentives, which are used to persuade customers, including contests and loyalty clubs, and also permitting access to free information and products like software and other digital items that can attract and increase the number of users (Thomson, 1996). For examples (see *newsnet5.com* or *clevelandmetroparkszoo2009*).

It is known that advertising plays a protective role for a brand and tries to increase the brand's market share. While sales promotion attempts to destroy the competitor's brand and decrease their sales by offering new incentives at the point of purchase. A customer on a website looks for the brands which are most compatible with their past experience. Companies can motivate customers via promotional tools presented directly in line with server leads in their search or surf areas.

Providing unique opportunities for their own product or service, such as offering a coupon on the website, can change the user's intentions. However, there are some difficulties.

Although advertising is an important industry on the Internet, it seems that sales promotion has been less successful. The main reason may be the digital nature of the Internet, since advertising is an informational channel which is trying to broadcast a series of informational messages. Coupons, for example, as one of the important elements of sales promotion, has an exchange value and is used to draw a part of the target audience's attention, but the digital nature of the environment causes more coupons to be dispensed. In that case, sales promotion not only fails to leverage more sales, but also cannot fulfill customers' wants by way of the free coupons and may actually decrease sales. According to some studies, certain software may be an appropriate solution *(see Kumer [1998] for more details)*.

Personal Selling

Online advertising returns to the oldest form of commerce: buying and selling in the context of inter-personal relationships. The interactive process enables the marketer to offer customized service. Customers can e-mail questions regarding their informational search in the desire stage, or even take action by placing the order (Thomson, 1996). Online ads and online selling has demolished the intermediates in offline businesses *(see dell. com)*. In the offline environment, personal selling requires a seller and buyer in a specific place to discuss a specific purpose, while cyberspace has completely omitted the location element. The transaction venue has become a world in which all buyers and sellers can negotiate from opposite sides of the globe.

Personal selling is the most important advantage of Internet ads and e-business. Today, negotiation as a tool of personal selling has completely changed. Email, online negotiation, and inspiring confidence before any face-to-face sales effort are the new personal tactics that result in less time for buying/selling conversation.

Public Relations

In recent years, public relations has become a critical communicational tool which can perform numerous functions for conventional ads (Kleiner, 1989). Advertising cost in traditional media has severely gone up, resulting in fewer placements and thus less reach to target customers. Because the customer experiences increasing exposure to ad impressions, advertising efficiency has decreased, meaning the advertiser must be more inclined toward public relations techniques. Due to the role change of advertising from passive to active and the reactive element, it is expected that public relations efficiency will be more than advertising, particularly regarding classical ads (Lindic, 2006). As Kotler (2001) states about PR, "…involves a variety of programs that are designed to promote or protect a company's image or its individual products" (p. 294). PR is marketing communication function that is able to execute defined programs in order to attract customer and public views (Hollensen, 2004).

Creating long-term communication with the media and journalists is a part of the PR function which can greatly influence a company's image. Utilizing the Internet in this context can improve a company's ability to obtain more advantages such as high speech communication, immediate product delivery, interaction, high productivity, access to ideal forums and appropriate management of publications. Furthermore, the Internet has changed the information distribution channels for different publics so that practitioners can easily communicate and interact with key publics (media, journalists, customers, suppliers, employees) to solve a crisis and negotiate the handling of all subjects. To improve public relations efficiency as a sub-function of the promotion mix, organizations can utilize a variety of devices which are discussed in the following section. They are also able to use consultant organizations such as the Public Relations Society of America (*prsa.org*).

Professional Websites

Companies can broadcast their promotional information by establishing **professional websites**. One example is Cisco at www.newsroom.cisco.com. Establishing a website expertise in PR has many advantages. A website can provide the public with news, current and archived information. This might include information on a company's product or service, company structure, company administration, market share, achievements, balance sheet, history, clips and contracts. It also enables the public relations department to receive comments, alerts and news from external sources regarding the company's makeup. Chat rooms also help a company's public relations to be accessible 24/7. For more information (see *media. daimlerchrysler.co* or *newscenter.verizon.com*).

Blogs

The second tool that can be used in public relation and marketing management is weblogs or blogs. The only difference between a blog and a website is that weblogs are considered unofficial. This means that they don't use conventional literature in their contents, pay little attention to grammar and writing rules, and do not obey current structures. Weblogs are a good opportunity for public relations to enter a more colloquial environment to inform its publics about an organization and its products or services. This has been intensified by the emergence of a new version of blogs called cooperative blogs (Albrycht, 2004). Cooperative weblogs are widely employed; in fact, according to a study by *PRWEEK.com* in 2005, more than seven percent of CEOs have their own blogs. This statistic has escalated after a change in the form of information gathering among journalists, since the new procedure revealed that journalists get their information mostly from blogs (RSCG Magnet, 2005) as they trust the individual bloggers more than an organization's PR staff. Weblogs are also a powerful device for harmonizing inter-organizational advertising strategies. Outstanding companies which host a great number of branches throughout the world can utilize weblogs to integrate dissemination strategies. As a free device, weblogs can help the PR staff to receive and publish the company's advertising purposes online on a daily basis. Some benefits provided by weblogs are receiving information about product defects, answering customer questions, which helps to decrease product failures, creating a place for sharing ideas and creating a professional weblog for each public. For instance, Nokia undertook this method for N90. After great success, it is going to use it for its other products like N71, N91 and N97 *(See thenokiablog.com.).*

Other Methods

There are other methods by which PR departments can distribute their publicity messages. One of them is an RRS feed or "Really simple syndication." RSS is a member of web feeds and is used to update areas like news titles, blogs and audio. The other device used by PR departments is podcast. Just like RRSs, podcasts allow subscribers to get their favorite feeds from a PR website. The main difference between podcasts and audio and video is not in their content but in their delivery form. Using podcasts, the CEOs can establish a relationship with other PR professionals. Providing a podcast in meetings relevant to decisions made by the company and giving it to other publics can be a remarkable asset for informational subjects. Through developments in the Internet and public relations methods, companies can fulfill their technical and strategic needs. *Instituforpr.org* is one organization which provides various strategies on the Internet.

Although the main players in the industry have changed and now focus more on new media, public relations manpower should not be neglected. Scrutinizing all websites, uploading files, analyzing environmental events, integrating and distributing timely publications in harmony with the organization, on-time lobbying, and a few other measures are undertaken by the PR staff. They constantly consider and scrutinize competitors, deal with statistical organizations like *Nilesen.com*, challenge journalists and provide reports to be broadcasted from one of these media. In short, a PR staff is an extremely important part of an organization's overall marketing effort.

WEB: THE NEW ADVERTISING CHANNEL

When the Internet and the World Wide Web are studied from a marketing communication point of view, we realize that together they have become a media channel, one that can be used to introduce a product and transfer the message to consumers. TV, radio and print media are among other media channels used for marketing purposes. As shown in Figure 5, media frequently used for marketing are combined with the Internet and vice versa.

The following model shows that Internet is now considered as a main media channel. While the Web is just a simple Internet service, it can be utilized to communicate with customers and convey messages. For example, advertising can be done via e-mail or instantly in a separate media. It can be placed into different categories based on function. Other services also are available on the Internet, such as Internet messaging (software for online chatting) and WAP (a protocol for wireless applications and newsgroups). Popular websites that can be placed in these models are Google (a search engine), Disney.com (an entertainment website), the *New York Post* (an online newspaper), Gmail.com (an E-mail service provider), and Altavista.com.

The impact of dissimilar media contexts on advertising effectiveness has been studied in TV

Figure 5. Media channels and the new digital media

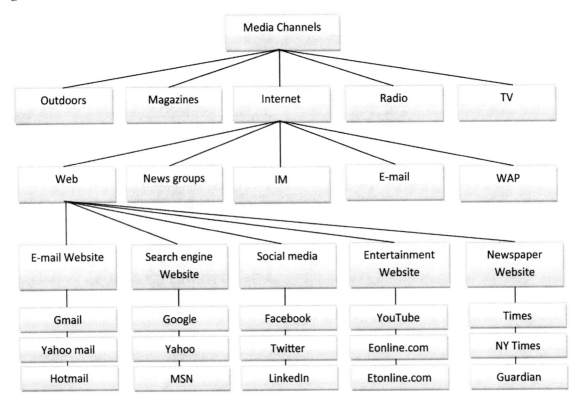

and print. The context in which an advertiser could put the ad or commercial was considered as effective in advertising (De Pelsmacker, Geuens, & Anckaert, 2002). According to studies, the inter-relationship of advertising and media and its relevant factor is obvious. Studies tried to choose the media factors which mostly effect recognition and recall. As Nowland et al. (1962) and Politz (1962) showed, different media channels can have the same effect on the target group, even with the same form of advertising. Since all media channels share the same amount of effect, it is important to select the one which can best affect the audience. Other researchers (Harmon & Coney, 1982; Sternthal, Dholakia, & Leavitt, 1978; Sternthal, Phillips, & Dholakia, 1978) have proved that besides the source of exposure, the ad content and message are also important.

When comparing different forms of advertising, interesting results are found. For example, TV commercials are displayed in a sequence-like form. When a commercial is aired, the commercial break interrupts a program's content. In radio, we face the same result where commercials come in serial form. However, when it comes to the Internet, great changes happen. In Internet advertising, advertisements are displayed parallel the website content.

Why We Use Internet Advertising

The most important merit of online advertising is interactivity. This allows the user to click on an ad and enter the website. That is a direct way of gathering more information about the consumer, and that is a considerable point because advertising on the Internet is the only media that facilitates this advantage. Some advantages of online advertising include:

- **Migrating Audience to the Internet:** The UCLA Center for Communication Policy (2004) found that Internet users are spending time online that they previously spent viewing television. Turban et al, 2006, agreed that worldwide, Internet users are spending significantly less time watching television and more time using the Internet at home Since access to the Internet is allowed via high bandwidth, and occupations are rapidly changing to the online world, it is believable that people spend more time on the Internet than watching TV.
- **Appropriate user:** It is a reality that the majority of Internet users have a comfortable income and are highly educated, which makes them a proper segment for online marketing.
- **Measurability:** When an advertiser calls a traditional media source for information, he cannot estimate properly that how many audiences will see his message. With Web advertising, the number of users and each user's time spent viewing the message is fully registered.
- **Personalization:** The Internet is capable of personalizing any audience and company's interests for delivering a customized service. While gathering these leads, Web advertising will broadcast according to any IP connection, as discussed in Chapter 4.
- **High exposure potential:** Internet advertising can easily be published together with text, image, sound, animation and video clips. Moreover, online games and entertainment can also be included.
- **Low cost:** Designing, creating, revising and publishing Internet advertising is inexpensive compared to conventional offline advertising.
- **Updating:** Revisions and modifications in online advertising can be performed in a short time.
- **Unlimited access:** Since Internet advertising is broadcasted from different Internet channels such as wireless connections and GPS, it can be seen from the anywhere—work, cinema, sports stadium—anywhere! There are also other advantages of Internet advertising, some of which are shown in Table 1.

INTERNET ADVERTISING REVENUE

According to IAB (2011), "Internet advertising revenues in the U.S. hit $7.3 billion for the first quarter of 2011, representing a 23 percent increase over the same period in 2010." Internet advertising revenues up to 2010 show a constant growth except during 2008 (probably due to the recession). Randall Rothenberg, President and CEO of the IAB, believes: "The consistent and considerable year-over-year growth we're seeing demonstrates that digital media is an increasingly popular destination for ad dollars, and for good reason. As Americans spend more time online for information and entertainment purposes, digital advertising and marketing has emerged as one of the most effective tools businesses have to attract and retain customers." According to studies, the biggest proportion of the revenue belongs to these types of companies and websites:

- Online retail 25%
- Financial services 15%
- Computing 11%
- Automotive 12%
- Telecommunications 8%
- Leisure travel 7%
- Media 6%

Table 1. Comparison of different advantages in different media (Barker & Gronne, 1996)

Measuring	Cost	Information Capacity	Feedback	Targeting	Reach	
Low	High	Medium	Low	Medium	High	**Newspapers**
Medium	High	Medium	Low	High	Medium	**Magazines**
Low	Low	Very low	Very low	Low	High	**Radio**
Low	High	Low	Very low	Low	Very high	**TV**
High	Low	High	Medium	Very high	Low	**Direct Mail**
Very high	Low	Very high	Very high	High	Low	**Online Ads**

- Consumer packaged goods 4%
- Entertainment 5%
- Pharmacy and health care 4%

Internet advertising formats will be discussed in Chapter 4. However, it is important to know how much each format has contributed to Internet advertising revenue. According to IAB (2008), each format's contribution is as follows (and see Figure 6):

- Lead generation 7%
- Classifieds 13%
- Rich media 7%
- Search engines 46%
- E-mail advertising 1%
- Sponsorship 3%
- Display Advertising 21%
- Digital video 3%

One factor that emphasizes the importance of Internet advertising is its quick growth. As shown in Table 2, internet advertising revenue strongly implies that a new advertising channel is flourishing, introducing products and services to customers. The channels and new methods of this media leave a substantial impact on other variables and factors in the market, which are discussed in detail in the following chapters. An appreciable point about revenue derived from advertising and Internet advertising is that, according to *zenithoptimedia.com* (2011), Internet advertising revenue

and the cost of advertising at the end of 2009 reached 54,230 billion dollars. On the other hand, magazine advertising had revenue of 43,856 billion dollars in 2009. That quick trend indicates that Internet advertising left its traditional competitors (radio, magazine, outdoor) behind in 2009. In addition, forecasting is showing that Internet advertising expenditures will catch on with newspapers by 2012 *(See Table 3)*.

COMMUNICATION

Communication allows senders and receivers to talk, transfer a message, exchange information, and interact. The purpose of stating communication patterns is that advertisements require distribution channels and competitive strategies in order to be introduced to prospects. Here we will introduce some communications patterns of the Internet and traditional media which are used to publish advertisements.

One-to-Many Communication

The pattern used by mass traditional advertising is one-to-many. This pattern is usually utilized by radio, TV and magazines. In this pattern, the sender delivers a message to a massive number of receivers through a designated medium. The one-to-many pattern is also called a passive one-to-many pattern (Figure 7). Through this pattern,

Figure 6. Internet advertising revenue (iab.net, 2011)

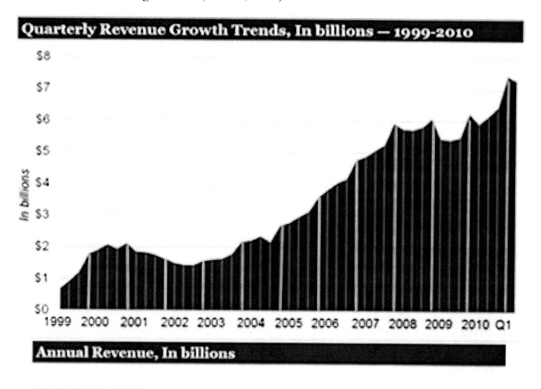

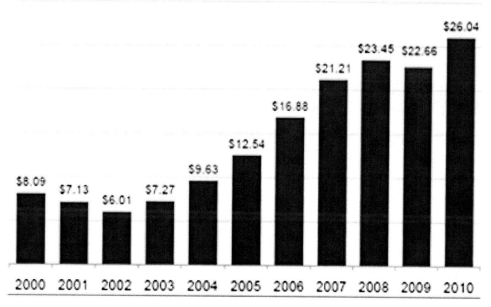

Table 2. Advertising expenditure by medium (zenithoptimedia.com, 2011)

US$ million	2009	2010	2011	2012	2013
Newspapers	97421	95235	93442	92552	**92133**
Magazines	**43856**	43622	42766	42502	42341
Television	165502	180315	189630	202154	214390
Radio	31672	31995	32528	33615	34756
Cinema	2091	2308	2451	2606	2764
Outdoor	28184	29456	31274	33413	35058
Internet	**54230**	63049	72174	82915	**94981**
Total	**422956**	**445980**	**464264**	**489756**	**516422**

the advertiser delivers his advertising message to one or more mass media which in turn displays the ad at different intervals to the receivers. In this way, advertisements are exposed to the customers.

Interpersonal Communication

With the emergence of the Internet, traditional communication patterns changed. The Internet is a hypermedia which allows advertisers to get a direct response from customers. The Internet also has formulated a new context in which users are able to create one-to-one communication with a website, expressing their real needs. Through the use of this model, advertisers can directly interact with their customers and learn about their needs. Interaction can be defined in many ways. The first definition was proposed by Barker and Gurron in 1996. They stated that when person A receives

a message from person B and in return sends a message back to person B, that constitutes feedback. If the exchange continues, it can be said that person A and person B are "interacting" (Figure 8). The major differentiation and main feature in interpersonal interactions, especially on the Internet, is that it has the capability of fostering a conference-based method which other media lack.

Computer Media-Based Communication

In Internet communication, there is the possibility to make many-to-many communication facilitated by chat rooms, online communities and forums. In this model, there are some message senders and some receivers. In interpersonal communication, personal interaction is distributed through the medium; however, in machine interactivity, the

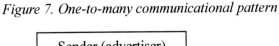

Figure 7. One-to-many communicational pattern

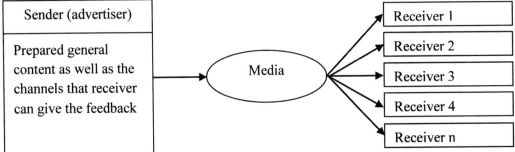

Figure 8. Interpersonal relationships

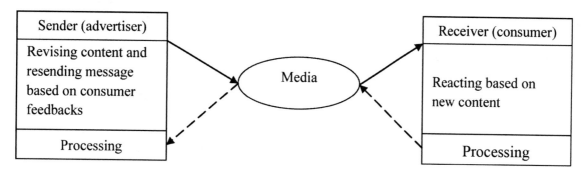

interaction can also be with the medium (Thomson, 1996). Interaction with the medium is a unique feature which permits advertisers to increase interactivity. In addition, the people involved can communicate with others through the website (Figure 9). Worldwide access is another advantage of this model. In fact, an advertiser can send his message to anyone and receive feedback.

There are three kinds of message sending in computer media-basal communication: shared content, research-based content and personalized content. In shared content, marketers put a highly popular message on websites like Facebook and Twitter in order to use a viral advertising philosophy to get more exposure. In pursuit of this goal, social networks such as Facebook let marketers have an exclusive place for sending their content. Research-based content includes all SEO and SEM activities, which are designed to lure more users to a website. In research-based content, we can find a highlighted role for suppliers for facilitating the communication process. As we will discuss in Chapter 12, by tracing and monitoring the actions and reactions of both parties, suppliers are trying to unsought noise. As we know from the nature of the Internet, user and marketer identities and specifically their behavior are not clear to each other; hence, it is natural for both parties to have unsought noise in the interaction process. Through **personalized content**,

Figure 9. Interactive pattern

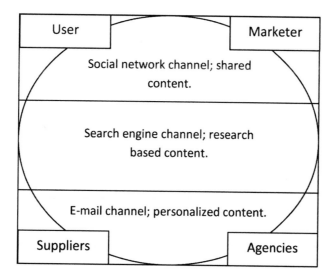

marketer and user send and receive content over an exclusive channel. However, to make this easier, marketers usually try to use segmentation in order to send their message to targeted groups of consumers.

SELECTING THE RIGHT WEBSITE FOR PLACING AN ADVERTISEMENT

One of the most important discussions in publishing ads on the Internet is the selection of an appropriate website. With so many websites available, care must be taken in selecting the most appropriate one. Considering the fact that the Internet is accessible all over the world, most marketers choose this media for publishing their ads and devote a significant portion of their budget to advertising in this medium. Regarding this situation, the need for using the Internet for publishing ads has increased and resulted in the change of the Internet advertising market from a one-way market, in which only a website was present as the provider, to a competitive market involving all providers and demanders. When the company decides to publish its advertisement and introduce its products and services via the Internet, one of the important requirements is selecting an appropriate website. Numerous websites can be considered for hosting websites by the advertisers. Each of these choices has unique characteristics which distinguish them from other websites.

As of 2006, the number of registered websites was more than 65.4 million domain names, including .com, .org, .gov, and .edu addresses (Zooknic Internet Intelligence, 2006). Considering the potential capacity identified on the Web, the number of businesses and organizations that accept a website as an important communication and dissemination channel has grown (Chen, Rodgers, & He, 2008).

According to IAB report (2008), display ads make up more than 24% of Internet advertisements. They are forms of advertising which need space on the host websites in order to be published (IAB, 2008). The point to be considered is what conditions the host website must have in order to be selected as the most appropriate website for publishing advertisements. Thus, identification and selection of an appropriate host is an issue which needs an efficient method of differentiation.

Nagi (2003) conducted a study concerning the selection of an appropriate website for positioning advertisements. In this study, Nagi, using the Analytical Hierarchy Process (AHP), offered the most appropriate website for publishing an advertisement in Hong Kong. Nagi identified five criteria for evaluation:

- Impression rate: how much the web page is seen by the user.
- Renting cost: monthly rent or every one thousand times of ad display on a website.
- Audience fit: compatibility of the age and education level of the user with the website content.
- Content quality: content which is published.
- Look and feel: elements designed and created on the website (Nagi, 2003).

Other variables also contribute to the selection of the right website. Having introduced the new concept of electronic satisfaction, we now discuss the model of selecting an appropriate website.

Electronic Satisfaction

While the subject of satisfaction has been discussed extensively in services and traditional retailing literature (Oliver, 1981; Parasuraman, Zeithaml, & Berry, 1988; Anderson, Fornell, & Lehmann, 1994), the exploration of dimensions and determinations of satisfaction within the e-commerce context is at a relatively early stage.

The success and failure of online sites depend on how well customers are satisfied (Chen, Rogers, & He, 2008), particularly in the online environments that present different experiences than offline ones (Wolfinbarger & Gilly, 2003). Wang et al. (2001) and Wang and Tang (2004) identify seven dimensions in their CIS instrument, including customer support, security and ease of use, which emphasize a cognitive rather than affective experience.

Many definitions exist of electronic satisfaction. Oliver (1997) defines satisfaction as "the overall subsequent psychological state following the appraisal of the consumer experience against the prior expectations." Anderson and Srinvasan (2003) suggest a definition of e-satisfaction as "the contentment of the customer with respect to his or her prior purchasing experience with a given electronic commerce firm." High customer satisfaction causes a customer to return to the website (Chen, Rogers, & He, 2008). Here, satisfaction is defined as any positive psychological state which results in the user's return to the website. This positive psychological state is directly related to the factors mentioned in the following core variables. However, there are also differences between satisfaction in traditional media and e-satisfaction. One of the most important differences is the replacement of human-to-human interaction with human-to-machine interaction. In this regard, researchers believe that there may be a need for new or modified approaches to conceptualizing and measuring e-satisfaction (Evanschitzky, et al., 2004).

In order to define customer satisfaction with a website, it is important to define satisfaction accurately so that the most compatible website can be identified from the perspective of satisfaction. For this purpose, more features have been investigated, revealing that electronic satisfaction has been formed by three main features.

Quality of Electronic Services

Quality of electronic services shows the degree to which a website can efficiently provide possibilities for buying, selling and delivering goods and services. E-SERVQUAL involves three concepts:

1. **WebQual**: Popular index calculated on the basis of user perceptions on dimensions of usability, information quality and service interaction quality; it has evolved via a process of iterative refinement (Barnes & Vidgen, 2000, 2003). The higher the quality of services offered, the higher the level of satisfaction.

2. **SoftQual**: The next element is **SoftQual**, which involves user satisfaction of e-commerce software and hardware such as download time, navigation, content, the amount of interaction and answerability designed in the website (Palmer, 2002).

3. **InfoQual**: The final element is **InfoQual**, which is the kind of electronic services offered by the website.

These services can be categorized into two categories of specialized and general services. *General services* include any kind of daily information that a website offers for increasing the general information of its users, such as news and weather reports. *Specialized* information services can include offering the results of new research related to a website.

In addition, online shopping allows methods of information gathering that are different from those of the traditional shopping experience, raising questions about user satisfaction with the Information Quality (IQ) and Software Quality (SQ) of EC applications resulting in discrepancies between prior expectations and perceived performance. In stock trading sites, other design principles such as convenience, reliability and technological advances have all been found to affect the level of user satisfaction and loyalty (Zviran, Glezer, & Avni, 2006). For EC there is no way of directly measuring the success of an application (Galletta & Lederer, 1989).

User-Oriented Design

User-oriented design has been identified as another influential factor in increasing costumer e-satisfaction (Zviran, Glezer, & Avni, 2006). This factor has been investigated by many researchers, and various reports have been published. User-oriented design or website usability includes the following points: structure, navigation, alignment, performance, categorization, searchability, online shopping, registration, and retailing.

According to a study conducted by Hise and Szymanski (2000), an appropriate website designed according to user needs and wants must consider three characteristics: preparing orderly and integrated home pages, designing easy search paths and providing high-speed display (Szymanski & Hise, 2000, p. 316). This categorization has been confirmed and assigned with other names by other researchers. For instance, Ranganathan and Ganapathy (2000) refer to these factors as facility of guiding, navigation time and display elements (Ranganathan & Ganapathy, 2002, p. 463).

Appropriate design of a website is more a qualitative influential factor. This means that the customer's first impression of the website is formed based on design. The more the design of a website coincides with the needs, interests and expectations of the target consumers, the more it will provide satisfaction for them. Higher satisfaction results in the presence of more users at the website which is a good opportunity for advertisers to use this high-traffic place.

Customer Interaction with the Website

The third factor increasing e-satisfaction is interactivity. The Internet, in comparison to other media, requires a higher level of interaction with its users (Ruggiero & Thomas, 2000). Since mutual activities or interaction is one of the distinctive features of the new media, the presence of such possibilities allows users to efficiently participate in the process of encouragement through control and supervision of advertisements, receiving required information and personal preferences (Hoffman & Novak, 1995). Interaction on a website is divided into six groups: 1) Complexity of selection; 2) Level of effort; 3) Answerability of media; 4) Ability for controlling media; 5) Ability for adding information; 6) Capability of interpersonal communication (Heeter, 1989).

Interactive systems can help consumers to process information, as they are able to easily reduce or eliminate unwanted or superfluous information and can organize that information in such a way that facilitates the process (Widing & Talarzyk, 1993). Consequently, the degree to which a website increases the possibility for interaction of consumers with the Web and each other directly increases the time a consumer stays at the website which is an indicator of e-satisfaction. Also, this satisfaction creates a positive attitude toward other variables of the Web. Therefore, this kind of website offers two unique features to the advertisers: first, advertising space with a high rate of traffic, and second, potential customers with a positive attitude.

Type of Business Model

Business models and their relationship with advertisements are comprehensively studied in Chapter 9, and a new categorization of various business models has been provided. However, in order to investigate and select an appropriate website for placing an ad, the Rappa model offered in 2005 is considered here. Generally, there are nine types of electronic business models according to this study which include *Brokerage, Advertising, Infomediary, Merchant, Manufacturer, Affiliate, Community, Subscription,* and *Utility*.

Figure 10. Right website model (RWM)

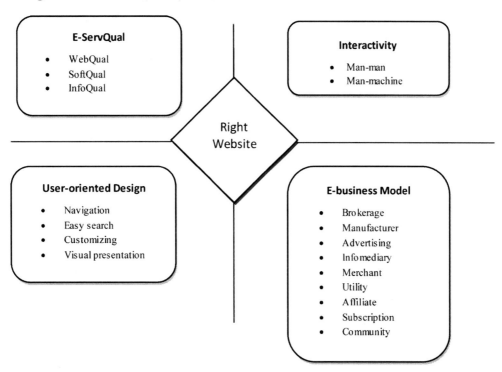

Right Website Selecting Model (RWSM)

As is indicated in Figure 10, there are generally four main features. The three features of E-ServQual, interactivity and user-oriented design are related to e-satisfaction and are from the perspective of the advanced user. The higher the quality of these features, the more satisfied is the audience on the website. For example, if the website has designed a forum or community, this will result in an increase of interaction on the website and the time an ad is displayed. Furthermore, appropriate adoption of these features will increase the intensity of the need for recheck which was discussed in a previous chapter. Thus, when an ad is seen for the first time (reach), the number of its displays increases (frequency) due to users' interest in returning to the website. In this way, the brand advertised on the website is seen by the users to the extent that they will remember the given brand compared to other brands.

The fourth feature, type of business model, is an independent feature and is more from the perspective of an advanced advertiser. The more the business model of a website is related to the type of advertised product or service, the more appropriate it will be. When the business model of a website is in line with the business model of the advertised product or service, the primary intention of the user to enter the website will be in line with the motive of designing the ads. Therefore, the kind of attraction represented in the ad will be the same as the motive that the website uses as the biggest advertisement format. A unique and specialized user will be exposed to the ad rather than any user with any kind of primary intention to enter into the website.

On the other hand, assume, for example, that a website has an advertisement business model. In this case, it not only accepts the ad, but also tries its best to increase the traffic of the website because it will raise more revenue by attracting more advertisements.

CONCLUSION

This chapter focused on Internet advertising, investigating the Internet and its history. The origin and history of online advertising was addressed, and some definitions were provided by researchers, and the position of Internet advertisement in marketing was presented. Also, the concept of pulling customers to the Web was explained. After that, the concept of the Promotion mix was discussed, and since the Internet has been added to information channels, four elements of this combination were defined in accordance with the nature of media. In the section related to advertisements as the first mixed element of promotion, the approaches considered by less familiar brands were discussed. In the section of Sales Promotion, it was noted that the main responsibility of sales promotion is to destroy competing brands, unlike advertisements which are responsible for supporting and enhancing the brand. The role of personal selling as the most important advantage of Internet advertising was emphasized, and online negotiation was explained as one of the new advantages of this media by reducing decision-making time. Then, the last mixed concept of promotion, public relation, was discussed, and the main determinants of this part of the Internet were revealed.

In addition, the major advantages of Internet advertising were mentioned. A comprehensive set of statistics regarding Internet advertising revenue was presented. Then, the reasons for utilizing Internet advertising were discussed. Next, the concept of communication and communication patterns—one-to-one, many-to-many and the interactive pattern—were discussed. Finally, a right website selection model was presented with the introduction of the concept of electronic satisfaction. Based on this model, an advertiser is able to identify the most appropriate website for placing an Internet advertisement.

REFERENCES

Alvin, J. S. (2001). The emerging position of the internet as an advertising mediumcrowdfunding In *Netnomics* (pp. 129–148). Dordrecht, The Netherlands: Kluwer Academic Publishers.

Anderson, R. E., & Srinivasan, S. S. (2003). E-satisfaction and e-loyalty: A contingency framework. *Psychology and Marketing, 20*, 123–138. doi:10.1002/mar.10063

Barker & Gronne. (1996). *Advertising on the world wide web*. Thesis. Copenhagen, Denmark: Copenhagen Business School.

Barnes, S. J., & Vidgen, R. T. (2003). Measuring web site quality improvements: A case study of the forum on strategic management knowledge exchange. *Industrial Management & Data Systems, 103*(5), 297–309. doi:10.1108/02635570310477352

Belk, R. W. (1975). Situational variables and consumer behavior. *The Journal of Consumer Research, 2*, 157–160. doi:10.1086/208627

Berthon, P., Pitt, L. F., & Watson, R. T. (1996). The world wide web as an advertising medium: Toward an understanding of conversion efficiency. *Journal of Advertising Research, 36*(1), 43–54.

Chen, Q., Rodgers, S., & He, Y. (2008). A critical review of the e-satisfaction literature. *The American Behavioral Scientist, 52*(1), 38–59. doi:10.1177/0002764208321340

Coolsen, F. G. (1947). Pioneers in the development of advertising. *Journal of Marketing, 12*(1), 80–86. doi:10.2307/1246303

Darroch, J., Miles, M. P., Andrew, J., & Cook, E. F. (2004). The 2004 AMA definition of marketing and its relationship to a market orientation: An extension of Cooke, Rayburn & Abercrombie. *Journal of Marketing Theory & Practice, 12*(4), 29–38.

Dibb, S., & Simkin, L. (1991). Targeting, segments and positioning. *International Journal of Retail and Distribution Management, 19*(3), 4–10.

Dréze, Z. (1997). Testing web site design and promotional content. *Journal of Advertising Research*, 77–91.

Duncan, T., & Moriarty, S. E. (1998). A communication-based marketing model for managing relationships. *Journal of Marketing, 62*(2), 1–13. doi:10.2307/1252157

Dyer, G. (1982). *Advertising as communication*. London, UK: Routledge. doi:10.4324/9780203328132

Evanschitzky, H., Hyer, G. R., Hesse, J., & Ahlert, D. (2004). E-satisfaction: A re-examination. *Journal of Retailing, 80*, 239–247. doi:10.1016/j.jretai.2004.08.002

Galletta, D. F., & Lederer, A. L. (1989). Some cautions on the measurement of user information satisfaction. *Decision Sciences, 20*, 419–438. doi:10.1111/j.1540-5915.1989.tb01558.x

Harmon, R. R., & Coney, K. A. (1982). The persuasive effects of source credibility in buy and lease situations. *JMR, Journal of Marketing Research, 19*(2), 255–260. doi:10.2307/3151625

Harvey, M. G., Lusch, R. F., & Cavarkapa, B. (1996). A marketing mix for the 21st century. *Journal of Marketing Theory & Practice, 4*(4), 1–15.

Heeter, C. (1989). Implications of new interactive technologies for conceptualizing communication-crowdfunding In Salvaggio, J., & Bryant, J. (Eds.), *Media Use in the Information Age* (pp. 217–235). Hillsdale, NJ: Erlbaum.

Hoffman, D. L., & Novak, T. P. (1996). Marketing in hypermedia computer-mediated environments: Conceptual foundation. *Journal of Marketing, 60*(3), 50–68. doi:10.2307/1251841

Hoffmann, D., & Novak, T. (1995). *Project 2000: Research program on marketing in computer-mediated interactive advertising bureau: IAB internet advertising revenue reported, 2007.* Retrieved from http://www.iab.net.

IAB. (2009). *Internet advertising revenue report, 2008 full-year results March 2009.* Retrieved from http://www.iab.net.

Keller, K. L. (2001). Mastering the marketing communications mix: Micro and macro perspectives on integrated marketing communication programme. *Journal of Marketing Management, 17*, 819–847. doi:10.1362/026725701323366836

Lee, J. W., & Lee, J. K. (2006). Online advertising by the comparison challenge approach. *Electronic Commerce Research and Applications, 5*, 282–294. doi:10.1016/j.elerap.2006.05.002

Lutz, R. J., & Kakkar, P. K. (1933). In Murchison, C. C. (Ed.), *The psychological situation as a determinant* (2nd ed., pp. 94–127). Handbook of Child Psychology Worcester, MA: Clark University Press.

McInnis, D. J. (2005). Marketing renaissance: Opportunities and imperatives for improving marketing thought, practice, and infrastructure. *Journal of Marketing, 69*, 14–16.

Meeker, N. (1997). *The internet advertising report.* New York, NY: Morgan Stanly Corporation.

Morris, J. D., & Moo, W. C. (2003). Internet measures of advertising effects: A global issue. *Journal of Current Issues and Research in Advertising, 25*(1), 25–43.

Ngai, E. W. T. (2003). Selection of the best web site for online advertising using the AHP. *Information & Management, 40*, 233–242. doi:10.1016/S0378-7206(02)00004-6

Nilsson, C. P. (2006). *Attention to advertising.* PhD Dissertation. Umeå, Sweden: Umeå University.

Nowland. (1962). *The effects of media context on advertising: A study conducted for life.* New York, NY: Nowland and Company.

Oliver, R. L. (1997). *Satisfaction: A behavioral perspective on the consumer.* New York, NY: McGraw-Hill.

Palmer, J. W. (2002). Web site usability, design, and performance metrics. *Information Systems Research, 13*(2), 151–167. doi:10.1287/isre.13.2.151.88

Papatla, P. (2001). Identifying locations for targeted advertising on the internet. *International Journal of Electronic Commerce, 5*(3), 23–44.

Parasuraman, A., Zeithaml, V. A., & Berry, L. L. (1988). SERVQUAL: A multiple-item scale for measuring customer perceptions of service quality. *Journal of Retailing, 64,* 12–40.

Parasuraman, H., Zeithaml, A., & Berry, L. L. (1988). SERVQUAL: A multiple-item scale for measuring customer perceptions of service quality. *Journal of Retailing, 64,* 12–40.

Pelsmacker, P., Geuens, M., & Anckaert, P. (2002). Media context and advertising effectiveness: The role of context appreciation and context/ad similarity. *Journal of Advertising, 31*(2), 49–61.

Politz, A. (1962). *A measure of advertising effectiveness: The influence of audience selectivity and editorial environment.* New York, NY: Alfred Politz Research, Inc.

Ranganathan, C., & Ganapathy, S. (2002). Key dimensions of business-to-consumer web sites. *Information & Management, 39,* 457–465. doi:10.1016/S0378-7206(01)00112-4

Rappa, M. (2005). Managing the digital enterprise. *North Carolina State University.* Retrieved from http://digitalenterprise.org /index.html.

Richards, J., & Curran, C. M. (2002). Oracles on advertising: Searching for a definition. *Journal of Advertising, 31*(2), 63–77.

Rogers, E. M. (1995). *Diffusion of innovations* (4th ed.). New York, NY: Free Press.

Ruggiero, T. E. (2000). Uses and gratification theory in the 21st century. *Mass Communication & Society, 3*(1), 3–37. doi:10.1207/S15327825MCS0301_02

Russell, R. J., Feuer, K. R., Meeker, M., & Mahaney, M. (2001). *Correction: Does internet advertising work? Yes, but.* New York, NY: Morgan Stanley Dean Witter.

Schramm, W. (1955). How communication workscrowdfunding In Schramm, W. (Ed.), *The Process and Effects of Mass Communications* (pp. 3–26). Urbana, IL: University of Illinois Press.

Shaw, M., Subramaniam, C., & Gardner, D. (1999). Product marketing on the internetcrowdfunding In *Handbook of Electronic Commerce.* Berlin, Germany: Springer-Verlag.

Sterne, J. (1997). *What makes people click: Advertising on the web.* Indianapolis, IN: Que Corporation.

Sternthal, B., Dholaika, R., & Leavitt, C. (1978). The persuasive effect of source credibility: A test of cognitive response analysis. *The Journal of Consumer Research, 4*(4), 252–260. doi:10.1086/208704

Sternthal, B., Phillips, L., & Dholakia, R. (1978). The persuasive effect of source credibility: A situational analysis. *Public Opinion Quarterly, 42*(3), 285–314. doi:10.1086/268454

Subramanian, C., Shaw, M. J., & Gardner, D. M. (1999). Product marketing on the internet. In M. Shaw, R. Blanning, T. Strader, & A. Whinstone (Eds.), *Handbook on Electronic Commerce.* New York, NY: Spring-Verlag.

Szymanski, D. M., & Hise, R. T. (2000). E-satisfaction: An initial examination. *Journal of Retailing, 76,* 309–322. doi:10.1016/S0022-4359(00)00035-X

Thomsen, M. D. (1996). *Advertising on the internet.* Masters Dissertation. Westminster, UK: University of Westminster.

Turban, E., King, D., Viehland, D., & Lee, J. K. (2006). *Electronic commerce: A managerial perspective.* Upper Saddle River, NJ: Prentice Hall.

Vakratsas, D., & Ambler, T. (1999). How advertising works: What do we really know? *Journal of Marketing, 63*(1), 26–43. doi:10.2307/1251999

Wang, Y., & Tang, T. (2004). A validation of the customer information satisfaction instrument for digital market context. *International Journal of Electronic Business, 2,* 567–582. doi:10.1504/IJEB.2004.006126

Wang, Y., Tang, T., & Tang, J. E. (2001). An instrument for measuring customer satisfaction toward web sites that market digital products and services. *Journal of Electronic Commerce Research, 2,* 89–102.

Widing, R. E., & Talarzyk, W. (1993). Electronic information systems for consumers: An evaluation of computer interaction – Assisted formats in multiple decision environments. *JMR, Journal of Marketing Research, 30*(2), 125–141. doi:10.2307/3172823

Xavier, D. (2003). Francois-Xavier Hussherr, internet advertising: Is anybody watching? *Journal of Interactive Marketing, 17*(4), 8–32. doi:10.1002/dir.10063

Zeithaml, V. A., Parasuraman, A., & Malhotra, A. (2000). *E-service quality: Definition, dimensions and conceptual model.* Working Paper. Cambridge, MA: Marketing Science Institute.

Zeithaml, V. A., Parasuraman, A., & Malhotra, A. (2002). Service quality delivery through web sites: A critical review of extant knowledge. *Journal of the Academy of Marketing Science, 30,* 362–375. doi:10.1177/009207002236911

Zenithoptimedia. (2009). *Internet advertising expenditure report: Press release.* Retrieved from http://zenithoptimedia.com.

Zooknic Internet Intelligence. (2006). *History of gTLD domain name growth.* Retrieved December 4, 2006, from http://zooknic.com /Domains/counts.html.

Chapter 3
Online Advertising vs. Offline Advertising

ABSTRACT

In this chapter, the authors first study the differences between traditional advertising and Internet advertising by focusing on their implicit meaning. Next, the consumer's elaboration model and consumer's involvement model that are applicable both in traditional and modern media are discussed. 28 advantages of Internet publicity are presented, and finally, the authors deal with the changes occurring in the consumer's information environment.

INTRODUCTION

Due to the increasing growth of Internet accessibility, companies are moving toward the use of this medium as an advertising environment. Since the advertising broadcasting has changed from unilaterally static to bilaterally dynamic, researchers expect to soon witness a fundamental change in the factors contributing to the efficiency of ads. Many studies have been conducted to clarify the differences between traditional and modern types of advertising. To have a better understanding of these differences, advertising methods and solutions functioning alike on the Internet and traditional media have to be identified

(Coupey, 1999); then the findings of the studies on traditional media can be applied to advertising on the Internet. However, where traditional and modern methods are shown to be different, more studies should be conducted on Internet advertising requiring new theories. From a theoretical point of view, it is vitally important to identify those methods through which the new medium has changed customers' data environment.

IMPILICIT MEANING

Advertising efforts for a brand often involve implicit concepts such as dignity and cheerfulness (Ringold, et al., 1989). These elements can

DOI: 10.4018/978-1-4666-0885-6.ch003

be visual or auditory, or the implicit meanings of words or sentences (Toncar & Munch, 2001). Audiences use such information to comprehend the message. Advertisement-evoked association and implicit meaning are mentioned by different names in research fields. For instance, when measuring the degree of influence of a particular advertisement, the ad influence over a special type of product is controlled by a descriptive checklist of implicit meanings that also checks the cognitive response (see Figure 1).

Brand image includes some associations (Keller, 1993) that cannot be conveyed explicitly through words. Moreover, the ads should be believable if they are supposed to establish a relationship with consumers. This can be fulfilled by applying implicit meanings (Dahlen, 2004).

Advertisements are full of implicit meanings (McQuarrie & Mick, 1999). According to a study conducted by Toncar and Munch (2001), implicit meanings are significantly influential when establishing relationships and creating advertisements. As far as implicit meanings are concerned, print

and Internet ads have common points. One of these points is the consumer's control over whether he pays attention to the ad or not. In printed advertisements, a consumer's control over ads is the intonation by which the message is read (Lee, 2000). In Internet advertisements, a user clicks on pages or information linked to the ad, and moves up and down on the website voluntarily. Both traditional and Internet advertisements require active participation (Dahlen, 2002), because it is the customer who decides about the length of exposure. However, the major difference between these two advertising methods is that the Internet is a live medium presenting more opportunities for interaction and more consumer motivators (Coyle & Thorson, 2001). In this way, Internet advertising is can better associate implicit meanings than traditional methods of advertising (see Figure 2).

Empirical studies revealed that communication and clicking rate increases via Internet advertising (Dahlen, 2000). Before 2000, the general belief was that the Internet is a rational medium and thus implicit concepts were not used in this me-

Figure 1. One sample of the implicit meaning in advertising

dium or in online advertisements, and most researchers suggested that Internet advertising should be used for those products that consumers were actively looking for and gathering data about (Dahlen, 2001). In that view, there was no need to apply implicit meanings in those advertisements. That is, according to these researchers, Internet advertising was suitable for accepted brands with high consumer involvement. However, the research conducted on print advertisements revealed that implicit meanings are useful when the involvement level is low (Toncar & Munch, 2001). For better identification of implicit meanings and the way they are used in Internet advertising and print advertisements, most researchers present three perspectives: product elaboration; WWW usage and advertisement processing; consumer's tendency toward the brand.

PRODUCT INVOVLEMENT

It has been reported that product involvement is a key determinant of a consumer's attitude toward an advertisement (Laurent & Kapferer, 1985). When the product has a high level of involvement and the customer is highly involved, custom-

ers will actively process the advertisement and spend more time on the ads, mainly focusing on data presented about the product. Several models have been presented to demonstrate elaboration or involvement of consumers with an advertised product or service. In this section, models related to customers and their behavior when confronted with advertising is introduced, focusing on traditional models first and then online context.

Conventional Models of Advertising

Not surprisingly, there is not just one model used by scholars that explains advertising. On the contrary, there are many such models which focus on different aspects of advertising, depending upon the author's area of interest. The advertising models have similarities and dissimilarities, and a few of these models will be considered in detail when comparing traditional and new models of advertising with respect to attention and attitude (see Figure 3).

Figure 4 illustrates a typical hierarchic model of advertising effects. The sequential process starts from the left in the model where the attributes of the advertisement are listed. Stimulation refers to the advertisement's ability to motivate the senses

Figure 2. Samples of implicit meaning in advertising

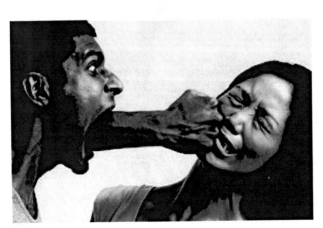 

of the consumer, including vision, hearing, or more uncommonly, smell, taste, and touch. The purpose of an advertisement is to stimulate a consumer, and that is why advertisements are sometimes referred to as stimuli. Credibility relates to how believable the message is perceived; this is subjective since different individuals will have contrasting views about whether the advertisement is credible or not. Moreover, personal relevance, preferences and familiarity are important variables that have an influence on advertising effect.

The next step in the model is attention, which is described as the amount of time devoted to the advertisement by the consumer. After that comes memory, which is a measure of how well the consumer remembers the advertisement. From an advertiser's point of view, it is naturally preferable that the target group remembers the advertisement. Attitude towards the advertising and attitude towards the brand lead to the final stage, namely, buying intention, which is the conative component where the consumer acts upon the advertisement and initiates a purchase (Nilsson, 2006) (see Figure 5).

The model provides an overview of important concepts in advertising broadcasting. When talking about advertising effects, it is often a matter of measuring the variations in these constructs and their relationship to each other. As shown in Figure 4, the model is naturally sequential, and it is thought that there is none or limited interaction or feedback between the different stages. In advertising literature, this model has been widely used (Thorson, et al., 1992). Thorson et al. (1992) found that advertisement attributes did indeed affect purchase intention, but the effects were both direct and partially mediated. However, this mediation did not flow through attention and memory to attitudinal and conative responses. Instead, some characteristics such as credibility and liking operate through attitude towards the advertisement and attitude towards the brand to buying intention. Moreover, attention affects neither buying intention nor attitude toward the advertisement. As a result, conative reactions are not driven by attention. In addition, the measure of recall was not a suitable index of persuasion (Nilson, 2006). Hence, paying attention to an advertisement makes audiences remember it better, but it has no influence on whether audiences like the advertisement or the brand. Aligned with the above-mentioned logic, Gibson (1983) criticized the use of recall measures to evaluate advertisements, saying that can have little or no correlation to consumer selections in the market. Still, none of the five advertisement characteristics drive attention or memory despite the fact that they drive attitude toward the advertisement, attitude toward the brand and buying intention.

The impact of advertisement characteristics on attitude toward the advertising and attitude toward the brand is an important, often debated

Figure 3. Sample of conventional advertisement

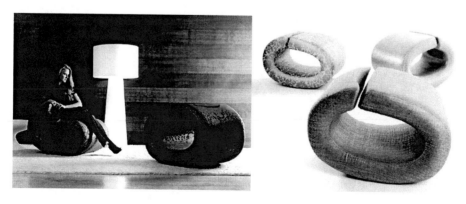

Figure 4. The classic hierarchic model of advertising effects (Thorson, Chi, & Leavitt, 1992)

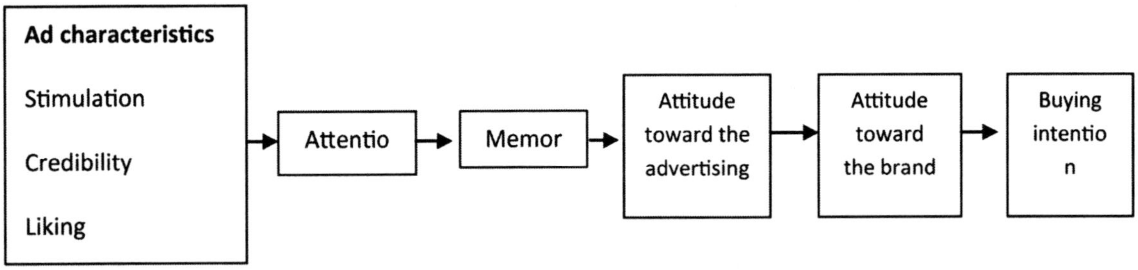

Ad characteristics					
Stimulation	Attentio	Memor	Attitude toward the advertising	Attitude toward the brand	Buying intentio n
Credibility					
Liking					

Figure 5. Sample of conventional advertisement

research discipline (Brown & Stayman, 1992), because the purpose of advertising is n to influence attitudes. In advertising fields, attitude has generally been described as a learned tendency to respond in a consistently favorable or unfavorable manner to advertising in general (Lutz, 1985). In the above-mentioned model, attitude toward the advertisement and attitude toward the brand is, not surprisingly, part of the sequence and has also been subjected to extensive research. Attitude toward the ad and attitude toward the brand are two measures that are being studied as favorable or unfavorable, or as a composite of other beliefs such as informational value and entertainment (Mehta, 2000). Millar and Tesser (1987) demonstrated how thoughts prior to an attitude assessment influences the correlation between attitude and behavior. In other words, thoughts prior to an attitude assessment can both increase and decrease the correlation between attitude and behavior. Stimulation and credibility drive attitude toward the advertisement; credibility, liking and familiarity drive attitude toward the brand; and credibility and personal relevance drive buying intention (Thorson, et al., 1992).

Two other advertising models, slightly different from the previous model, are derived from the traditional model but they have two routes instead of one single route from advertisement characteristics to purchase intention. They also focus on advertising from an emotional/non-emotional perspective.

Figure 6 illustrates the two-route hierarchic model of advertising effects (see Figure 7). These two models differ from the classical model in the sense that they have two distinct routes. In this model, there is one route that is influenced by the advertisement characteristics and a second route that is not. In the second model (Figure 8) both routes are influenced by the advertisement characteristics. These two models have in common the main route comprised of the attitude toward the advertisement, attitude toward the brand and buying intention.

The attention- memory sequence in the models is treated differently for emotional commercials compared to non-emotional commercials. The reason for this is that an advertisement that elicits an emotional response in the audience is supposed to create an enhanced memory engram as opposed to a non-emotional condition (Squire, 1986). It is more likely that there is a direct link between memory and attitudes for emotional advertisements than for non-emotional advertisements (Thorson, Chi, & Leavitt, 1992). In the non-emotional version of the advertising model, there is no link between memory and the other constructs except for its input from attention. In the first model (Figure 6), the attention construct does not correlate with the advertisement characteristics, and in the second model (Figure 8), the memory construct does not correlate with the attitude toward the advertisement construct, indicating that marketers cannot reach an integrated model. Instead, different models apply to different kinds of stimuli, i.e. commercials (Nilsson, 2006). The question becomes whether it is possible to separate attention and memory from attitude formation as in these models. Without any kind of attention to an object and without short-term, long-term, verbal, or pictorial memory, it becomes difficult for the consumer to have any knowledge or attitude towards a specific advertisement and its characteristics (see Figure 9).

In the above-mentioned models, attention and memory are described as processes not intrinsically related to the attitude toward ad, attitude toward brand and buying intention. At the same time, data does not supported the classic hierarchy of the advertising effect model where attention and memory are part of the main sequence. Considering that attention is a construct that is inherently connected to whether input will reach the central nervous system or not, it is indeed disturbing that the attention and memory constructs have a subordinate route or sequence such as can be seen in Figures 6 and 8. At the same time, data in some studies does not support the classic hierar-

Figure 6. The two-route hierarchic model for emotional commercials (Thorson, Chi, & Leavitt, 1992)

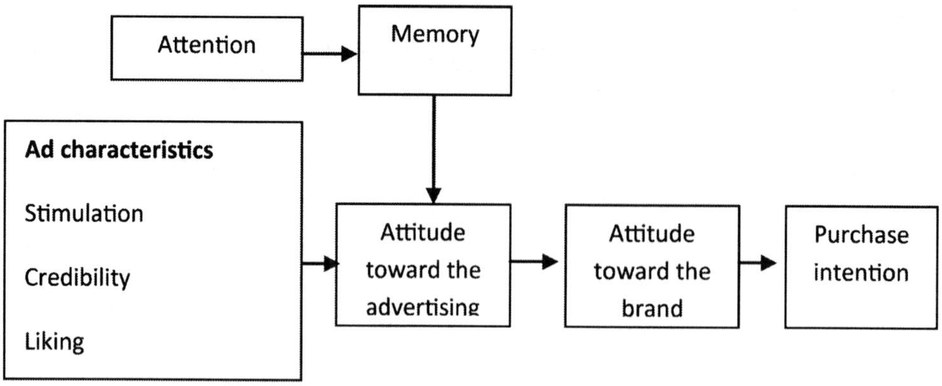

Attention
Memory
Ad characteristics
Stimulation
Credibility
Liking
Attitude toward the advertising
Attitude toward the brand
Purchase intention

Figure 7. Sample of conventional advertisements

The Art of a Good Softener

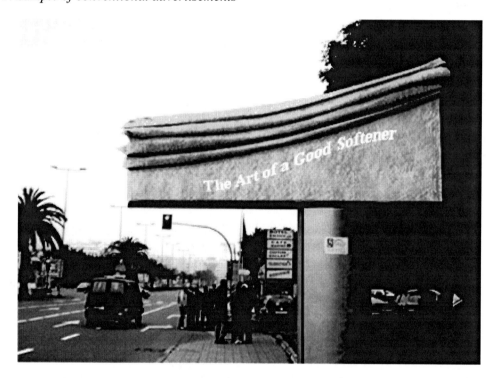

Figure 8. The two-route hierarchic model for non-emotional commercials (Thorson, Chi, & Leavitt, 1992)

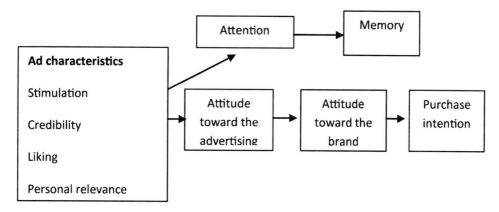

chic advertising model. The reason why attention and memory are modeled aside of the main route is because data has not shown any correlation between attention and memory, and the other constructs (Nilsson, 2006).

Elaboration Likelihood Model

The ELM model is a framework that shows us two routes to motivate a consumer: the peripheral route and the central route. These two routes of involvement and elaboration show us the way a consumer's attention is attracted to an advertisement so that a new behavior is established. Through

Figure 9. Samples of conventional advertisements

a peripheral route, a consumer's belief and n behavior are changed which results in a change in the consumer's belief. However, through a central route, the data is first processed by cognitive response, then little by little the consumer's belief is changed, and that changes the consumer's behavior. According to the elaboration likelihood model, advertisement processing is performed either through the peripheral route or the central one. The peripheral route is developed when the level of involvement is low. In this instance, consumers focus on external signs (such as those used in an ad to attract attention), not the brand. They do not focus on the brand claims (such as: our product is the best). The central route is developed when the consumer is highly involved with the product. In that case, consumers use a lot of energy to believe the ads. They focus on the content and claims, and investigate them carefully (see Figure 10).

What features dictate the route taken by the consumer? What are the relative impacts of consumer characteristics versus the message itself? Petty and Wegener (1998) categorized the antecedents and mediating processes involved in attitude change. They identified four basic antecedent factors (recipient characteristics, message, source and context) that affect the outcome of attitude change through three interrelated mediating processes (affective, cognitive and behavioral processes). As there are few detailed reports on the working process of ELM, this section will scrutinize the ELM model carefully.

Recipient Characteristics

Recipient characteristics refer to any generally enduring aspects of the receiver (Petty & Wegener, 1998). There are three usual types of variables related to recipient characteristics. Attitudinal variables, such as attitude accessibility and issue-relevant knowledge, affect the strength of attitude change. The accessibility of an attitude can specify the direction of attitude change, serve as a peripheral cue or increase the amount of scrutiny given to a persuasive message. Prior knowledge may also act as a peripheral cue, affecting the extent of elaboration and biasing information processing. The second type of recipient characteristic is demographic, such as gender and age. Gender usually gains much attention as research showed that women were more susceptible to being influenced than men. The variable of age, however, is related to the vulnerability of given populations, especially young children. Vulnerability to influence in these groups becomes a social responsibility issue (Rodriguez, 2006) (see Figure 11).

Figure 10. The elaboration likelihood model of persuasion (Cacioppo & Petty, 1984)

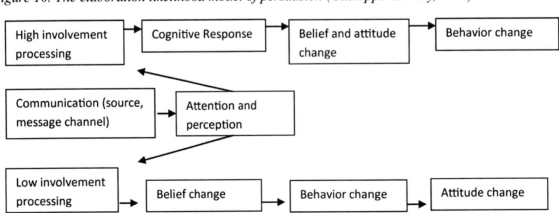

The individual's personality or skills comprise the third type of recipient characteristics. These include intelligence (Rhodes & Wood, 1992), self-esteem, self-monitoring, and the need for cognition. A number of individual differences have been examined to determine which personality characteristics are susceptible to persuasion. As an example, Rhodes and Wood (1992) believed that increased intelligence was associated with decreased persuasion. They stated that there is a curvilinear relationship between self-esteem and persuasion, positive when the individual is receptive and negative when the person is not receptive to the persuasive message. Self-monitoring is the sensitivity of individuals to socially appropriate behaviour versus reliance on internal beliefs. Attitudes serve different tasks for different levels of self-monitoring; each group should be more persuaded by messages that match the function served by their attitudes (Petty & Wegener, 1998). Individuals with a high need for cognition have a higher motivation for cognitive elaboration because they enjoy thinking compared to cognitive misers who think only when they are in a situation that forces them to do so (Cacioppo, et al., 1996). As with all individual difference variables, there may be interactive effects with other variables (i.e., mere thought effect and primacy/recency effect) (Rodriguez, 2006).

Message

The message refers to aspects of the communication itself (Petty & Wegener, 1998). There are three common characteristics related to the message, including message topic/position/style, the content of the message and the message organization. Regarding the message topic, position, and style, four elements are considered: issue relevance/ importance, the position taken, conclusion drawing and the use of rhetorical questions. Issue-relevance/importance indicates that some people care about certain issues more than others (Crano, 1995). Issue-relevance/importance

can be viewed as a recipient characteristic, but since the influence agent can affect the message to increase personal relevance, it is also considered to be part of message characteristics (Petty & Wegener, 1998). Personal relevance increases message elaboration, increasing persuasion with strong arguments, but decreases persuasion when arguments are weak (see Figure 12).

The position taken plays a prominent role in persuasion based on whether the recipient of the message finds the message agreeable or disagreeable. Some scholars have studied message discrepancy, or how far the message position is from one's own attitude (Petty & Wegener, 1998). One group of researchers proposed that attitude change should be a function of message discrepancy. Another group believed that the recipient's latitude of acceptance (or range of acceptance) would moderate the effects. Based on the ELM (Petty, et al., 1992), message discrepancy could serve different functions based on the level of elaboration likelihood.

Conclusion drawing involves presenting the message position either implicitly or explicitly. Research has shown that stating the position explicitly is more persuasive, but persuasion is stronger if the recipients draw their own conclusions. When presenting the message implicitly, however, there is a concern that the recipient will be unable or unwilling to draw the correct conclusion. Therefore, only if the recipient is highly motivated will an implicit message be more effective. The use of rhetorical questions also impacts attitude change as they may serve as a positive source cue if the speaker appears more likeable or a negative source cue if the speaker appears less confident. They may also serve as an indicator of high-quality arguments. Because rhetorical questions require the recipient to think, they may enhance cognitive processing if the elaboration likelihood is low, or may disrupt processing if the elaboration likelihood is already high (Petty & Wegener, 1998).

Figure 11. Advertising based on recipient characteristics

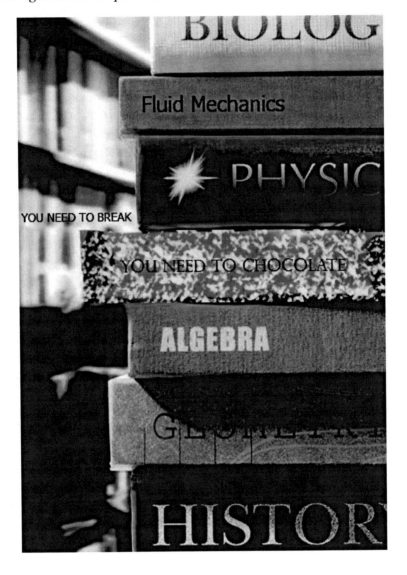

The content of the message is the second type of message characteristic and the one most studied (Petty & Wegener, 1998), with variables including argument quality, argument quantity, positive versus negative framing of arguments, fear/threat appeals, emotion versus reason in messages, and one-sided versus two-sided messages. An argument involves offering some consequence that is likely to occur if the advocacy is adopted. The quality of the argument depends upon the recipient's perception that the consequences are likely and desirable (Rodriguez, 2006). Research has shown that the importance and novelty of the consequences may also impact persuasion effectiveness. Research on argument quantity has shown that in low elaboration conditions, increasing the number of arguments in a persuasive message increases persuasiveness. In high elaboration conditions, increasing the number of strong arguments increases persuasiveness, but increasing the number of weak arguments actually decreases it. The effect of framing arguments depends upon the individual's level of motivation. When motivation is high, negatively framed arguments have greater

Figure 12. Sample of message-focused advertisement

impact, whereas when motivation is low, positively framed arguments are more effective. Individual difference variables may also play an important role in framing effectiveness (Rodriguez, 2006).

A fear or threat appeal has shown to be effective if the recipient is convinced of the severity or undesirable effects of the consequences and believes that there is a high likelihood of the consequences occurring if the suggested actions are not taken. Fear/threat appeals may also serve as a simple cue, bias message processing and determine the extent of message scrutiny. In determining whether emotion or reason in messages is more effective, current research has suggested that it depends on the basis of the attitude under challenge (Petty & Wegener, 1998). In one set of studies, matching attitudes was considered as the best, while in another set of studies, mismatching was determined to be the best. Conflicting results suggest that the issue would benefit from more research. On the issue of one- versus two-sided messages, is important to distinguish between two-sided messages that are refutable and those that are non-refutable (Petty & Wegener, 1998).

The third type of message characteristic is message organization. Common variables influence whether one should start or end with the strongest argument and whether the source should be presented before or after the message argument. Another variable of interest is the temporal ordering of the message or the placement of one's side of the argument first or second. Temporal ordering has been suggested as a moderator of the primacy/recency effect (Petty & Wegener, 1998). Primacy suggests that the first placement would result in the strongest persuasion, whereas recency indicates that the most recent, or the second placement in this case, would be more effective (Haugtvedt & Wegener, 1994; Rodriguez, 2006).

Source

Source variables refer to aspects of the person or entity presenting the persuasive message (Petty & Wegener, 1998). Some sources are explicit (i.e., a candidate makes a speech about an election) and others are implicit (i.e., a voice-over talking about the attributes of the brand in a commercial).

Based on Kelman's (1958) taxonomy, there are three common types of characteristics related to the source: credibility, attractiveness, and power (see Figure 13).

Credibility is the first type of source characteristic. Petty and Wegener (1998) found that there were indications that source credibility does not operate the same in all circumstances (Petty & Wegener, 1998; Rodriguez, 2006). As an example, Hovland and Weiss (1951) discovered that the effect of source credibility was more pronounced for topics that were less likely to directly impact the subjects than for topics that were highly relevant to the subjects. Two of the more frequently examined types of source credibility include the perceived expertise of the source (knowledge) and the trustworthiness of the source.

Source expertise can operate as a peripheral cue so that in conditions of low (rather than high) personal relevance, expert sources lead to more persuasion than inexpert sources (Petty, Cacioppo, & Goldman, 1981). Source expertise effects, moderated by other variables, also relate to the amount of scrutiny given to persuasive messages. Finally, source expertise has a biasing impact under high elaboration conditions.

The processing of persuasion messages can be affected by trustworthiness as trustworthy sources are more persuasive than untrustworthy sources (Eagly, Wood, & Chaiken, 1978). In addition, people who prefer not to process a message will accept a message from a trustworthy source without scrutiny (Priester & Petty, 1995).

The second type of source characteristic is attractiveness. Attractiveness includes not only the physical aspects of the source, but also perception of the source as likeable. Source attractiveness/ likeability primarily serves as a peripheral cue, having a greater effect on persuasion when elaboration likelihood is low rather than high. However, if endorser attractiveness acts as an argument by relating directly to the attributes of the product (i.e., a supermodel endorsing a beauty product),

then attractiveness may influence evaluations in high elaboration conditions (Shavitt, et al., 1994).

The third type of source characteristic is power. The power of the source over the message recipient includes having control over the positive or negative sanctions, and the ability to monitor whether or not the recipient accepts the source's position (McGuire, 1969; Petty & Wegener, 1998). Powerful sources are more persuasive than weak sources; however, power may interact with other variables (i.e., distraction, relevance and reactance).

Context

Context refers to any factors related to the setting of the communication (Petty & Wegener, 1998). This is a wide category of variables that includes distraction, audience reactions, forewarning, anticipated discussion or interaction, channel/ message modality, mood and repetition of the message. Any of these factors can influence the outcome of a persuasion attempt (see Figure 14).

Distraction influences attitudes by disrupting one's thoughts. The term "forewarning" refers to an instance in which an individual receives a persuasive message after learning about the position that will be taken or the persuasive intent of the source (Petty & Wegener, 1998). Researchers believe that the forewarning of an advocated position gives the individual time to develop anticipatory counterarguments. Forewarning of persuasive intent without knowledge of the topic interacts with personal relevance in determining attitude change. A concern for a favorable social impression arises when individuals anticipate discussion or interaction. An individual's resulting attitudes are affected by the importance of the issue, their knowledge of the opinions of the audiences and their already-established attitude towards that issue. The communication mode (print, audio or audiovisual) in which the persuasive message is presented also affects persuasion because some modes require more scrutiny than others (Petty & Wegener 1998).

Figure 13. Sample of implicit-oriented advertisement

Mood, or the way one feels at a particular point in time, can serve multiple roles. When elaboration is low, mood will act as a peripheral cue (Gorn, 1982, Petty, et al., 1993). When elaboration is moderate, mood will impact the extent of elaboration. A happy mood will disrupt processing (Bohner, 1991), whereas a negative mood will increase processing (Schwarz, 1990). Happy people cognitively process to the extent that they will remain happy. When elaboration is high, mood influences the nature of the thoughts that come to mind. Happy moods create favorable thoughts and favorable attitudes. When the argument includes a proposition for avoiding a negative consequence, individuals in negative moods process information in an attempt to correct or improve their situation. Repetition of a message has been shown to enhance persuasion up to the point where the individual becomes irritated or bored and processing becomes biased. If the message argument is strong, low levels of

repetition serve as an aid for further processing of the message, whereas if the message argument is weak, persuasion is decreased. To reduce the monotony of the increased repetition of the same message, introducing variations of the message is recommended (Rodrigue, 2006).

Advertisement Involvement Model

Presented in 1986 by Vaughn, the other model a planning model and illustrates how advertising works. This model presents four standard groups considering the level of consumer involvement with the products and services. The first group includes those products or services where consumers spend a lot of time before purchase. These consumers are inclined to take the time to know more about these products and gather information. These products and services are purchased on the basis rational purchasing. Some of the items included in this group are homes, cars

Figure 14. Sample of context-focused advertisement

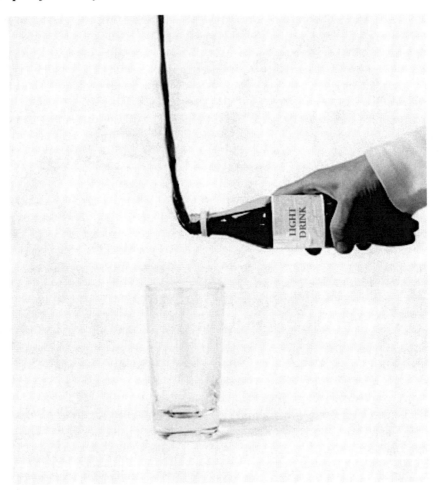

and furniture. The second group includes those services and products with which the consumers are highly involved. These products are more related to consumers' emotions, and consumers spend a lot of time before deciding to buy them; however, the amount of time is shorter than that of the first group. This group includes products such as jewelery and clothing, and is referred to as psychological purchasing. The next two groups include products with which consumers show a low level of involvement. One of these two groups is called social purchasing and include products that are required at home in daily life. The next group includes items purchased to satisfy personal needs and is called responsive purchasing.

The advertisement involvement model initiated by Vaughn is supported by many studies. When the product involvement is low, consumers are less likely to believe the contextual claims of the brand, and they usually focus on graphic motivators. Actually, to believe the contextual claims of the brand, more cognitive effort is required compared to believing graphic elements (Chattopadhyay, 1998), and customers are not motivated enough to spend the energy for cognition when involvement level is low versus when involvement is high, and this is when they are more likely to believe the contextual claims of the brand.

Therefore, it is more important to advertise products of low involvement. Thus, the belief that the Internet is only suitable for products of high involvement is rejected. Implicit meanings are communicated through external elements of advertisements, so advertising for products of high involvement should differ from advertising for products of low involvement with respect to cognition of implicit meanings. According to Dahlen et al. (2004), advertising is less effective for cognitive implicit meanings when the product is of high involvement, because consumers process these types of ads precisely and focus more on brand claims than external elements. The reason is that the Internet includes more motivators because it is online and establishes mutual communication. In other words, compared to printed advertisements, Internet websites include more lateral convincing elements and are more suitable for ads with low involvement. Such a difference is evident for products of low involvement but the difference is not that great for products of high involvement.

Internet-Based Models of Advertising

Figure 15 illustrates a detailed model that takes into consideration additional aspects of the advertising phenomena as opposed to the previously discussed models. This model is in fact an adaptation of a general advertising model that was presented by Rossiter and Percy (1997) and is dissimilar to the previously studied models in the sense that it is specifically designed to model Web advertising. Rossiter and Bellman argue that Web advertising has different characteristics than other kinds of advertising, mainly because the consumer is actively skipping about searching for interesting items of information, often pausing to be entertained and perhaps missing or deliberately bypassing content that the advertiser thinks is important (Rossiter & Bellman, 1999, p. 15). This is an excellent observation that captures a general picture of Web surfer behavior. What they are describing in essence is the attention system in action, which is constantly involved in selecting, including and excluding information when traversing a website where advertisers are competing for attention. This behavior is not unique for the World Wide Web. In fact, it is similar to surfing through printed materials, such as newspapers and magazines.

The situational factors in Rossiter and Bellman's model are moderators affecting the Web ad schema and advertisement processing where the concept of attention can be identified. Even though the model mentions these constructs, it is not specifically targeting the interrelation between attention and context represented as a task environment.

Consumer's Tendency toward the Brand

Consumer's tendency towards the advertised brand is an influential factor that determines the efficiency of an advertisement (Dahlen, 2001). It has been observed that when consumers have a positive attitude toward an advertised brand, they can remember the ad for a long time and thus believe it will have more value (Rice & Bennett, 1998). They are also more likely to investigate the contextual claims (Chattopadhyay, 1998). A brand that is desirable for consumers has two advantages over one that is not. First, the advertisement of these brands is recognized more easily because of a history with and preference for the brand that helps the consumer distinguish the brand without making a cognitive effort. Second, it is easier for the consumer to believe the brand information. A brand of less popularity, on the other hand, may not attract a consumer's attention and even if it does, the consumer may not believe it easily (Janiszewski & Meyvis, 2001). As stated above, compared to graphic elements, contextual claims of a brand require more effort in order to be believed. Thus, consumers with a positive attitude towards a brand focus on the brand claims more than those with a negative attitude, and this latter group focuses more on graphic elements.

Figure 15. Model of web advertising effects (Rossiter & Bellman, 1999)

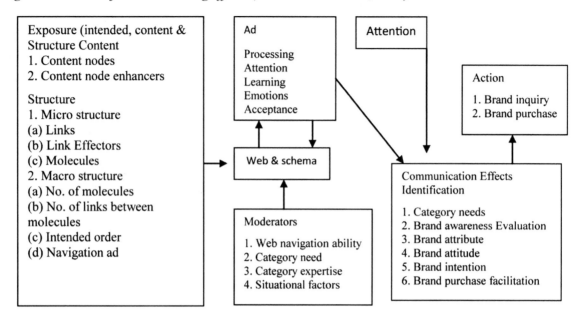

When designing advertisements for those consumers whose attitude toward a brand is negative, more attention should be paid to graphic elements, while this is not the case with those consumers whose attitude toward a brand is positive. On this basis, the Internet includes more motivators than traditional media; that is, the Internet has more inherent potential for making use of these elements. Compared to printed advertising, Internet advertising provides consumers with negative attitudes with a better understanding of implicit meanings. However, these two advertising methods do not differ in with regard to consumers with positive attitudes (Dahlen, et al., 2004) (see Figure 16).

WWW Usage and Advertisement Processing

Recent studies revealed that light and heavy Internet users process and believe Internet advertising differently (Bruner & Kumar, 2000). Light users are mostly affected by websites and tricky motivators, while heavy users are more focused on central points and tend to eliminate external elements to merely search for their goals (Dahlen, 2001).

Light users focus on every existing motivator of a website and examine each one; consequently, they spend a lot more time on Internet advertisements. However, heavy users are mostly focused on processing the searched data (Bruner & Kumar, 2000; Dahlen, 2000). This means that light users are more targeted by Internet advertising because they process the executive elements of different advertisements. On the other hand, only a few of these elements are properly considered by heavy users as they eliminate the peripheral signs and focus their attentions more on related data including the contextual claims of the brand. Thus, compared to heavy users, light users understand the implicit concepts of an Internet advertisement better than those of printed advertisements. For heavy users, there is not much difference in their cognition of those implicit concepts presented on the Internet and those presented in printed media (Dahlen, et al., 2004).

Advantages of Internet Advertising

According to a study conducted by the Interactive Advertising Business (2007), Internet advertising has 28 advantages over other advertising methods. There is also a multi-variable categorization of media and advertising. As shown in Figure 17, each medium has advantages and disadvantages.

Advertising on Social Networks

If Facebook were a country, it would be the third largest in the world because it currently reaches 710 million users, raising the questions: Are your customers on Facebook? Moreover, are they able to hear your sounds, pock your clues and wake up by your hints? Is there any way to trace your customers on Facebook? To gather some insights into this issue, Facebook developed a tool entitled the "Facebook Advertising Platform" where marketers can place small display advertisements as sidebars on Facebook and profile pages.

Social network advertising offers an online marketing practice that closes the loop between sales and advertising with smarter lead, which are obtained from tracing consumer reactions. We know that Facebook has grown from a collegiate social network in 2004 to become a site frequently used by 7.3% of the world's population (Kessler, 2011), and has also evolved into a marketing tool. However, new trends show that advertising on Facebook cost more but received fewer click-through in 2010 compared to 2009, and performed about half as well as traditional banner ads (Wasserman, 2011).

Webtrends (2011) conducted a study on Facebook to try and establish benchmarks for brands looking to advertise on the platform. According to the findings of this study, the average Click-Through Rate (CTR) for Facebook ads in 2009 was 0.063% compared to 0.051% in 2010. The Cost Per Click (CPC) was $0.27 and $0.49 for those periods, respectively. By considering these statistics, we can conclude that the Web world does not follow a constant trend. As a unique user-generating and user-acquisition trend forms, it may lose its momentum by competing with other emerging technologies (like Google +). Nonetheless, Facebook is projected to post $4 billion in advertising this year (Webtrends, 2011). It is clear that Facebook ads may not get many click-through, but for the moment, friends' recommendations give them longer "shelf life." In addition, marketers are familiar with Word-Of-Mouth (WOM) in judging advertising effectiveness. Does word of mouth work on Facebook?

Web 2.0 helps social networking sites like Facebook to become ubiquitous and to provide a network of communication among its users (Katona, et al., 2010). Social networks like Facebook and Twitter gather millions of people into a new online world with new ways of reciprocal communication and exclusive user identification. Along with customer identification, consumer profiles are also voluntarily provided, and friends are linked by an explicit pattern of communication. In the last five years, social networks have become popluar all over the world. Currently, Facebook has 687 million members worldwide (insidefacebook.com, 2011). Kantona *et al.* (2010) reported that "the assumption underlying all these 'network marketing' techniques is that network information can help identify influencers and predict consumers' adoption probabilities" (p. 3).

Changing business themes and internet-only technologies allow marketers to offer customized service to their consumers, requiring up-to-date data -based marketing and CRM (Villanueva & Hanssens, 2007). As mentioned before, social network marketing, such as on Facebook, must consider the impact of word-of-mouth in the marketing mix. Previous efforts to evaluate whether or not WOM works in a positive way believed that WOM has a powerful effect c (Richins, & Root-Shaffer, 198 & Joshi, 2007), and ignoring ing the social network variable need a new comprehensive defii

Figure 16. IAB's 28 reasons to use interactive advertising (iab.net, 2007)

A Marketer's Potential Uses of the Internet	How to Measure Performance
1. Increase brand awareness	• Pre/post (or exposed vs. unexposed) brand awareness tracking
2. Generate trial	• Increase target audience • Track first-time buyers
3. Increase usage of the brand	• Track frequency of purchase • Field usage study
4. Up-sell customer to premium product or service	• Track purchase behavior over time
5. Encourage customer to buy more per purchase occasion	• Track amount by per-purchase occasion
6. Improve customer's attitudes/image of the brand	• Track customer's perceptions or attitudes about brand over time, including purchase consideration and intent
7. Cross-sell other brands from the same company	• Track customer's purchase behavior of specific brands • Measure the effects of co-marketing promotions
8. Co-market with non-company brands	• Track customer's purchase behavior of specific brands • Measure effects of co-marketing promotions
9. Increase repeat purchase	• Track number of customers making repeat purchases
10. Encourage brand loyalty/increase customer's involvement with brand	• Repeat purchase • Share of requirements • Track customer's perceptions or attitudes about brand vs. competitive brands • Track purchase intent of brand vs. competition
11. Provide in-depth information about the brand and/or do product demonstration	• Clicks • Length of visit • E-mail inquiries and/or requests for additional information • 800# calls
12. Develop database of customers and prospects/collect sales leads	• Number of sales leads collected online • Quality of sales leads
13. Provide/improve customer service	• Track number of visits online versus offline inquiries • Track customer satisfaction over time • Track costs of customer service online vs. offline
14. Reduce obsolete/excess inventory via promotions	• Track sales of obsolete/excess inventory • Compare selling costs versus offline alternatives
A Marketer's Potential Uses of the Internet	How to Measure Performance
15. Reduce marketing costs	• Compare online marketing costs and effectiveness to traditional marketing costs
16. Test different copy concepts	• Purchase intent • Pre/post (or exposed vs. unexposed) brand awareness • Pre/post (or exposed vs. unexposed) attitude

Figure 17. Advantages and Disadvantages for Promotional Target

Media	Advantages	Disadvantages
Newspaper	• Potentially large coverage area • Low cost relative to other media • Immediate/timely (daily or weekly) • Access to many socioeconomic groups • Targeting of specific audience via specialty section • Visibility of product (i.e. pictures) • Flexibility in ad size and cost	• **Inconsistent reproduction** • **Typically one-day exposure** • **May be limited to text or black and white** • **Lack of movement and sound** • **Can be expensive**
Radio	• Specific audience (demographics) • Immediate/timely/multiple exposures • Possible high entertainment value Celebrity endorsement or pitch • Time and content flexibility	• **Time limitation** • **Need for repetition** • **Ad recall is low**
Magazines	• Potentially large coverage area • Targeting of specific audience • Flexibility in size and cost • Visibility of the product (i.e. pictures) • Possible use of coupons to measure effectiveness • Large repeat and secondary exposure	• **Clutter (can be lost among others)** • **Cost associated with repeat exposure** • **Lack of movement and sound** • **Not immediate; publication may be weekly, monthly or less frequent**
Television	• Large coverage area • Targeting of specific audience • Uses both visual and auditory stimulants • Large repeat exposure	• **Can be costly to produce and air** • **Time limitations restrict message** • **Need for repetition/short ad recall**
Direct Mail	• Targeting of specific audience • More opportunity to educate on product/service benefits	• **Expensive** • **Difficult to obtain clean mailing list** • **May be perceived as junk mail and be discarded/unopened**
Point of Sale	• Can influence impulse purchasing • Helps product to stand out among competition • Customer has opportunity for direct response at the time of ad presentation (i.e. purchase)	• **Can be expensive** • **Clutter (ad can be lost among other point-of-sale materials)**
Outdoor or billboard	• Large audience exposure depending on placement • Can provide information and directions • Continuous exposure	• **Limited message length** • **Initial production and preparation costs** • **Ideal sites are difficult to acquire**
Internet	• Customers access at their convenience • Relatively cost-effective • Targeting of types of viewers • Messages can be timely • Advertisements can be interactive • Ability to use coupons to measure effectiveness	• **Technical maintenance necessary** • **Not effective as stand-alone strategy** • **Difficult to gauge impact** • **Costs of development and maintenance can vary**

network's WOM. Hennig-Thurau *et al.* (2004) believed eWOM communication is "any positive or negative statement made by potential, actual, or former customers about a product or company, which is made available to a multitude of people and institutions via the Internet" (p. 38), but we need to have a more narrow definition. In pursuit of this goal, we should consider the communication advantages that social networks give to marketers (see Figure 18).

The communication patterns of social networks allow users to upload their personal photos. In this regard, the concept of having an unfamiliar consumer disappeared. By observing users' photos, the consumers' relationships and emotions are seen in a much more real way. When a user contacts another user, the parties are already known by their user IDs as well as their photos, profiles, interests and priorities. Keeping this in mind, WOM may be defined as follows:

Social network WOM is any action or reaction made by a social network's members when trying to show emotion formed from exposure to a social network-based advertisement.

The action or reaction can be seen in the form of "poking" or making that ad visible to others. We should not assume that talk alone will suffice, as the tools people use to convey concepts on a social network are more than the words or voices as with traditional media; inside these networks, the social climate is somewhat different. Users have the ability to employ some unique devices for communication such as "poking," "adding to favorites" and "send to friends." These are the realization of WOM on the social networks. Consequently, we can conclude that WOM has changed, since people have changed the way they communicate via new technologies. Marketers can find better positions in these networks if they can build good relationships with the owners of these social sites in order to launch a campaign based on users' interests and profiles.

INFORMATION ENVIRONMENT

Information environment is comprised of all data relevant to products which are within easy reach of consumers (Bettman, 1979). It such as the type and amount of available information, offering methods and data-organizing methods.

There seems to be no major difference between the Internet and traditional mass media in terms of the type of available content, because both provide awareness, image-making and reliability for a brand (Jones & Slater, 2003). One major difference is that the Internet allows marketers to broadcast extra information freely on their own websites (Faber, Lee, & Nan, 2004). The value of such free information is highlighted when one considers the cost of placing the same messages through traditional mass media. The value becomes even clearer when potential customers react to this free information. The Internet also enables marketers to post traditional audio and video clips on their websites, although this is still restricted in some countries by bandwidth and the speed of downloading per second.

Another feature of a consumer's information environment is organizing information. In mass media, organizing is performed by brand; mass media broadcasts brand advertisements on the basis of a desired subset of each brand in turn. An audience must stay in front of the media to receive the information or other related promotional messages. Hence, decision-making becomes difficult for the audience because they hear different voices in a short time period (Bettman, Johnson, & Payne, 1991). Nevertheless, advertising in the online environment is to some extent targeted in comparison to traditional media. When online users choose an advertisement and clicks on its banner, embedded programs recognize their wants and redirect them to the related promotional message. Thus, the audience simultaneously searches their information and receives related advertisements.

The final issue which must be compared between the information environment of online and

Figure 18. The history of social networks

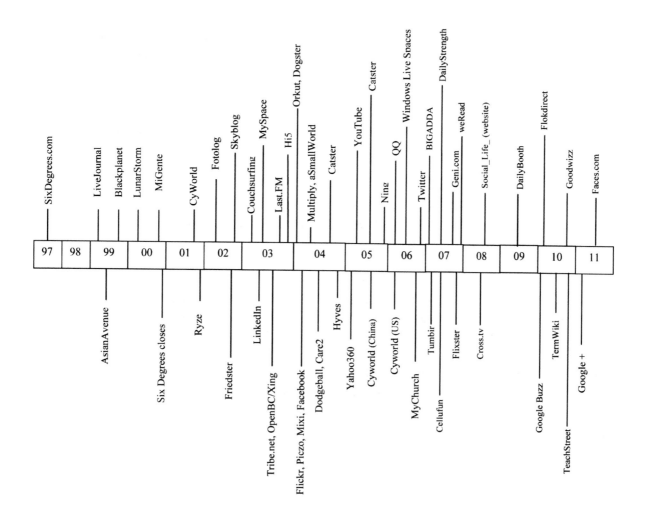

traditional advertising is flexibility and the degree of information "accessibility." Flexibility in the new media means that both senders and receivers of messages can locate information and remove inappropriate information during the process of information seeking. In other words, flexibility in the online environment allows this media to create a reciprocal relationship, unlike traditional media which offers only unilateral communication. Accessibility enables potential customers to gather a product's related information and have control of that information. In comparison to traditional media, accessibility in the online environment has

provided ways for its users to gain more information, such as a simple but valuable "click," and other avenues like search, chat, mail and direct negotiation (video connections).

CONCLUSION

Advertising efforts often involve implicit concepts, and these can be visual, auditory, or the implicit meanings of words or sentences. The audience uses such information to realize the message. Implicit meanings are a critical factor in brand advertising as brand image includes some associations that cannot be conveyed explicitly in words. There are some differences in the perception of implicit meanings in both traditional and online advertising. For a better identification of implicit meanings and the way they are used in Internet advertising and print advertisements, the subject must be considered from three points of view: product elaboration, WWW usage and advertisement processing, and the consumer's attitude towards the brand.

Product elaboration is the main determinant of a consumer's attitude toward an advertisement (Laurent & Kapferer, 1985). When the product has a high level of elaboration and the customer is highly involved, customers actively process the advertisement and spend more time on the ads. Several models were discussed in detail for the elaboration or involvement of consumers with the advertised product or service. As an example, ELM or the Elaboration Likelihood Model, is a framework that shows us two routes to motivate a consumer: the peripheral route and the central route. The peripheral route is developed when the level of involvement is low. In this situation, consumers focus on external signs (such as those used in an ad to attract attention), not the brand. They do not focus on what brand claims (such as: our product is the best). The central route is developed when the consumer is highly involved with the product and uses a lot of energy to believe the ads. They focus on the content and claims, and investigate them carefully. These two routes of involvement and elaboration show us how a consumer's attention is attracted by an advertisement so that a new behavior is established. The ELM was examined via four critical features including recipient characteristics, message, source and context.

The second issue which must be considered in understanding implicit meaning is the consumer's attitude toward the advertised brand, which is an influential factor that determines the efficiency of an advertisement. It has been observed that when consumers hae a positive attitude toward an advertised brand, they can remember the ad for a long time and thus believe it has more value. They are also more likely to investigate the contextual claims.

WWW usage and advertisement processing is the third issue of implicit meaning. Light users are mostly affected by websites and tricky motivators, while heavy users focus more on central points and tend to eliminate external elements to merely search for their goals. Compared to heavy users, light users understand the implicit concepts of an online advertisement more deeply than printed advertisements. The last issue discussed in this chapter was social network advertising. A framework of the history of social networking was studied, followed by an exclusive definition of WOM for social network advertising. Challenges were presented with possible appropriate answers.

In summary, this chapter provided some insights into the advantages and disadvantages of advertising in both offline and online media.

REFERENCES

Bettman, J. R., Johnson, E. J., & Payne, J. W. (1991). Consumer decision making. In Robertson, T. S., & Kassarjian, H. H. (Eds.), *Handbook of Consumer Behavior* (pp. 50–84). Englewood Cliffs, NJ: Prentice Hall.

Bettman, J. R., & Kakkar, P. (1977). Effects of information presentation format on consumer information acquisition strategies. *The Journal of Consumer Research*, 3(4), 233–240. doi:10.1086/208672

Brown, S. P., & Stayman, D. M. (1992). Antecedents and consequences of attitude toward the ad: A meta-analysis. *The Journal of Consumer Research, 19*(1), 34–51. doi:10.1086/209284

Bruner, G. C. II, & Kumar, A. (2000). Web commercials and advertising hierarchy-of-effects. *Journal of Advertising Research, 40*(1/2), 35–42.

Cacioppo, J. T., & Petty, R, E., Feinstein, J., & Jarvis, W. B. G. (1996). Individual differences in cognitive motivation: The life and times of people varying in need for cognition. *Psychological Bulletin, 119*, 197–253. doi:10.1037/0033-2909.119.2.197

Cacioppo, J. T., & Petty, R. E. (1984). The elaboration likelihood model of persuasion. *Advances in Consumer Research. Association for Consumer Research (U. S.), 11*(1), 668–672.

Chattopadhyay, A. (1998). When does comparative advertising influence brand attitude? The role of delay and market position. *Psychology and Marketing, 15*(5), 461–475. doi:10.1002/(SICI)1520-6793(199808)15:5<461::AID-MAR4>3.0.CO;2-5

Coupey, E. (1999). Advertising in an interactive environment: A research agenda. In Schumann, D. W., & Thorson, E. (Eds.), *Advertising and the World Wide Web* (pp. 197–215). Mahwah, NJ: Lawrence Erlbaum.

Coyle, J. R., & Thorson, E. (2001). The effects of progressive levels of interactivity and vividness in web marketing sites. *Journal of Advertising, 30*(3), 65–77.

Crano, W. D. (1995). Attitude strength and vested interest. In Petty, R. E., & Krosnick, J. A. (Eds.), *Attitude Strength: Antecedents and Consequences* (pp. 131–157). Mahwah, NJ: Erlbaum.

Dahlen, M. (2002). Learning the web: Internet user experience and response to web marketing in Sweden. *Journal of Interactive Advertising, 3*(1).

Dahlen, M., & Bergendahl, J. (2001). Informing and transforming on the web: An empirical study of response to banner ads for functional and expressive products. *International Journal of Advertising, 20*(2), 189–205.

Dahlen, M., Ekborn, Y., & Mörner, N. (2000). To click or not to click: an empirical study of response to banner ads for high and low involvement products. *Consumption. Markets & Culture, 4*(1), 57–76. doi:10.1080/10253866.2000.9670349

Dahlen, M., Malcolm, M., & Nordenstam, S. (2004). An empirical study of perceptions of implicit meanings in world wide web advertisements versus print advertisements. *Journal of Marketing Communications, 10*, 37–45. doi:10.1080/1352726042000177391

Eagly, A., Wood, W., & Chaiken, S. (1978). Causal inferences about communicators and their effect on opinion change. *Journal of Personality and Social Psychology, 36*, 424–435. doi:10.1037/0022-3514.36.4.424

Faber, Lee, & Nan. (2004). Advertising and the consumer information environment online. *The American Behavioral Scientist, 48*(4), 447–466. doi:10.1177/0002764204270281

Gibson, B. S. (1996). Visual quality and attentional capture: A challenge to the special role of abrupt onsets. *Journal of Experimental Psychology. Human Perception and Performance, 22*, 1496–1504. doi:10.1037/0096-1523.22.6.1496

Gibson, L. D. (1983). Not recall. *Journal of Advertising Research, 23*(1), 39–46.

Gorn, G. J. (1982). The effects of music in advertising on choice behavior: A classical conditioning approach. *Journal of Marketing, 46*, 94–101. doi:10.2307/1251163

Haugtvedt, C. P., & Wegener, D. T. (1994). Message order effects in persuasion: An attitude strength perspective. *The Journal of Consumer Research, 21,* 205–218. doi:10.1086/209393

Hennig-Thurau, T., Gwinner, P. K., Walsh, G., & Gremler, D. D. (2004). Electronic word-of-mouth via consumer-opinion platforms: What motivates consumers to articulate themselves on the internet? *Journal of Interactive Marketing, 18*(1), 38–52. doi:10.1002/dir.10073

Hovland, C. I., & Weiss, W. (1951). The influence of source credibility on communication effectiveness. *Public Opinion Quarterly, 15,* 635–650. doi:10.1086/266350

IAB. (2007). *IAB's 28 reasons to use interactive advertising.* Retrieved from http://www.iab.net.

Insidefacebook.com. (2011). *Facebook now reaches 687 million users – Traffic trends and data at inside Facebook gold.* Retrieved June 6, 2011, from http://www.insidefacebook.com /2011/06/10/facebook-now-reaches-687-million-users-traffic-trends-and-data-at-inside-facebook-gold-june-2011-edition/.

Janiszewski, C., & Meyvis, T. (2001). Effects of brand logo complexity, repetition, and spacing on processing fluency and judgment. *The Journal of Consumer Research, 28*(1), 18–32. doi:10.1086/321945

Jones, J. P., & Slater, J. S. (2003). *What's in a name: Advertising and the concept of brands.* Armonk, NY: M. E. Sharpe.

Katona, Z., Zubcsek, P. P., & Miklos, S. (2010). *Network effects and personal influences: The diffusion of an online social network.* Unpublished Paper. Retrieved May 15, 2011, from http://www.cs.bme.hu /~zskatona/pdf/diff.pdf.

Keller, K. L. (1993). Conceptualizing, measuring, and managing customer-based brand equity. *Journal of Marketing, 57,* 1–22. doi:10.2307/1252054

Kelman, H. C. (1958). Compliance, identification, and internalization: Three processes of attitude change. *The Journal of Conflict Resolution, 2,* 51–60. doi:10.1177/002200275800200106

Kessler, S. (2011). *The history of advertising on facebook.* Retrieved June, 29, 2011, from http://mashable.com /2011/06/28/facebook-advertising-infographic/.

Laurent, G., & Kapferer, J. (1985). Measuring consumer involvement profiles. *JMR, Journal of Marketing Research, 22*(1), 41–53. doi:10.2307/3151549

Lee, Y. H. (2000). Manipulating ad message involvement through information expectancy: Effects on attitude evaluation and confidence. *Journal of Advertising, 29*(2), 29–43.

Lutz, R. J. (1985). Affective and cognitive antecedents of attitude toward the ad: A conceptual framework. In Alwitt, L., & Mitchell, A. (Eds.), *Psychological Processes and Advertising Effects Theory, Research and Applications.* Hillsdale, NJ: Erlbaum.

McQuarrie, E. F., & Mick, D. G. (1999). Visual rhetoric in advertising: Text-interpretive, experimental, and reader-response analyses. *The Journal of Consumer Research, 26,* 37–54. doi:10.1086/209549

Mehta, A. (2000). Advertising attitudes and advertising effectiveness. *Journal of Advertising Research, 40*(3), 67–72.

Millar, M. G., & Tesser, A. (1987). Attitudes and behavior: The cognitive-affective mismatch hypothesis. *Advances in Consumer Research. Association for Consumer Research (U. S.), 17,* 86–90.

Nilsson, C. P. (2006). *Attention to advertising.* PhD Dissertation. Umeå, Sweden: Umeå University.

Petty, R. E., Cacioppo, J. T., & Goldman, R. (1981). Personal involvement as a determinant of argument-based persuasion. *Journal of Personality and Social Psychology, 41,* 847–855. doi:10.1037/0022-3514.41.5.847

Petty, R. E., Gleicher, F., & Jarvis, W. B. G. (1993). Persuasion theory and AIDS prevention. In Pryor, J. B., & Reeder, G. D. (Eds.), *The Social Psychology of HIV Infection* (pp. 155–182). Hillsdale, NJ: Erlbaum.

Petty, R. E., & Wegener, D. T. (1998). Attitude change: Multiple roles for persuasion variables. In Gilbert, D. T. (Ed.), *The Handbook of Social Psychology.* Oxford, UK: Oxford University Press.

Priester, J. R., & Petty, R. E. (1995). Source attributions and persuasion: Perceived honesty as a determinant of message scrutiny. *Personality and Social Psychology Bulletin, 21,* 637–654. doi:10.1177/0146167295216010

Rhodes, N., & Wood, W. (1992). Self-esteem and intelligence affect influenceability: The mediating role of message reception. *Psychological Bulletin, 111,* 156–171. doi:10.1037/0033-2909.111.1.156

Rice, B., & Bennett, R. (1998). The relationship between brand usage and advertising tracking measurements: International findings. *Journal of Advertising Research, 38*(3), 58–66.

Richins, M. L., & Root-Shaffer, T. (1988). The role of involvement and opinion leadership in consumer word-of-mouth: An implicit model made explicit. *Advances in Consumer Research. Association for Consumer Research (U. S.), 15,* 32–36.

Ringold, D. J., Calfee, J. E., Cohen, J. B., & Pollay, R. W. (1989). The informational content of cigarette advertising: 1926–1986: Counting advertising assertions to assess regulatory policy: When it doesn't add up: Filters, flavors. . . flim-flam, too! *Journal of Public Policy & Marketing, 8,* 1–39.

Rodrigue, S. C. (2006). *The impact of masking of persuasive message effectiveness.* PhD Dissertation. Baton Rouge, LA: LSU.

Rossiter, J. R., & Bellman. (1999). A proposed model for explaining and measuring web ad effectiveness. *Journal of Current Issues and Research in Advertising, 21*(1), 13–31.

Rossiter, J. R., & Percy, L. (1997). *Advertising communications & promotion management* (2nd ed.). New York, NY: McGraw-Hill.

Schwarz, N. (1990). Feelings as information: Informational and motivational functions of affective states. In Higgins, E. T., & Sorrentino, R. M. (Eds.), *Handbook of Motivation and Cognition: Foundations of Social Behavior* (pp. 527–561). New York, NY: Guilford.

Shavitt, S., Swan, S., Lowery, T. M., & Wänke, M. (1994). The interaction of endorser attractiveness and involvement in persuasion depends on the goal that guides message processing. *Journal of Consumer Psychology, 3,* 137–162. doi:10.1016/S1057-7408(08)80002-2

Squire, L. R. (1986). Mechanisms of memory. *Science, 232,* 1612–1619. doi:10.1126/science.3086978

Thorson, E., Chi, A., & Leavitt, C. (1992). Attention, memory, attitude and conation: A test of the advertising hierarchy. *Advances in Consumer Research. Association for Consumer Research (U. S.), 19*(1), 366–379.

Toncar, M., & Munch, J. (2001). Consumer responses to tropes in advertising. *Journal of Advertising, 30*(1), 55–65.

Van den Bulte, C., & Joshi, Y. V. (2007). New product diffusion with influentials and imitators. *Marketing Science, 26,* 400–421. doi:10.1287/mksc.1060.0224

Vaughn, R. (1986). How advertising works: A planning model. *Journal of Advertising Research, 26*(1), 57–66.

Villanueva, J., & Hanssens, D. M. (2007). *Customer equity: Measurement, management and research opportunities: Foundations and trends in marketing.* Boston, MA: Now.

Warrington, P., & Shim, S. (2000). An empirical investigation of the relationship between product involvement and brand commitment. *Psychology and Marketing, 17*(9), 761–782. doi:10.1002/1520-6793(200009)17:9<761::AID-MAR2>3.0.CO;2-9

Wasserman, T. (2011). *Facebook ads perform half as well as regular banner ads.* Retrieved January 31, 2011, from http://mashable.com/2011/01/31/facebook-half-click-throughs/.

Chapter 4
Internet Advertising Formats

ABSTRACT

Just like the traditional type of advertising that has its own methods of transmitting messages, online advertising applies various methods to transmit its messages via a unique distribution channel and environment. The type of advertising and method of disseminating depends on many factors (see Chapter 11). In this chapter, the authors introduce different methods by which the Internet advertising channel transmits advertisers' messages to consumers.

INTERNET ADVERTISING METHODS

Banners

Banners are the most common methods of Internet advertising. A Banner is a graphic element 1.2 cm in width and 12.5 cm to 15.5 cm in length. A pixel is the unit used to compute and assess the digital content of banners. A banner usually includes the company name, product name and a short message (Figure 1).

DOI: 10.4018/978-1-4666-0885-6.ch004

Banners motivate website visitors to click on their advertising message in order to transfer the visitor to the company's or product's main website. There are two entities who participate in publishing a banner. The first is the advertiser, who attracts visitors to the company's or product's website, and the second is the internet publisher who places the banner on the pages of the host website and is paid for this service. The banner is frequently placed at the top of the website's page horizontally and may includes audio-visual clips. Clicking on a banner activates the A/V element,

Figure 1. Standard size banner (12×2.5)

which loads and quickly displays the site linked to it.

Various Types of Banners

- **Keyword Banners:** These banners appear when a user searches for a special word or keyword via a search engines.
- **Random Banners:** These banners introduce a new product, cannot be accessed from a link, appear on website pages randomly, and do not follow a special pattern.
- **Fixed Banners:** These banners are permanently placed on a page and cannot move to other pages of the website.

Advantages and Disadvantages of Banners

Advantages: Banners are easily customized for a special user, and since they are small in size, they can be loaded within a short time, thus attracting and entertaining the user. From a statistical point of view, banners are visible for a long period. However, the main advantage of banners is their ability to be linked to their company's host website from a simple click, and that they provide the user with more comprehensive information about the product and the advertiser.

Disadvantages: Placing a banner on a popular website as a marketing effort may significantly deplete an advertising budget. In addition, the limitations imposed by the host website may impede transmitting messages to online customers. To alleviate these possible roadblocks, advertising

designed two methods for placing banners on a website which enable them to display their banners with the least trouble (Amiri & Menon, 2003).

Placing Banners on a Website

Swapping Banners: Exchanging banners is one of the most cost-effective methods for placing a banner on a website. In this method, Company A displays a banner of Company B and vice versa. There are some major problems with this method, including the situation when the traffic of website A is heavier than that of website B; in that case, the former one will usually display the banner of the latter under some terms and conditions. This is termed the Sound Marketer Problem. Based on this, another method titled "Interchanging or Exchanging Banners" was developed.

Exchanging Banners: This method involves companies placing banners on various websites. There are some banner-adapting companies who specialize in interchanging banners. Assume that Company A can properly display the banner of Company B, while Company B cannot display the banner of Company A properly, but instead it can display the banner of Company C, and Company C can display the banner of Company A. Such broadcasting ability is determined by website traffic and the relationships among business models. On the Banner Interchange method, a company that is a member of a multi-company market displays another company's banner and receives credit depending on the time it displays the banner. The repetition of banner broadcasting continues until a time when the host company (the website displaying the banner) gains enough credit for its banner to be displayed on another website. Then the company's banner will be displayed on a website chosen from those of other market members. This eliminates the condition of heaviness or lightness of website traffic by replacing that with a monetary standard. Additionally, if a company decides it wants its banner to be displayed before gaining enough credit, it has to pay a designated amount to compensate for the credit shortage.

There are patterns for banners to be displayed on web pages; these are differentiated from each other based on the advertising management process.

Banner Advertising Models

There are models for banners to be displayed on web pages; these are differentiated from each other based on the advertising management process and include:

- Broker Model
- Portal Model
- Advertiser Model

Broker Model

A Broker model involves an advertising broker or mediator who links publishers to advertisers (Figure 2). The advertising broker is the host's mediator and undertakes all advertising activities, including introducing the advertisements to the publishers or directly to the end users (Double-Click, 2004). Moreover, an advertising broker chooses the publishing site based on the content and type of advertisement and even aligns the advertiser's geographical location with that of the publisher. Ultimately, the broker appears as an advertising agency and gains profit from marketing activities. Since 1995, several companies were established based on this model; among the most influential are DoubleClick.com and Real Media. com (Bilchev & Marston, 2003).

Double-Click's Broker Model

DoubleClick claims that its Internet advertising approach targets its customers one by one. The developed model on which DoubleClick bases its services is the broker model. In this company, a network is established based on broker management of advertising comprised of more than 500 companies. The network has its own server. When a visitor visits members' websites, the server identifies their IDs or bugs by inspecting their browsers. Then it utilizes intelligent agents to record visitors' interests and behaviors. For each website, the server records the advertisement to which visitors reacted most and creates a separate profile for each user. When a user visits one of the websites in the network, the server identifies the visitor by these profiles and sends the visitor's particulars, interests and behaviors to the home website. For instance, if a visitor has mostly clicked on athletic advertisements, the host website will mostly display such advertisements (Figure 3; a hypothetical model shows how Doubleclick's network works).

Portal Model (Publisher)

In a portal model, the publisher leads the advertising. This model is mostly followed by those publishers who are large enough to provide advertising services, and the traffic on their pages is heavy. Some of the privileges of this advertising model are its ability to store users' behaviors and interests in a customized server, and to provide them with customized services. User data is the key that enables the publisher to be in touch with more advertisers (Figure 4).

Advertiser Model

In an advertiser model, the advertiser himself leads the advertising. This model is mostly used by major online retailers comprised of several interconnected organizations (Figure 5). These

Figure 2. Broker model of publishing advertisement (Kazienko & Adamski, 2007)

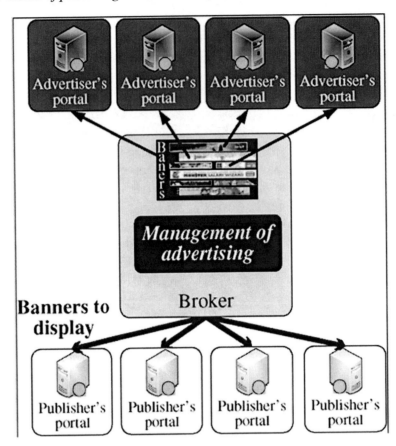

stores include many links that enable them to influence their customers directly, and that is the reason they use this model. One of the most prominent advertising portals for this model is that of the Poland Company (Figure 6).

POP-UP AND POP-UNDER

Pop-ups are the most famous type of Internet advertising. Known as ad spawning, pop-ups automatically appear in a new window on the browser at the front side of an opened page (Figure 7). On the other hand, Pop-under advertisements are placed beneath opened pages and appear as soon as the page is closed.

The history of pop-ups dates back to 2001 when advertisers sought new alternatives for Internet advertising due to a reduction in the rate of clicking on banners and the absence of a proper standard for evaluating the efficiency of advertising efforts (Cho, Lee, & Tharp, 2001). This resulted in the creation of Rich Media, a powerful tool that has evolved Internet advertising significantly because of its ability to use animating software. Pop-ups and pop-unders are examples of the Rich Media advertisements. containing motivating messages. By applying Java scripts and flashes, these messages can also move. In 2007, the Dynamic Logic Institute declared that of the total income gained through internet advertising, the share of pop-ups and pop-unders was 53%.

Figure 3. A hypothetical model for doubleclick networks

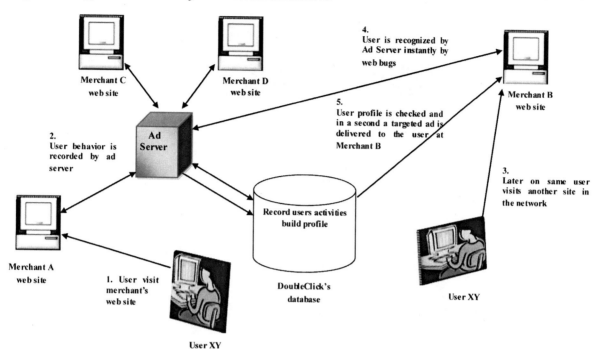

Pop-Up Publishing Techniques

There are some techniques by which advertisers publish their advertisements in an intrusive way.

- **Disabling mouse**: This technique causes the user to be unable to exit the page or close it until the end of the ad's exposure.
- **Unlicensed download**: In this technique, the advertisement hides behind download-ing software, sometimes even adapting it-self to the software. Then as the software is being downloaded, it enters the user's browser and runs the page without asking for the user's permission to do so.
- **Keeping the user on the main site** *(farm-ing)*: Using this technique, the advertiser keeps users on the main page even though they want to visit other pages on the site. This way, the user will be exposed to the advertisement for a longer time.
- There are some other techniques for broad-casting such advertisements, some of

which include explicit or hidden spawning of ads or adoption of a forged name.

Regulations and Procedures

To improve interaction between advertisers and customers, the Interactive Advertising Bureau has published a set of regulations and procedures specifying how advertisers can use pop-ups. Their research endeavor was aimed at improv-ing customers' attitude toward pop-ups so that broadcast advertisements can be adapted for the users. This procedure is formulated in three basic parts: user consistency, specification, and label-ing. These guidelines improve advertisers' and advertising agencies' ability to customize ads based on customers' demands. Also, application of these procedures makes pop-ups more reliable for customers, improves the efficiency of Internet advertising and increases the possibility of online purchase.

The following guidelines are the result of many continuous studies and researches conducted

Figure 4. Publisher's portal model (Kazienko & Adamski, 2007)

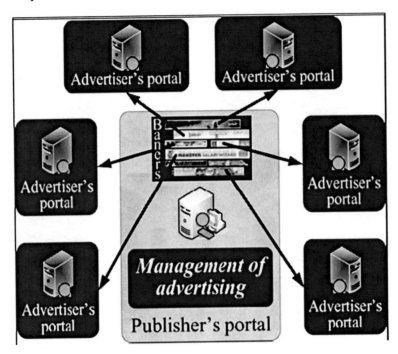

throughout the world to assess the efficiency of advertising and identify customers' requirements. Another study was conducted in 2007 by the IAB to identify the key challenges of Internet advertising faced by Rich Media as to advertising agencies, users, marketers, publishers and providers of the technology for Internet advertising. A summary of the findings is presented in Figure 8.

Pop-Up Blocker

Sometimes users cannot see pop-ups. Such advertisements distort the search process and thus are blocked by certain software that prevents them from entering into the user's system (see Figure 9). To obtain comprehensive information download the pertinent software, refer to *Sopzilla.com and Panicware.com.*

EMAIL ADVERTISING

Before the emergence of Web pages, emailing was considered a new communication method and with many advocates. According to Berkowitz's report issued in 2004, the annual expense of emailing is between 1.2 to 2.1 billion dollars, and that was expected to increase to 6 billion dollars in 2008. Once Web pages and new email facilities and transaction methods were introduced, email advertising showed rapid growth.

In email advertising, marketers send information about their services and products to potential customers through email. The message can include images, animation or links the customer can click on for more information. In this method, advertisers try to motivate customers by motivating them to pursue the main idea of the advertisement. In 2004, DoubleClick issued a report showing the daily increasing popularity of emailing. Thus, email can be one of the most important methods for Internet advertising (Figure 10).

Figure 5. Portal model for advertising (Kazienko & Adamski, 2007)

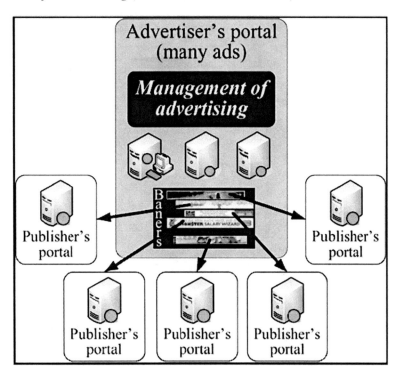

For advertisers to be able to send their ads to potential customers, they need a list of customers' email addresses. One method for gathering this information is to design space on the home website offering a benefit such as "free access or free download." For example, if the user visiting the site is a student, the information provided free might be electronic textbooks.

After clicking on the offer, a page opens that asks the student to insert personal information, including an email address, in order to receive the free download. An email is immediately sent to that address welcoming the student as a member of the website. The student is then asked to click on the address link within the welcome email. Returning to the site via this link, the user chooses an ID and a password. This way, the advertiser's website can gather the email addresses of users visiting the website and can send them ads via email on a daily basis. It is of a significant importance to have a list of customers' email addresses. There

are some companies who sell such lists, such as *Topiaca.com, Liszt.com*, and *Worlddata.com*.

Advantages of Email Advertising

Low expense: Email advertising is cost-effective and provides companies with the opportunity of being in touch frequently with their target customers. Email advertising is highly efficient because it does not involve finding a host site or paying rentals for the site, and the money spent for this type of advertising provides optimum results because the ads are displayed to those individuals who are more apt to buy that special type of product or service.

Long period of exposure to ads: When a user's mailbox opens, there is a waiting time of a few seconds in which to study received messages; this is when the ad is exposed and attracts a user's attention. If a customer tends to study one of the received messages a little longer, the ad is still

Figure 6. Portal model used by poland.com (Kazienko & Adamski, 2007)

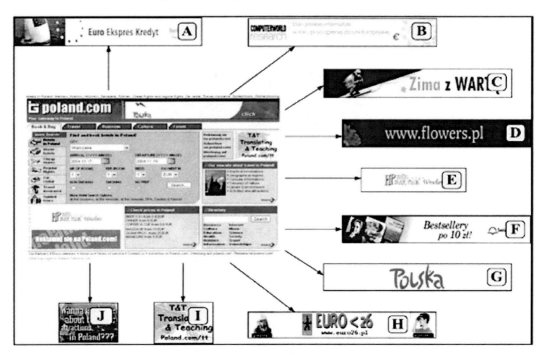

Figure 7. A pop-up example appeared in the middle of the page visited by the user

Figure 8. Pop-up broadcasting procedure (Interactive Advertising Bureau, 2007)

Def.	Any advertising experience that utilizes a web-browser initiated additional window to deliver an ad impression either directly above or below the existing browser experience.				
Freq.	Each user should be exposed to no more than one pop-up ad for each visit to an online site.*				
Labeling	Both pop-ups and pop-unders should be clearly labeled with the name of the Network / Advertiser – Publisher – Browser Type (if applicable): *Example:* UndertoneNetworks.com - CBS MarketWatch - Microsoft Internet Explorer				
Specifications	Unit Type	Unit Size (WxH in pixels)	File Weight	Audio/Video Initiation	Close Box
	Pop-Under	720X300	50k images 50k flash	User intitiated	Mandatory
	Pop-Up	250X250 300X250	30k images 40k flash	User intitiated	Mandatory
	Pop-Up Large	550X480	30k images 40k flash	User intitiated	Mandatory

Figure 9. Basic challenges of pop-ups (Interactive Advertising Bureau, 2007)

Key Issues	Methodology	Key Conclusions
Buyer Needs	• Agency & Marketer Tours • Sales Team feedback	• As some advertisers employ these ad types, we must sustain the viability of this ad type.*
User Acceptance	• Lab studies • Live Testing • Web Surveys	• Consumers do not distinguish pop-ups from pop-unders.** • More than 90% of consumers find pop-ups annoying or objectionable.*
Ad Effectiveness	• Historical analysis • AEF research	• More than 50% of users cited a 'very negative affect' to brands using pop-ups. 70% cited same for brand using pop-unders.**
Publisher Requirements	• Industry Forum • Inventory Modeling	• Labeling is key way to manage consumer service issues • Standard sizes are key to managing consumer expectations

Figure 10. Email advertising (yahoomail.com)

being exposed on the page below. Because of its small size, the ad opens earlier than the received messages, increasing exposure.

According to the report of Emarketer.com (2005), in the near future, email advertising will be the most outstanding method of advertising: it targets customers in a more precise and subtle manner compared to other advertising methods; it is a nonstop way of advertising; and it is incredibly inexpensive. With email advertising, companies may provide the chance for face-to-face communication, and if used in the right way, this method can increase customer confidence in a company or its products and services.

Unsolicited Commercial Emails (Spam)

It is easy obtain an email list. For this purpose, advertisements can be simply designed by one of the existing dynamic programming languages.

Since it is a time-consuming process to prepare a targeted list of email addresses, some companies apply send an advertisement to all members by adding receivers' names to the top of an email page. This method results in some negative consequences, and such emails are called spam or unsolicited commercial emails. Gopal conducted a study in 2006 revealing that this method is mainly used by those companies who do not consider the negative effects of such advertisements. The products and services offered by most of these companies are usually illegal and questionable. Reputable companies avoid this method because breaking into users' privacy may be irritating and unpleasant, and that response does not lead to purchase. According to a report issued by IDC in 2004, unsolicited advertisements are a prevalent problem. Each day more than 12 billion emails of this type are transmitted across the Internet. According to statistics, AOL filters about 1.4 billion of such emails each day. FTC is a company that studies these types of emails. In 2002, FTC reported that more than 8.3 million emails were received from users asked to identify unsolicited emails, meaning that the company had received 15,000 emails per day. The two models used for sending advertising emails include:

- **Opt-in model:** In this model, which customers find acceptable, an advertisement is sent to those customers who had previously shown some interest in the company's products or services and agreed to receive such ads.
- **Opt-out model:** This is a model customers find irritating because they receive irrelative, unsolicited emails.

ADVERTISING IN A SEARCH ENGINE

Most search engines allow companies to register their Internet address, providing the companies with some advertising advantages. Such a registration is free, and anyone can register an Internet address in a search engine. Users looking for special types of products or services can receive a list of pertinent manufacturers or service providers. However, a company's odds of being placed on the first 10 pages of the search results is almost zero. To increase that chance, some simple measures should be taken, such as making changes in the wording of the website text, adding key sentences to the title representing the types of products or services, and eliminating those words not compatible with the types of products or services. Moreover, some websites are designed to increase the chance of early exposure by providing companies with some solutions. Some Internet websites active in this field are *Keywordcount.com, Webpositiongold.com,* and *Searchenginewath.com*. Search engines often rent space on their first page where advertisers can introduce their products and services (Figure 9).

Advertising by Google

Google provides an advertising system called Adsense which provides publishers websites with targeted advertisements. To improve conformity among advertisements, publishers' websites, and users, the websites are periodically inspected by Google. To post advertisements in Google, basic data must first be entered on a page named "Ads by Google." Next, Google displays an advertisement using this information. These ads serve a double purpose: "Google Adsense" first displays the advertisement on a publisher's website and then searches to complete the advertising program. At this stage, a Google Search box is placed on the publisher's website to allow visitors to search through the website. The fee paid to the website owner by Google depends on the number of visitors who click on the box. Google links advertising images and texts to a user's "search page." This is possible even for companies who are just introducing their websites, products, and services to Google Ads.

VIDEO ADVERTISING

Together with video programs, video advertising has also been transferred from TV to the Internet, mobile devices, and even games. Today, only a small part of advertising budgets are allocated to video advertising accounts, and TV is no longer considered an exclusive outlet for video advertising. According to statistics provided by Jupiter in 2005, 24% of existing online advertisements are displayed through online videos. Video advertisements allow marketers to attract more users' attention and are clearly distinguishable during time of heavy traffic. Video advertisements can decidedly influence customers' attitudes more than moving banners or text, although the expense of video advertising is five to 10 times more, and there are some difficulties as to execution. A study performed by Advertising.com in 2007 reported that even being exposed within a short period, video advertisements influence customers' attitudes more than other types of advertisements. Does this mean that video advertising is the best advertising method? (see Figure 11)

Although statistics are encouraging, we cannot ignore previous advertising methods in favor of a newly emerging one. While we cannot be assured about the continuous influence of video advertising, more research is required to see whether the influence is only fleeting or if it is ongoing. This is not the first time when an Internet advertising format has entered the market in outburst burst of glory; RichMedia was extremely fascinating at first. Advertisers should consider what method suits what situation, product or service. The potential efficiency of this method can be actualized if it is used properly. Important principles to consider about such advertisements and how to improve their efficiency include:

- Creativity in production and exposure
- Simplicity of ads and short period of exposure
- Exposure period of not more than 30 seconds
- Focus on one key message

To transmit a message efficiently, two principles should be observed:

- **Sequential exposure:** Since a message should be delivered to the audience within a short period of time, it is better to display parts of the message sequentially during the exposure period in order to convey the message more efficiently.
- **Shortening:** It is better to display a short part of the video first and provide the audience with a URL or other link the complete video.

Taking into account that people are getting access to broader bands, the future of Internet advertising is expected to belong to this type of advertisements.

BUTTONS

Buttons are squares measuring 50×50 pixels in area, normally placed at the bottom of a web page. This type of Internet advertising can be clickable or simply used to introduce a product/service or a brand (Figure 12).

SKYSCRAPERS

As an Internet advertising format, a skyscraper is almost like banner. The only difference is that skyscrapers are narrower and placed vertically on the right or left side of the page (in the shape of a building skyscraper).

A study conducted in 2006 by Kelli on the popularity of various advertising methods revealed that skyscrapers are the most popular. Another study conducted about skyscrapers by iMedia discovered that the method is being applied by advertisers in an unexpected way. The advertisers put their logos where these types of advertisements are usually placed, in a way that the logo seems to be a type of ad (iMedia, 2002). It was also found that those advertisers who use this method are more successful if they expose their brands at the top of the ads, because customers are not inclined to scroll too far down the page to see a brand.

HALF-PAGE SKYSCRAPERS

Large skyscrapers are called half-page skyscrapers measuring 300×600 pixels. Usually they are exposed for 15 to 20 seconds, and then the ad theme changes. Although they are much larger than other types of Internet advertisements, they can be loaded easily because their size is only about 40 kilobytes. These types of skyscrapers

Figure 11. Advertising in the search engine

are usually placed at the bottom of the page or on the right side. They can be exposed without clicking because when the page is completely loaded, these ads are exposed automatically. The content of these skyscrapers include layers developed by dynamic programming and flash technology (see Figure 13).

ADVERTISING IN CHAT ROOMS

Chat rooms are virtual public places where people can ask questions about anything from medical advice to information about a purchased product. It is also a place where people can share their emotional feelings and exchange information and therefore is a perfect place for advertising purposes (Figure 14).

The methods mentioned above are the most prevalent types of Internet advertising and are used throughout the world. There are also other types of Internet advertising methods, but they are less common and less effective; examples include:

INTERSTITIALS

In his E-commerce book published in 2006, Turban specified that the term *"interstitial"* is derived from the word *"interstice,"* meaning a narrow split between two objects. **Interstitials** are advertisements placed inside a browser's window. They appear when a user moves from one page to another; the interstitial appears before this new page is loaded and disappears upon completion of loading. This type of advertisement belongs to the pop-up family. Interstitials are the most irritating types of Internet ads because they demand forced exposure (Cho, 2000). Commercial ads

Figure 12. Different types of buttons

displayed on TV are of the same type because they also force the viewer to abandon a program and watch the ad instead. Voluntary Exposure is just the opposite and occurs in traditional print media such as newspapers and magazines. These print ads do not prevent readers from studying the text and so are less invasive, much like banners in Internet advertising.

TRANSITION ADS

The size of Transition Ads or Changing Ads measures 640×480 pixels, and the theme alters continuously during exposure. The nature of these ads is the same as electronic billboards in sports stadiums or street billboards (with a different format). The theme of these ads changes continuously to introduce a special group of products (Figure 15).

LARGE RECTANGLES

Large rectangles are another type of Internet advertisement. They are used more frequently compared to other types introduced in this chapter, and are usually visible at the bottom and right corner of websites (Figure 16).

LARGE BUTTONS

Large buttons are similar to standard buttons mentioned earlier and measure 160×120 pixels. Studies conducted on the efficiency of Internet advertising reveal that the size of an ad is one of the main influential factors in attracting users' attention (Bruner, 2006). Bigger ads proved to be more efficient; therefore, new types of buttons have emerged that are much larger than the original ones (Figure 17).

SUPER OR LEADER BANNERS

A super or leader banner is a member of the banner family. A super banner is measures 728×90 pixels and can include animation. These types of banners are mainly used to promote products where the manufacturers want immediate consumer reaction. Sometimes a new brand is added to the company's product line, and the company tries to introduce the brand within a short period of time; these super banners are helpful for this purpose. Usually advertisers place super banners in portals of heavy traffic and pay a high rental (Figure 18).

Figure 13. A half-page skyscraper and an example of a skyscraper

TILES

Tiles are rectangular ads placed at the bottom of a web page on the left side and usually measure 120×120 pixels. Tiles or slabs (a material used to cover floors or walls), as the name implies, are designed so that most of the time, users think that the tile is a part of the website. Hence, it attracts users' attention and is clicked on more. Reputable broadcasters or Internet hosts should act meticulously when selecting those ads designed in the form of a tile, because improper ads, especially those advertising an unpleasant or offensive product, may have an adverse effect on the user and consequently degrade the credibility of the host website. That is why hosts should adopt an attentive attitude toward broadcasting tile ads (Figure 19).

EARLUGS

The term Earlug is a combination of *Ear* (meaning hearing) and *Lug* (meaning bunch). This type of Internet advertising is created in a GIF (Graphic Interchange Format) and is able to broadcast both image and sound. According to a study conducted by Thorson & Leavitt in 1986 and reviewed by Rogers and Thorson in 2000, motion and sound are recognized as two factors contributing to the efficiency of advertisements. These types of ads should be used more on those websites that are not easily related to the type of product advertised. Clear examples of websites where earlugs can be used are news websites which broadcast events and news, and each second a new theme is added to the content. Sound and animation are the best ways to attract the user's attention on these types of websites (Figure 20).

Figure 14. Advertising in chat-rooms

SPONSORSHIP ADVERTISING

Sponsorship is an indirect method of advertising that allows organizations to market their products and services on a webpage where the key content is somehow related to of the company's products and services. These ads appear as a part of a list of sponsored links. By clicking on these links, users access desired websites. One of the benefits of this type of advertisement is the small space they occupy.

CLASSIFIED ADVERTISING

The share of this method compared to all other Internet advertising methods was 17% in 2007, according to statistics issued by the Interactive Advertising Bureau. These ads can usually be observed in online magazines or newspapers (Figure 21).

HYPERLINKS

Hyperlinks are often linked to hypertext. They include a word, a term, or a chart that enables the user to transfer to the advertising website via a simple click. Hyperlinks are small in size and can be placed inside text like a sponsorship advertisement, but they are not limited in number and they can be placed anywhere on the page. Artistic designing can significantly increase their efficiency. These types of ads target those users searching for data who usually study the searched items carefully. Therefore, when proper key phrases, sentences and words that are related to the subject are placed in a user's favorite text in the form of a link to an advertising website, the user's existing demand can be transferred to the advertiser's product or solution. These types of ads are especially useful for websites with business models similar to those of Encyclopedia and Communities, because in these websites,

Figure 15. Different types of transition ads

members gather information for one another and are sensitive to certain words. Establishing links for these key words can change the community business model to a combining model called the advertising community. Hyperlink advertising is a tool that allows communication between two websites and can be an advertising interchange between prominent, heavy traffic websites.

WEBSITES

A website is the biggest method of Internet advertising because a website—whether commercial, cultural, political, or educational—is established to promote and introduce a specific subject. Unlike other types of Internet advertising, websites are free from size or expense limitations and can include any advertising message. The factor that differentiates a website from other methods of advertising is consumer behavior, because users search for websites to satisfy their demands. Other ads are exposed when a user is surfing websites. As a matter of fact, websites adopt a *pull strategy* because they publish messages directly to their audiences. Other advertisements adopt a *push strategy* because, as you will read in Chapter 8. Since all advertisers need to guide consumers

Figure 16. A large rectangle

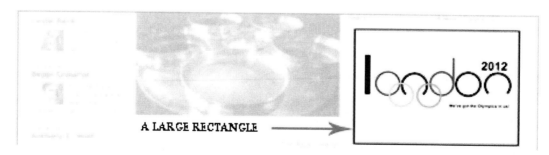

Figure 17. Three types of large buttons measuring 160×120 pixels

Figure 18. A super banner

Figure 19. A tile at the left corner of the website

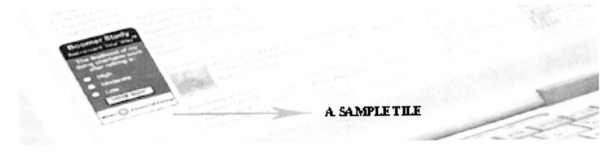

Figure 20. One example of an earlug

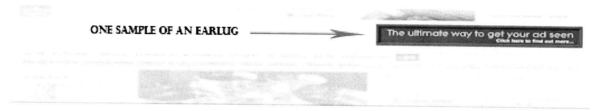

to their own websites, they create a gateway by broadcasting various types of advertisements. These types of advertisements are actually short, involving users mentally and motivating them to click (the role of branding should not be ignored in this regard). It is not the mission of a banner to broadcast a comprehensive message that results in a behavioral reaction; it is the website that fulfills this task.

As the most comprehensive type of Internet advertising, a website has the means to motivate the customer to buy. Unlike other types of advertisements, the efficiency of a website is not short-term. The mission of a website includes keeping the user on the website for a long period of time and guaranteeing a return visit in the fu-

ture. Factors that are effective in increasing the stay time include appropriate design and facilities for online interaction with website owners and other members. However, to make a customer remember the site for a long-time is a challenge faced by this method. Some factors are influential in this regard, such as aligning a user's mental involvement with product involvement, creating a positive attitude about the website; as this mental involvement increases, it automatically reminds the user of issues that can be solved by returning to the site.

Figure 21. Classified ads on the left side of an online hypothetical newspaper

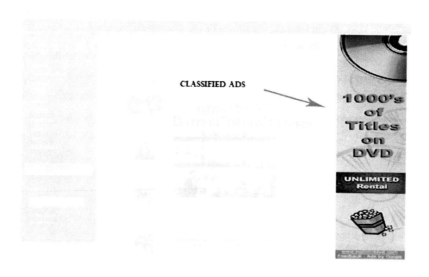

ADVERGAME

Product placement is a method in which companies pay movie display their ads in films. This method is extended to the Internet via advergame, which allows advertisers to introduce their brands to users in an entertaining way—inside a video game (Hairong & Leckenby, 2004). This placement is performed at three levels: Associative Integration, Illustrative Integration and Demonstrative Integration. Associative Integration is the lowest level where the brand is placed into a background, an activity or an event. Illustrative Integration is the second level where the brand is placed in an outstanding and obvious location. Demonstrative Integration is the highest level of integrating a brand into an advergame. For example, the first character of a game is designed in a way that suggests that the character's incredible movements are due to the shoes it wears; the shoe brand belongs to an advertiser who paid a the most money.

CONCLUSION

In this chapter, we introduced different methods through which Internet advertising channels transmit advertisers' messages to consumers.

Banners are the most common method of Internet advertising. Their goal is to motivate visitors to click on advertising, which transfers the visitor to the main website. Various types of banners include: keyword banners, random banners and fixed banners. There are also different ways to placing banners on websites such as swapping banners and exchanging banners. To publish a banner advertisement, a marketer must use one of these three models: broker model, advertiser model or portable model. The second formats for Internet advertising are pop-ups and pop-unders. Pop-ups are the most common type of Internet advertising and are known as ad spawning. Pop-ups automatically appear in a new window on the browser at the front side of an opened page. Pop-under advertisements are placed behind opened pages and appear as soon as the page is closed. There are some techniques through which advertisers publish their advertisements in an intrusive or trespassing way like: disabling the mouse, unlicensed downloads, and keeping the user on the main site *(farming)*. The third format is email advertising, where businesses send information about their products and services to potential customers through email. The message can include images, animation, or visual clips on which the customer can click for more information. For email advertising, there are two models used for sending which include: the opt-in model and the opt-out model. The fourth method is advertising in a search engine. Most search engines allow companies to register their Internet addresses, providing the companies with some advertising advantages. Such a registration is free of charge, and anyone can register his Internet address in a search engine. Google has provided an advertising system called Adsense, which provides publishers' sites with targeted advertisements. To improve conformity among advertisements, website of publishers and users, the site is periodically inspected by Google. In this chapter, we also investigated other Internet advertising formats like video advertising, buttons, skyscrapers, half- page skyscrapers, chat rooms, interstitials, transition ads, large rectangles, large buttons, super or leader banners, tiles, earlugs, sponsorship advertising, classified advertising, hyperlinks, websites, and advergame. The main objectives of this chapter were introducing Internet advertising formats and understanding the target markets for each.

REFERENCES

Advertising.com. (2007). *Banner audio/video guidelines*. Retrieved from http://www.platform-a.com /search/node/video%20advertising.

Age, A. (2007). *How to make effective online video ads.* Retrieved from http://www.adage.com.

Amiri, A., & Menon, S. (2003). Efficient scheduling of internet banner advertisements. *ACM Transactions on Internet Technology, 3*(4), 334–346. doi:10.1145/945846.945848

Berkowitz, D. (2004). *Responsys responds to email challenges.* Retrieved April 9, 2011, from http://www.emarketer.com.

Bilchev, G., & Marston, D. (2003). Personalized advertising, exploiting the distributed user profile. *BT Technology Journal, 21*(1), 84–90. doi:10.1023/A:1022460428681

Bruner, E. R. (2006). *Best practices for optimizing web advertising effectiveness.* Retrieved from http://www.doubleclick.com.

Chen, J., & Ringel, M. (2001). *Can advergaming be the future of interactive advertising?* Working Paper. Retrieved from http://www.locz.com.b r/loczgames/advergames.pdf.

Cho, C., Lee, G. J., & Tharp, M. (2000). Advertising responses to different forced exposure levels on the www. In *Proceedings of the 2000 Annual Conference of the American Academy of Advertising.* American Academy of Advertising.

Cho, C. H., Lee, J. G., & Tharp, M. (2001). Different forced-exposure levels to banner advertisements. *Journal of Advertising Research, 41*(4), 45–56.

Doubleclick.com. (2004). *Online advertising.* Retrieved from http://www.doubleclick.com /us/products/online_advertising/.

Emarketer.com. (2005). *Email advertising report.* Retrieved from http://www.emarketer.com.

Green. A. (2007). *The promise of online video, dynamic logic market norms.* White Paper. Retrieved from http://www.dynamiclogic.com.

Hairong, L., & Leckenby, D. L. (2004). *Internet advertising formats & effectiveness.* Retrieved from http://www.kaschassociates.com /49101web/LIB2004AdvertingFormatsEffectivness.pdf.

IAB. (2007). *Pop up guidelines & table.* Retrieved September 16, 2011, from http://www.iab.net.

Idc.com. (2004). *Worldwide email usage 2004-2008 forecast: Spam today, other content tomorrow.* Retrieved August 26, 2011, from http://www.idc.com.

Imedia.com. (2002). *Logo placement affects skyscraper success.* Retrieved November 11, 2010 from http://www.imediaconnection.com /news/958.asp.

Przemysław, K., & Adamski, M. (2007). Adrosa—Adaptive personalization of web advertising. *Information Sciences, 177,* 2269–2295. doi:10.1016/j.ins.2007.01.002

Turban, E., King, D., Viehland, D., & Lee, J. K. (2006). *Electronic commerce: A managerial perspective.* Upper Saddle River, NJ: Prentice Hall.

Chapter 5
Advertising Agencies and Interactive Media

ABSTRACT

Advertising generally refers to the promotion of products, services, activities, and ideas. According to marketers, advertising is an important part of a promotional strategy. However, other elements of promotion, noted in Chapters 1 and 2, include sales promotion, personal selling, and public relations. Advertising involves the process of designing a message to promote a product, idea, or even a service. Advertising is a difficult task since it is the arrow that targets customers in order to attract them and change their beliefs, attitudes, and behaviors.

For advertising to be efficient, various methods are used. Forming emotional or rational attractions, characterizations, animation, developing memorable mottos, and propaganda are some methods that allow an advertisement to achieve more success. To design a dynamic advertisement, a department should be organized inside or outside of an organization, with a staff demonstrating outstanding marketing skills. This chapter provides a detailed analysis of advertising agencies. It first presents a perspective of advertising agencies, and follows with the nature of the industry, work environment, and other involved elements. Next it deals with the role of advertising agencies in the new media and introduces concepts that have emerged due to changes made in the agency environment. Moreover, two groups of interactive agencies which play a significant role in online interactions are discussed: network advertising and lead generation.

NATURE OF THE INDUSTRY

Advertising agencies are different due to the capacity and size of their transactions; however, the advertisement production process is the same for all. Generally, advertising agencies have two tasks to fulfill. The first task is the procurement of all advertising requirements such as artistic, graphic, written and audiovisual aspects, and the second task is strategic placement. Strategic placement is a comprehensive effort to find the right media, the right exposure time and the right space for the ads. Advertising agencies produce advertisements for other companies, and design activities to improve those companies' customers' mental

DOI: 10.4018/978-1-4666-0885-6.ch005

images and interests. Moreover, these industries are responsible for finding the right media for advertisement placement. The right media is a message distribution channel where marketers are able to reach, communicate and deliver advertisements to target audiences with minimum repetition. When searching for the right media, some advertising agencies act more skillfully in market niches. A market niche for advertising agencies is a market which is considered smaller than other markets with few competitors. For example, some companies are more skillful in outdoor advertising such as billboards and electronic exposures, and some are more proficient in advertising on buses, or inside metro stations, taxi stations, and airport terminals. When online advertising finally proved itself to be a necessary method, committees were established inside advertising agencies to meet the demand. These new work groups' objectives were to shift and redirect users from a small advertisement to a larger one. Advertising agencies design small online advertisements like banners to motivate users to click on them and thus lead the users toward the advertiser's website or larger advertisement. This larger advertisement provides the users with all the specifications of the product, including the brand name, company records, and various types of other products. It is noteworthy radio, TV, newspaper, and website companies who sell or rent time and space for advertisements play no role in the production of an advertisement; employees of these organizations are more involved with preparing the information and laying the groundwork required to sell the time and space.

Organizations believe that advertising can improve their sales and revenue by publicizing their products/services. Thus, proper design of an advertisement is a prerequisite to achieving this goal. However, most organizations do not have employees skillful enough to produce an efficient advertisement. Moreover, since some advertising activities are transient, company owners can hardly satisfy such experts and retain them. To meet their

advertising demands, most companies contact advertising agencies for bids on an advertising project. The advertising agencies then present their estimates and ideas, and if a mutual agreement is reached, a contract is agreed upon between the two parties. This is when the agency's various committees (Research, Innovation, Production, and Media) begin their work aimed at increasing their customer's sales.

In large companies, a public relations department is able to effect decision-making in governments, businesses, and institutes. Generally, public relations agencies can provide resources that their customers are unable to provide, including high levels of knowledge, experience, skill and innovation in a certain field. Customers of public relations agencies could be businesses, institutions, merchants and public interest groups. To improve customer satisfaction and to gain more clients, advertising and public relations agencies have incorporated marketing to increase the variety of their services

ADVERTISING AGENCIES

Advertising agencies play an important role in producing modern advertisements. They require a proper level of knowledge and experience in order to provide efficient services. An advertising agency principally is skilled in advertisement design, production and placement. The Association of Advertising Agencies of America (AAAA) defines advertising agencies as independent commercial institutions consisting of innovative individuals and commercial experts who produce ads and find proper media for publishing (for sellers or advertisers who seek customers). Advertising agencies work with a variety of different methods and have distinctive ways of communicating with their clients. We first examine the history of these agencies, and then we discuss the different types of ad agencies.

History of Advertising Agencies

First Period

The first advertising agency was registered in the United States in 1841 and was founded by Olney B. Palmer. Palmer first established an advertising newspaper and an agency that was paid by commission. In 1849, he established some branches for this agency in New York City, Boston, Baltimore and Philadelphia. At that time, there were no guidelines for the cost for space sold to advertisers. As the founder of an informative organization, Palmer dealt with this issue and smoothed the way for the next generation of advertising organizations. Generally, the organization founded by him was in the business of selling space to publishers. Palmer received 25% of the sales price as a commission. Sometime later, publishers found out that this method was much more efficient than direct selling, and advertisers wanted it to expand to other regions. However, when the method became widespread, publishers began to have direct interaction with advertisers, and the space price became a bargain. This made the business of advertising agencies stagnant; they were in dire need of a new method for their survival (Bergen, Dutta, & Walker, 1992).

Wholesaling Period

The second period in advertising agency history, known as the wholesaling period, refers to the years between 1865 and 1880. George P. Rowell, who founded his advertising agency in 1865, presented a new competitive tool to increase the efficiency of advertising agencies. Rowell signed contracts with 100 newspapers; each newspaper had to sell one column to Rowell to be used as advertising space. Through this method, agencies could remain the sellers of publishing space.

Semi-Service Period

The wholesaling period ended in 1880 with the establishment of sale committees by publishers. Some of these committees sold space directly to advertisers and some to advertising agencies. During this period, agencies had two main tasks: selling space for publishers and buying space for advertisers. In the semi-service period, advertising agencies returned once more to their main task: producing and placing advertisements as ordered by advertisers.

Service Period

Agencies' services developed gradually so that from the 1917 onward, advertising agencies evolved into service organizations. In this period, advertising agencies were promoted to the position of advertising and marketing counselors.

The emergence of other media such as radio, TV, and the Internet made the tasks of these agencies more complicated and specialized. Advertising alternatives went beyond newspapers and direct mail, and it was not possible for an advertising space was to be sold easily as in previous periods, because it seemed irrational to sell space directly to the advertisers. Due to various alternatives that existed for the advertisers (as a result of the emergence of new advertising space in newly emerging media) and due to advertisers' ignorance about the advantages and weaknesses resulting from choosing media for advertising, the necessity arose to delegate the sales task to an intermediate agency (Gagnard & Swartz, 1988).

DIFFERENT TYPES OF ADVERTISING AGENCIES

Advertising agencies are divided into small, single-bureau organizations, multinational organizations and multi-agency organizations depending on their size and the amount of services they provide. Some agencies, such as those that design and pursue marketing and advertising in search engines (Search Engine Marketing, SEM, and Search Engine Optimization, SEO), are experts in a special type of advertising. In fact, all advertisements are not produced by advertising agencies; there are some companies that produce their own advertisements fulfilled by in-house organizations.

To introduce the various types of advertising agencies, this chapter deals with each separately.

Comprehensive Advertising Agencies

These agencies provide a set of marketing services including production of sufficient number of advertisements, distribution, packaging and product design; they also do the artistic work required. An example of these is the *Oho* Company (*see oho.com*). These types of agencies are known as Digital agencies because most of their strategies and activities are concentrated on the Web. We will discuss them in this chapter and will mention some of their business models.

Modular Agencies

Modular agencies are service providers who offer specific services. That is, an advertiser may ask the innovation unit of such an agency to do one advertising activity while requesting other services from other agencies. A customer or an advertiser may ask the media unit of an agency to publish an advertisement produced by another company. In this case, the price of the service is a matter of mutual agreement and depends upon the amount of work performed at each stage.

In-House Agencies

Most organizations that prefer close supervision over their advertising efforts use in-house agencies. These types of agencies are fully governed by the advertisers. They perform all the tasks performed by independent agencies with some differences. In-house advertising departments are responsible for providing advertising functions such as:

- Fitting promotional goals with advertising cues, appeals, and message.
- Designing the first prototype of advertising and providing some of its requirements.
- Communicating and negotiating with publishers.
- Selecting the right media in order to reach more of the target audiences with fewer placements.

In-house agencies have to do tasks delegated by their single organization, while independent agencies can provide their services to various types of clients. In-house agencies can use evident or implied attributes of an organization, such as its social status and ties, to develop their advertising activities. In these agencies, the organization applies meticulous control over expenses and timetables while the agencies can provide the organization with increased profits due to the services they provide.

Creative Boutiques

Creative boutiques are service-providing agencies whose task is to present innovative designs. They do artistic work and provide incentives, animations and other elements that can increase the efficiency of an advertisement.

Mega Agencies

Mega agencies emerged at the beginning of the 1980s. They provide their services by merging several advertising companies, usually worldwide. One of these agencies is Saatchi and Saatchi, *saatchi.com,* established in 1986 in London. It is considered as one of the greatest agencies in the world.

Specialist Agencies

There are some advertising agencies that have a special field of activity and are skillful in providing one or several types of services. An example of these agencies is *complaintsboard.com* that focuses its activities more on outdoor advertising.

ORGANIZATIONAL STRUCTURE

Like any other social group, advertising agencies also have an exclusive internal framework of activities, which are divided into four groups:

- Customer management
- Innovation department
- Purchasing media
- Research

These groups do their tasks separately, yet they are coordinated with each other and interact during the production of advertisements.

Customer Management

Customer management deals with customer affairs and accounts and is a major part of an advertising agency's structure. Personnel in the customer affairs department deal directly with potential and current customers. This is a part of an agency that registers customers' orders and demands, identifies a customer's business and introduces it to the agency to adopt the correct advertising message. The main member of this group is the account manager as that person interacts most with the customer The account manager or account planner is responsible for long-term cooperation with clients and is fully aware of market changes, and customers' attitudes towards a client's products and services, and he knows the client's competitors. The account manager is in contact with senior managers in the client's organization and is responsible for the agency's

performance. Moreover, the account manager is responsible for long-term planning, personnel appointments and the profitability during the client's relationship with the agency. "Account manager" is a term principally applied to a customer's representative in an advertising agency; an account manager seeks the best methods for introducing a client's products to customers and develops a better understanding of the product. Previous "planners" are now strategists who develop brands and branding actions. They have become mass media strategists. Using customer information, these strategists predict where and how people are more inclined and ready to receive the advertising message (Gummersson, 1994).

Other Roles

An account manager is an employee who introduces an advertising agency to clients. He identifies advertising and sale problems of the client and chooses an advertising orientation. In the advertising industry, the term "account" applies to the client. Account refers also to the relationship formed between the client and the agency. Each agency has several clients and designates a team of employees to deal with a client's affairs. This team is headed by the account manager. An account manager may lead a number of clients of different in different fields of business (Waller, 2004). The account manager performs a series of tasks with the cooperation of different specialist teams. First, an innovation and creative group will create the foundation and concepts of the advertising. Then, a media group will propose the appropriate media so that the advertisement has more reach. At the same time, a research group is responsible for gathering data from advertising trends and click streams in order to make an educated decision. There also are other teams working with an account that include design copywriting and reproduction groups which work along with other groups to create an efficient product for the customer.

Interactive Agencies

After developing a general understanding of the advertising industry, this chapter now focuses more on agencies that perform their advertising activities through the Web. These interactive agencies generally provide these four major services to online advertisers:

- Strategic consulting
- Media purchasing and planning
- Website creation and design
- Analysis of business information

Some interactive agencies provide all of the above services, and some specialize in one field. For instance, some agencies focus their attention on gathering and analyzing market information for their clients, while other agencies focus more on creating and developing websites.

Strategic Consulting usually includes two major activities: 1) analyzing customers, their products, and their competitors' status; and 2) planning to optimize the marketing budget. The analyzing stage usually includes examination of the industry, users and competitors. After conducting an upward or downward analysis, the agency proposes a special type of marketing or online advertising for the client (email, search engine advertising, branding, or a mix of different marketing channels).

Media Purchasing and Planning involves a broad range of services usually divided into some subsidiary activities such as:

- Development of a media strategy and production of an advertisement
- Execution of advertising activities (media purchasing and distribution of advertisements)
- Analysis and optimization of advertising activities

At the planning stage, the agency estimates the general perspective and goals of the client and designs a proper strategy to help the client achieve those goals. This strategy determines the degree of reach, number of repetitions and leads. At the same time, there is a team responsible for design and production of online advertisements (banners, rich media and advertising promotions). At the second stage, the agency enters into negotiations to purchase advertising space for search engines, display ads, email lists and advertising networks. At the analytical stage, the agency studies advertising data (such as brand lift) and applies that to improve its knowledge and performance for future activities.

Website Improvement includes Web designing, content management and making lateral plans. To improve a website, most advertising agencies focus more on the Web designing aspects instead of the programs used. The Web has made improvements for different purposes such as developing a base for e-commerce, interactive marketing, and intranet and extranet facilities. Website improvement usually includes the following stages:

- Strategic planning: through identification of a firm's target audiences, all website activities and contents are planned.
- Improving data architecture: organizing the content and data of a website and intranet to increase usability and traceability.
- Set-up and execution of a new website design.

When the website is designed, the agency optimizes the website to optimize the opportunity for the customer's goals to be attained. Moreover, the agency also provides the required tools to manage the website and increase its operational efficiency.

Business Information Analysis is becoming a differentiating factor that distinguishes interactive agencies from one another. This analysis and its pertinent tools are used to support strategic planning, media purchasing, the planning process and website improvement. This analysis process includes tasks such as analysis of activities, Web analysis, analysis of coequal industries, database analysis, goal-setting and pursuing media. Hence, agencies that acquire more sophisticated reporting tools and software, and present more accurate analysis, provide their services at a higher quality level because this activity has a direct effect on other activities of an agency (To see the 50 top interactive agencies around the world, *so to adgae.com.*).

INTERACTIVE AGENCIES AND CHANGING OF USER TRENDS

Changing of users' habits and activities has changed the perspective of advertising agencies so that these agencies have made significant changes in the alternatives they propose to advertisers. Although traditional agencies used to resist such changes, the advertising industry has accepted the new technologies and found strategies and business models appropriate for the new advertising opportunities that are based on the new technology.

Large holding companies active in all marketing and advertising aspects played the main role in the emergence of new advertising channels. According to a report issued by the Internet Media Institute (2007), large holding companies own more than 60% of the total income earned by interactive companies. Advertising agencies have less chance to achieve success because advertisers do not have to refer to an agency to meet their advertising demands; rather, they can simply search for key words referring to advertising agencies and register orders by visiting the pertinent websites. The place where the website is established is not a matter of importance because advertisers can ask advertising agencies in other countries to produce ad copy and publish it on websites. Since advertisers seek advertising agencies in search engines, small agencies have less chance to be selected because one criterion used

to rank website links on the first page of search results is the number of visitors clicking on their links. Hence, larger companies have more of a chance to attract new accounts

NEW ISSUES FOR INTERACTIVE AGENCIES

Advertisers always look to interactive agencies for a complete chain of services such as finding the right media, designing and developing a website, Search Engine Marketing (SEM) and market analysis. From a holistic point of view, such agencies are appropriate alternatives for providing advertising services and can develop insights about the efficiency of a marketing channel. As predicted by the Internet Media Institute (2007), most advertising agencies will merge to form a perfect combination of services for their users. New services presented by interactive agencies include:

Engagement Marketing

While advertisers of traditional media have long used engagement marketing, the Web as an interactive medium intrinsically focuses more attention on customer participation than traditional media. Web designing is the first stage of engagement marketing that deals with users' passive attitude towards Web content. The second stage is Web improvement and developing interactive transactions and user-generated content. Engagement marketing may take place in different forms such as interacting with an online advertisement, interacting with a website (such as customization of a product) and polling (Rashtchi, et al., 2007). Involving users with the brand is a key point to consider. It is also important to understand that the advertising activity is user-driven and not advertiser-driven.

Improving Main Content

In the new Internet world (Web), advertisers have to apply more interactive tools, including online videos and games. However, it is not enough to simply place offline activities online. Agencies have to make an investment in focusing on the serious content (Internet Media, 2007). In this respect, interactive agencies display five-second online videos instead of 30-second TV commercials. These videos are easily displayed inside the content, requiring no special time or speed. In comparison with offline ads, online ads should be more associated with a customer's wants as the Web is a flexible medium and has the capacity to indicate customer preferences and tracing. Traceability allows advertisers to change and improve their content quality. Content quality comes from a process in which there is a purpose: "user-oriented broadcasting." Creating new changes aligned with customer click streams is the main activity that ensures content quality. Before using new technologies to make some improvements, it is important to know: what caused customers to click on an ad and enter a website. What cues or appeals have attracted customers' attention and kept them online? What deficiencies cause customers to exit a website quickly? We can define content quality as follows:

Content quality is the process of identifying, grouping and forming appeals and cues, and delivering associated services (content) to customers in a flexible and customized way to deliver the highest electronic satisfaction for customers.

Interactive agencies attempt to develop content quality and create user-oriented advertisements for their clients.

Virtual Marketing

Virtual marketing was designed to earn maximum profit from a minimal marketing/advertising budget. Virtual marketing is not based on traditional marketing methods; it is quicker and is presented covertly in an unconventional method. In the past few years, advertisers used virtual marketing methods increasingly to improve the Web and user-generated content. A virtual marketing method used on the Internet is amateur-looking websites and user-generating content including blogs and online videos. Virtual marketing played a significant role in the success of some fast-growing Internet companies like *Google, MySpace,* and *Youtube.* Although many advertising agencies and advertisers try to apply virtual marketing, this method is a difficult way of producing a successful advertisement, and only one out of 10 advertisements produced through this method achieves the predetermined goals (Rashtchi, et al., 2007). To achieve success, interactive agencies must develop their potentials and capabilities of virtual activities.

USING INTERACTIVE AGENCIES

Interactive agencies are usually expert in one of the following fields of activity:

- Online branding
- Performance-based marketing (direct response and searching)
- Relationship marketing

Online Branding

For online branding, interactive agencies try to increase customers' knowledge about an advertiser or a specific product. They usually conduct a study about brand image, then produce an advertisement based on the study results, target proper users and ultimately analyze the results. Since advertising activities are performed to publicize a brand, it is difficult to assess the Return On Investment (ROI). Interactive agencies do so by measuring the improvement of a brand's status, and they sometimes pursue the online or offline behaviors resulting from such publicizing activities.

Performance-Based Marketing

In performance-based marketing, advertisers can measure the efficiency of advertising efforts, and they can also calculate ROI. Some advertisers prefer performance-based marketing because it can target determined goals and directly account for marketing expenses. Performance-based marketing includes direct marketing, search, lead generation, and online promotions.

Relationship Marketing

The changes made reveal that service marketing is relationship-oriented. Having been realized since the 1980s, this approach is titled relationship marketing and opens new horizons for transactional relationships among the partners (Triki, Redjeb, & Kamoun, 2007). Relationship marketing defines marketing as the focal point of relationships and a network of long-term interactions (Gummesson, 1994). Relationship marketing focuses more on retaining existing customers than attaining new ones. One of the clear advantages of relationship marketing is that the cost of customer retention is only a fraction of the cost of attaining a new customer. Since organizations tend to analyze the life value of a customer, the role of relationship marketing has become more vital. Interactive agencies tend to make advertisers increase their use of relationship marketing by providing services such as email, data mining, CRM software, joint promotions and plans to improve customer loyalty.

ADVERTISING SERVICES AND TECHNOLOGIES

The type of technology used and the extent of usage is another issue to be considered by an interactive agency. The role of technology and services is limited in traditional advertising; however, the role of technology is determinant and tangible in its economic growth. That is why

with the emergence of interactive agencies, many other types of advertising agencies have vanished or have limited business. Most of these agencies changed the model of their business to compensate this limitation (one of the largest companies that covered the distance was Double Click). Due to customers' tendency toward online activities and the need for doing an exact analysis about such activities, a new route had to be defined for this group of interactive agencies. On this basis, search engine marketing has been added to the activities of advertising agencies as a new field of work. Interactive agencies are developing their services and technologies so that they can improve their core competency and merit system by increasing the amount of services provided. In general, there are three major service-providing and marketing groups:

- Search engine marketing companies
- Analytics companies
- Ad-serving companies

Moreover, there are two other types of interactive companies that play an intermediating role:

- Ad networks
- Lead generations

Search Engine Marketing (SEM)

Search engines are the most important tools with which people retrieve data or pages on the Internet (Hochstotter & Koch, 2009). Search engine innovations such as geographical and demographic goal- setting have significantly increased the complexity of companies working in the field of search engine marketing. While most advertisers are still managing the keywords of their organizations, the development of search engines has made such issues even harder to be managed, and advertisers may face high costs to advertise their websites. Along with the development of search engines, interactive agencies have offered new software and are trying to increase the ROI resulting from this method of marketing. As search engine marketing includes a set of strategies used by advertisers to attract more users for their websites via search engines, they offer some services to improve these strategies. Some of these services that provide the advertisers with a higher added value are as follows:

Keyword Management also known as "bid management" or "pay-per-click management," keyword management allows interactive agencies to help advertisers to experience an optimum process of advertising through search engines and to select the most appropriate bid, keyword and search engine for their advertisement.

Search Engine Optimization (SEO) is an effort to improve the rank of the key phrase of a website in outstanding search engines such as Yahoo and Google. Agencies do so usually by code updating and analyzing, and through improving HTML architecture and website content. An agency usually tries to identify factors effective in improving a website's rank, such as external links, content, or keywords.

Paid inclusion is the money paid to the search engine by the website to register the page on the search engine's list. It does not guarantee placement, the search engine only takes the subscribed webpage into account at the time of searching. However, some popular search engines like Google do not receive any money for inclusion.

Feed Management: Assigning the database of a website to the comparison shopping engine of a search engine or to comparative sites is called feed management. This usually includes receiving unstructured data from websites and changing them into customized data to feed a comparison shopping engine. Feed management is important for advertisers because it ensures them that their retailing data is included in the comparison shopping engine. It is noteworthy that feed management does not guarantee a special rank. According to the report of SEMPO (the Search Engine Marketing Professional Organization), SEM agencies'

income in 2005 was to about $345 million. From this amount, 47% was earned from SEOs, 40% from the bids, 10% from technology, and 3% from paid inclusions. Moreover, according to another report issued by the same organization, companies like *Atlas,* that produce the required software, earned about $33 million in 2005.

Most of the income resulting from search engine marketing are earned by independent or joint stock interactive agencies and search engine marketing experts such as *iCrossing* and *Efficient Frontier*. Major technology providers in the domain of SEM are *Atlas* one point (owned by *aQuantive*), *Bid Rank,* and *Send Traffic*. As to website analyzers who improve the rank of Web pages, *Web Side Story,* and *Omniture* outperform others. To view the top 20 companies active in the domain of search engine marketing, see *Ad-Age.com.*

WEB ANALYTICS

The key trends of web analytics are:

*   Central analysis development
*   Shifting to confidential and customized analysis
*   Multi-channel analysis
*   Gaining profit through developing online advertising and e-commerce

Central Analysis Development: Web analysis has changed from an online marketing spot solution to an online marketing strategic platform that combines analysis with online marketing capabilities including site-searching, bid management, content management, behavioral goal-setting, link marketing and email marketing. Within the framework of task development, applied programs of analysis have changed to activity centers, while they also assess and maximize the life cycle of digital marketing. Meanwhile, interactive agencies have resorted to Web analysis development so that optimization of products is considered important, and small agencies and organizations of this industry are constantly merging with one another. While most companies try to develop these tasks by integrating other marketing tasks, companies belonging to older software corporations such as ERP and CRM are developing their tasks to establish a digital marketing and analysis system. This analysis-oriented development will result in a tougher competition among those market players who seek superiority.

Shifting to Confidential and Customized Analysis: While most analysis approaches in the current market are common, some improvements have been made in software to provide customized services. For instance, *Science Visual* software produced by *Website Story*, providing real-time analysis about Web traffic, is currently offering separate copies for analysis of email, network security and financial transactions, and in this way, takes steps to improve its organization by expanding the range of professional analysis.

Multi-Channel Analysis: The Web analysis market was developed to allow businesses to be able to collect multi-channel and behavioral data online and offline. The market includes a telephone center and sales data. While analytical companies focus mainly on the Web, some other approaches have been developed to improve analysis and optimize customer transactions through other digital channels like mobile phones, video and on-demand video (a system enabling viewers to select their favorite films and watch them on their PCs or via an interactive TV system).

Gaining Profit through Online Advertising and E-commerce Development: Development of a Web analysis market is linked to online advertising and e-commerce. Usually the demand for web analysis is higher in online advertising; according to a report issued by Internet Media in 2007, the demand for analysis services provided by the Web is increasing. Also according to this report, the global market Web analysis in 2006 amounted to $ 417 million and is expected to rise to one billion dollars in 2011. The present market of Web analysis is governed by four companies: *Core Metrics, Omniture, Webtrend,* and *Web Side Story*. Although other companies are also active in this market, these four are the major market players. According to an estimation by the Piper Jaffary Institute, the market share of these four companies is about 60%. Google is also a Web analyzer, providing its services for free, limited to the advertising policy of its search engine.

Key Web Analytics Tasks

According to a report issued by the Web Analytic Association (2006), objective tracking, data collection, measurement, reporting study of quantitative data of the Internet for website optimizing, and marketing innovations are among the key tasks of Web analytics. Web analytics enables marketers to attract more users, retain current users and increase their sales. Web analytics generally enables organizations to fulfill the following tasks:

- Pursuing online marketing activities such as pay-per-click, keyword purchasing, banner advertising, emails and affiliation marketing programs.
- Pursuing website tracking by user.
- Analyzing change rate by product, price, customer source, search word and tracking route.
- Studying transfer trends.
- Identifying sources referring users to websites (site traffic source).
- Measuring efficiency of all processes.
- Identifying online processes of high transfer prices.
- Identifying products frequently visited and determining the correlation between data and customer behavior.
- Identifying those pages of a website frequently visited by users and validating the data with sales changes.

Figure 1 illustrates an analytic dashboard presented by Google in 2011 and some of the issues mentioned above.

ADVERTISING BROADCASTING

Publication of an advertisement includes four major activities:

- Moving toward a consolidated policy
- Pushing toward online videos
- Developing new advertising methods
- Optimizing technology

Moving Toward an Integrated Practice

There are two groups involved in publishing advertisements: publishers and advertisers. These two groups seek the tools they need for online marketing. For an advertiser, this may include an integrated practice for display advertising, search engine marketing and web analysis. For instance, *Atlas.com* has shown in its analysis that advertisers may achieve better results from search marketing if customers are exposed to display advertisements. The key factor that makes advertisers move toward integrated practice is the tendency to improve marketing methods and find out which marketing method can guide the business toward its goals. Publishers also look for ability of integrated analyzing, outcome management and behavioral targeting within a certain practice.

Pushing Toward Online Videos and Developing New Methods

Due to the increase in bandwidth, watching online videos and movies has become a major function of the Internet among users, especially in the United States. According to a study conducted by *ComScor.com* in 2006, 64% of American users watch online-videos.

Since the tendency toward watching and downloading online videos has increased significantly in the past few years, video advertising has been revealed to be promising. On this basis, online advertising is moving toward presenting new methods of online advertisements. These methods include on-demand TV and portable media devices. These new tools, channels and online videos can create another wave of Internet advertising. Hence, it is vital for technology providers to design approaches to improve these activities. One of the leading companies in this regard is *aQuantive.com*, which is now *Marketing Advertising*.

Optimization of Technology

Publishers and advertisers should focus on the optimization of technology. For advertisers, this will develop the potential for high rates of change and rapid return on investment. For publishers, optimization of technology increases the rates of pay-per-click and pay-per-thousand exposures (a method for paying for Internet advertising expenses that will be explained in detail in Chapter 6) that ultimately increases their revenue. A general rule for successful optimization is innovative optimization. Based on this rule, the advertiser tests and optimizes innovative advertisements to find out which one generates the best results. According to a study conducted by Piper Jaffary in 2007, the dollar value of publishing online advertisements had been $350 million in 2006, showing an annual growth rate of 30%. Advertisers and publishers have a 50-50 share in this amount. Agencies with higher shares, who are the main players in the market, are *Double Click* and *Real Media*, two established publishers, and *Double Click* and *Atlas* (belonging to aQuantive), two advertisers. Other key players include *Falk* (owned by Double Click), *Mediaplex* (owned by

Figure 1. An analytic dashboard offered by Google (google.com, 2011)

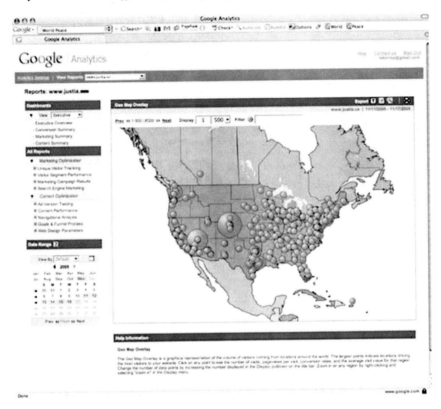

ValueClick), and *Acipiter* (recently purchased by aQuantive). Major online video advertisement publishers include *Eyebloster*, *Point Roll* and *Motif/Klipmart* (owned by Double Click).

Advertisement Publishing Method

Advertisement publication depends on the type of technology that put ads on the website. Technology sellers provide software that let agencies place advertisements and also lets publishers receive ads. Services provided by advertising agencies for publishers include systems that optimize the ads published on a website to maximize the publishers' revenue. These systems include daytime indicators and user location indicators, and are capable of making clear whether the user is new or not. The system is also capable of analyzing and pursuing consumer behaviors. Publishing technologies usually include inventory management, goal-setting potentials, and tools for analysis and reporting. Creation of an advertising server by an advertiser allows the advertiser's publishing tools to:

1. Plan activities
2. Execute activities (deliver advertisements)
3. Analyze the results and move toward optimization

Advertisement publishing and serving tools used by advertisers usually include planning, traffic study, ad serving, tracking, reporting and analysis. *Atlas.com* (affiliated with *aQuantive.com*) offers such a service. X-X presents a set of approaches including activity planning, media buying, creative management, message delivery, data collection, analysis and optimization accessible to advertisers.

So far we have talked about interactive agencies that have a direct relationship with advertisers and provide them with preliminary online marketing and advertising services. However, two other types of interactive agencies are also introduced in this chapter, which play an intermediating role and assist interactive agencies in providing more efficient services. The term "intermediate" as applied in interactive agency literature, differs in concept from the one used generally by the public. Those interactive agencies acting as mediators include ad publishing and lead generating networks. Ad publishing networks are investigated later in this chapter, and lead generation is will be discussed in detail in Chapter 12.

ADVERTISING NETWORKS

An advertising network is a mediator that collects or buys ads (banners, hypertexts, and rich media) from websites and sells them to agencies or advertisers. Advertising network websites have a mixed variety of content and are generally divided into groups of 10 to 20 categories. For instance, different channels include sports, technology, online games, men's favorite subjects, women's favorite subjects and youths' favorites. Advertising network channels are also classified based on other factors such as "targeting users," "geographical specifications," "demographic specifications," "certain times of day," and "behavioral analysis." Advertising networks also offer valuable services to advertisers, such as assisting them in defining a proper strategy, media planning, innovation, optimization, activity management, and reporting.

Advantages of Advertising Networks

Advertising networks play a valuable role in the online advertising market for both advertisers and publishers. Advertising networks enable advertisers to reach thousands of small publishers without any direct negotiation. When an advertiser is in need of widespread messages to make a brand known to the public, an advertising network can meet his repetition and access demands and introduce the brand via key portals and large vertical websites.

An advertising network is a cost -effective method for small publishers, allowing them to sell their website spaces for advertising purposes, and with the assistance of such networks, these publishers do not need to have a sales division. Large publishers also enjoy the assistance of such networks for selling empty space on their websites. Some of the most important privileges of advertising networks include:

- **Reach:** In the domain of brand marketing, advertising networks have reached millions of users. For instance, automobile manufacturers can use such networks to introduce new products by displaying these products in vertical websites and portals.
- **Pricing:** The prices offered by advertising networks are far cheaper than those offered by portals and websites, because most advertising networks obtain $1 to $2 per thousand exposures while the price obtained for displaying ads on vertical sites and portals is about $8 to $10 (Internet Media, 2007).
- **Targeting in Network:** Advertisers can use advertising networks to target special content channels existing in large vertical sites. Moreover, advanced goal-setting technologies such as behavioral analysis have increased the value of advertising networks for advertisers.
- **Optimization:** Optimization technology enables advertisers and ad networks to analyze which website offers appropriate service and which is the best advertising placement.

Key Issues in Advertising Networks

At first, the advertising network industry was ignored because they were focused on diagrams and thus not interesting to publishers. At the preliminary stages, the industry lacked proper goal-setting technologies and could not provide advertisers with the clarification they needed. However, such defects no longer exist, and advertising networks are now cooperating with high-quality sites. According to an Internet Media Institute's (2007) forecast, advertising networks will soon evolve into standard online supplements. Moreover, while the advertising space on vertical sites and portals has decreased, the number of advertisers seeking advertising networks is rising quickly. Now that advertising networks are equipped with behavioral analysis systems, advertisers can publish their ads on special vertical sites.

Targeting Technologies

By developing their targeting methods, advertising networks are adding value for their advertisers. These methods include studying demographics, activity at certain times of day and consumer behavioral analysis with today's targeting more focused on behavioral analysis. Generally, there are two types of behavioral analyses: cookies and buying intention. Cookies are tools by which the behavior of an online user can be traced, and in this way, advertisements are published based on the content of the websites visited by the user and also based on the user's gender. For instance, when a user first visits the site of a manufacturer of electronic devices and then visits a news site, electronic devices ads are displayed on the news site. Setting goals based on buying intention is an effort to identify and target customers based on the customer's stage in the buying cycle. Advanced targeting technologies enable advertisers to have a higher rate of return on investment, and also enables publishers and networks to receive more commissions, because according to a report issued by the Jupiter Research Institute (2006), 88% of advertising agencies who used behavioral targeting were fully satisfied with the results. Superior

targeting technologies can increase the revenue of advertising networks. There are companies that specialize in analyzing consumer behavior like *Revenue Science* and *Tacoda*. These companies are usually either partners of advertising networks or they have their own advertising networks.

Variety of Advertising Networks

During the first days of online advertising, most advertising networks focused their attention on a pricing model based on what advertisers were charged depending on a network's performance after ads were displayed one thousand times (pay-per-thousand exposures). However, today's advertising networks are trying to meet the demands of publishers and advertisers of different business models by presenting comprehensive approaches. For instance, *Valueclick.com*, a provider of advertising networks based on the pricing model defined above, obtained an advertising network from Web Clients Company in 2005, and this network charges customers based on the model of pay-per-thousand exposures. Currently, the company publishes ads based on both pricing models.

Market Size

The market also includes semi-advertising networks, and according to a report by Internet media (2007), more than 10% of the market share of display ads belongs to advertising networks. Considering that in 2006, 15 billion dollars was spent on display ads, Internet media estimates the share of advertising networks to be 1.5 billion dollars. Advertising space is vast, and networks work in a sectional way. Two large companies active in this domain are *Advertising.com* and *Valueclick. com*. Generally, advertising networks are divided into three groups, and most advertising networks are categorized under at least one of these groups:

- **Dynamic ad networks:** Advertising networks based on this model purchase advertising space in advance and then classify and select the best group for the advertiser. Then the classified spaces are sold at a higher price to advertising agencies or advertisers (see *Drivepm.com* and *Advertising.com*).

- **Traditional ad networks:** Advertising networks categorized under this title have contracts with publishers selling advertising space, but they do not guarantee to sell all of the space. Actually, in this model, the advertising network acts as the publisher's representative to sell all or part of advertising space (see *Value cclick.com* and *Realmedia.com*).

- **Ad representation:** Networks categorized under this title cannot be regarded as perfect networks. Based on this model, advertising companies present website advertising space to advertisers or agencies and earn a commission for finalizing a contract (see *WinstarInteractive.com* and *Specificmedia.com*).

According to Comscore.com (2006), the most superior advertising networks of the world are based on studies conducted by Internet institutes such as Media Post, iMedia Connection, and ComScore.

LEAD GENERATION

Lead generation is a process by which an advertiser can be aware of customers' future tendencies. Lead generation agencies actually provide advertisers with customer information such as their previous shopping habits, email addresses, telephone numbers or information specified in a registration form, and this way advertisers can publish ads that are more targeted. According to a report issued by the Online Lead Generation Association, online lead generation gathers customer data for the purpose of delivering a targeted product. Lead generation on the Web usually is accomplished by expert agencies that can provide customers with high-quality information by establishing a website or an advertising network to engage the customers.

Agencies procure the required customer information via various online advertising methods such as common registration. They display users' favorite issues in the form of ads on the websites most visited by the users announcing some sort of free product or service. When users click on the ad, they are re-routed to an ad landing page with a registration form which must be filled in to receive free offer. To prevent users from inserting imperfect or invalid information, an email is automatically sent to the email address provided by the user, who then clicks on the link placed in the email (Figure 2). The agency can purchase the information from advertising networks. Most agencies guarantee the information when selling it to advertisers, and they also make advertisers guarantee that they do not sell the leads to others.

According to a report issued by the Interactive Advertising Bureau (2009), 7% of online advertising incomes in 2008 were the result of lead generation. Since online advertising revenue in 2009 exceeded 23 billion dollars, it can be inferred that the revenue earned through lead generation in that year amounted to more than 1,644 million dollars.

Leads are priced on different bases; however, they are usually priced based on the difficulty of collecting the information, the expense of collection and the time spent for this purpose. The lead generation market is not an integrated one. Companies working in this regard are divided into two groups based on their field of activity. The first group is expert in financial resources and investment affairs, such as *Bank Rate, Lead Tree* and *House Value,* and the second group has a wide range of activities, such as *Web Clients, Azoogle Ads* (owned by Value Click), *Adteractive, CoregMedia,* and *QuinStreet.*

Figure 2. A sample of generating leads

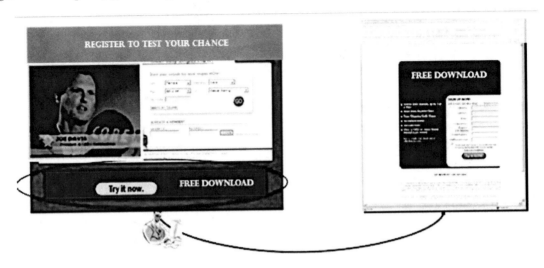

CONCLUSION

Organizations advertise because they believe that advertising can improve their sales by publicizing their products. Thus, proper design of advertisements is a prerequisite to achieving this goal. However, most organizations do not have employees skillful enough to produce an efficient advertisement. Therefore, a new complementary firm is needed—advertising agencies. Advertising agencies have two tasks to perform: the procurement of advertising requirements and strategic placement. Strategic placement is a comprehensive effort to find the right media, the right exposure time and the right space. Most advertising companies perform more successfully in market niches, which are markets considered less important than other markets and in which exist few competitors. The history of advertising agencies involves four periods: the first p, wholesaling, semi-service and service. This chapter also introduced different types of advertising agencies including comprehensive advertising agencies, modular agencies, in-house agencies, creative boutiques, mega agencies, and specialist agencies.

Agencies generally are structured around four departments: customer management, innovation, media purchase, and research. The person who is in touch with customer the most is the account manager. This account manager or account planner is the main person who plans for a long-term client relationship, and for this he encourages customer participation. The account manager is fully aware of market changes and customers' attitudes towards a client's products and services, and he knows the client's competitors.

After developing a general understanding about the advertising industry, this chapter focused more on those agencies who perform their advertising activities on the Web—interactive agencies. These agencies generally provide four major services to online advertisers: strategic consultation, media purchase and planning, website creation and design, and analysis of business information. Furthermore, new changes in the interactive agencies business were discussed which include: engagement marketing, improving main content, virtual marketing, online branding, performance-based marketing and relationship marketing. The chapter then introduced web analytics and advertising networks, and explained how these two issues are scrutinized. Finally, a brief perspective of lead generation as a type of interactive agency was presented.

REFERENCES

Adage.com. (2006). *Top 50 interactive agencies, agencies report 2006*. Retrieved from http://www.adage.com /datacenter/article?article_id=108866.

Adage.com. (2006). *Top 20 search engine marketing and optimization companies*. Retrieved from http://www.twistimage.com /.../advertising-age-gives-you-the-search-marketing-fact-pack-2006/.

Association of Advertising Agencies of America. (2011). *Website*. Retrieved from http://www.aaaa.com.

Atlassolutions.com. (2006). *Atlas ad serving platform*. Retrieved from http://www.atlassolutions.com /news_20061101.aspx.

Bergen, M., Dutta, S., & Walker, O. C. (1992). Agency relationships in marketing: A review of the implications and applications of agency and related theories. *Journal of Marketing, 56*(3), 1–24. doi:10.2307/1252293

Cagley, J. W. (1986). A comparison of advertising agency factors: Advertiser and agency perceptions. *Journal of Advertising Research, 26*(3), 39–44.

Comscore.com. (2009). *Leading ad networks company*. Retrieved from http://www.marketingcharts.com /interactive/top-25-ad-networks-in-april-platform-a-yahoo-lead-pack-9182/comscore-top-25-ad-networks-unique-visitors-april-2009jpg/.

Durkin, M., & Lawlor, M. A. (2001). The implications of the internet on the advertising agency-client relationship. *The Service Industries Journal, 21*(2), 175–191. doi:10.1080/714005026

Ellis, S., & Johnson, L. W. (1993). Agency theory as a framework for advertising agency compensation decisions. *Journal of Advertising Research, 33*(5), 76–80.

Fam, K. S., & Waller, D. S. (1999). Factors in winning accounts: The view of agency account directors in New Zealand. *Journal of Advertising Research, 39*(9), 12–32.

Gagnard, A., & Swartz, J. E. (1988). Top American managers view agencies and research. *Journal of Advertising Research, 28*(6), 35–40.

Gummesson, E. (1994). Making relationship marketing operational. *International Journal of Service Industry Management, 5*(5), 5–21. doi:10.1108/09564239410074349

Harris, J., & Taylor, K. A. (2003). The case of greater agency involvement in strategic partnerships. *Journal of Advertising Research, 43*(4), 346–352.

Helgesen, T. (1994). Advertising awards and advertising agency performance criteria. *Journal of Advertising Research, 34*(4), 43–53.

Hochstotter, N., & Koch, M. (2009). Standard parameters for searching behavior in search engines and their empirical evaluation. *Journal of Information Science, 35*(1), 45–65. doi:10.1177/0165551508091311

IAB. (2009). *Internet advertising revenue report, 2008 full-year results March 2009*. Retrieved from http://www.iab.net.

InfoCaptor. N. J. (2008). *InfoCaptor's pharmacy financial analytics dashboard*. Retrieved from http://www.dashboardinsight.com%2Fdashboards%2Fproduct-demos%2Finfocaptor-pharmacy-dashboard.aspx.

Jancic, Z., & Zabkar, V. (1998). Establishing marketing relationships in the advertising agency business: A transitional economy case. *Journal of Advertising Research, 38*(6), 27–36.

Jupiter Research Institute. (2006). *Behavioral targeting to transform online advertising*. Retrieved from http://www.marketingvox.com / jupiter_behavioral_targeting_to_transform_online_advertising-021979/.

Na, W., Marshall, R., & Son, Y. (2003). How businesses buy advertising agency services: A way to segment advertising agencies' markets. *Journal of Advertising Research*, *43*(1), 86–95.

Prendergast, G., Shi, Y., & West, D. (2001). Organizational buying and advertising agency-client relationships in China. *Journal of Advertising*, *30*(2), 61–71.

Rashtchy, S., Kessler, A. M., Bieber, P. J., Schindler, N. H., & Tzeng, J. C. (2007). *The user revolution, the new advertising ecosystem and the rise of the internet as a mass medium, investment research, internet media*. Retrieved from http://www.scribd.com.

Scribd. (2000). *Project report on advertising agency*. White Paper. Retrieved from http://www.scribd.com /doc/3671764/Advertising-agencies-project.

Sempo.org. (2005). *Revenue of search engine marketing*. Retrieved from www.sempo.org /.../research/sempo_research/...2005/SEMPO-12-05-05new.

Triki, A., Redjeb, N., & Kamoun, I. (2007). Exploring the determinants of success/failure of the advertising agency-firm relationship. *Qualitative Market Research: An International Journal*, *10*(1), 10–27. doi:10.1108/13522750710720378

Waller, D. S. (2004). Developing an account-management lifecycle for advertising agency-client relationships. *Marketing Intelligence & Planning*, *22*(1), 95–112. doi:10.1108/02634500410516940

Web Analytic Association. (2006). *Key web analytics*. Retrieved from http://www.webanalyticsassociation.org.

Chapter 6
Internet Advertising Pricing Methods:
How to Calculate Advertising Costs?

ABSTRACT

The Internet is rapidly turning into an advertising channel. According to available statistics, online advertising expenses in 2006 increased by 19 percent. However, offline advertising witnessed a two percent growth in the same period (Weisman, 2006). Just in the United States, Internet advertising revenues hit $7.3 billion for the first quarter of 2011, representing a 23 percent increase over the same period in 2010 (iab.net, 2011). Surprisingly, the trend showed that Internet advertising expenditure reached 49,994 million dollars at the end of 2008 (Zenithoptimedi, 2009), much earlier than expected. Beneficiaries of this investment and growth are search engines such as Google, Yahoo, and MSN, to which most of this chapter is dedicated.

Establishing and administrating a website requires visitors. Users visit the websites if they know them and find that their content fulfills their needs and wants. Administrators or owners of a website, commercial sites in particular, do not have the knowledge to introduce or advertise the website to potential users. Advertising a website and the products or services provided by it requires knowledge of the requirements and applications of advertising. One of the most important requirements involves advertisement pricing. In this chapter, the authors will discuss one of the effective issues of any E-business: payment and its methods. New methods, their application procedures and thee advantages and disadvantages of major websites will be examined in this chapter.

COST-PER-THOUSAND AND FLAT-FEE EXPOSURE MODEL

Flat Fee means paying a fixed amount for displaying an ad in a certain time period; this is the oldest method of online advertising pricing. The flat-fee method is often applied regardless of traffic guarantees in which the advertiser guarantees to show the ad during website prime time; this gives the advantage to the publisher. In this method, a flat fee is paid on a monthly basis; whether the ad is published during low or high traffic times.

Since information on high-traffic times of the website is available to the publishers, it is possible to change the flat-fee method to CPM. CPM or

DOI: 10.4018/978-1-4666-0885-6.ch006

Cost per Mille is a different way to advertisers for per-thousand exposure. If the information on traffic and the users of the website is available, the CPM and flat-fee methods can be interchangeable. CPM also can be promoted with guarantees of exposure time in a certain time period, thereby being more appropriate for the customers.

The greatest challenge of marketers is to recognize the business models that can be applied successfully in the online environment. Some advertisers support CPM and believe that this method includes an appropriate unit of measurement in which pricing is based on exposure and each publisher broadcasts the ad separately. The customers also believe that this is a rational way to advertise their products or services.

However, flat fee and CPM are in their infancy, because the Internet is different from traditional media. While traditional media enjoys a one-to-many communication model, the Internet and the Web, in particular, are based on a many–to-many communication model (Hoffman & Novak, 1995). These methods are derived from the most important advantage of advertising. Web interaction should not be ignored because CPM emphasizes banners rather than target communication. Target communication is a method in which a HTML-structured website is upgraded through technologies like Hyperlinks or JavaScripts, and creates online selling processes. In fact, target communication is the real marketing that advertisers try to gain from their users. When a customer places an advertising order and the ad is published by CPM, more visitors rush on to the website, and this is a considerable success because it is a one-to-many communication model which looks for the audience to read its message. Note that this is an interactive medium, and interaction among the members is one of the key factors for success. In fact, a long-term presence on a website results in increased learning and draws the user's attention to other factors; consequently, there will be a positive impression of the website in the user's mind. Applying CPM, however, endangers the

website. Some of the dangers emerge when the administrators decide to develop their own website. Their biggest problem would be a lack of users having homogeneous tastes and interests,, for the website's business model attracts non-homogeneous users; besides, this presence is temporary. In addition, in CPM, measuring and recognition of the interaction and pricing based on the value of interactive visits by the user is difficult; hence, this process is not favorable for the customer. In fact, the CPM model does not determine anything more than the number of users who have been exposed to the banner ads on certain websites. Since customer behavior on the host website is dependent upon the type of website and the customers' motive to visit the site which is readily measurable, merely recording the number of visits is not enough information to sum up the value relative to the advertising cost. In other words, direct comparison of the website according to the number of users exposed to the ad, regardless of other factors, is meaningless.

CLICK-THROUGH RATE MODELS

Advertising pricing based on a click-through rate is an attempt to develop a more responsible method for paying for online advertising. In this method, paying for ad exposure is based on the number of times the user has actually clicked on an advertisement. The price paid for one click on the ad is one to four percent of a dollar (Hoffman & Novak, 2000). However, note that few visits result in clicking on the advertisement. According to a study conducted by Double Click in 1996, only four percent of users who visit publishers' websites click on the advertisements when they observe them. In a study that was undertaken on network publishing of a banner advertisement, it was found that, on average, 25 percent of the advertising publishers had an eight percent click rate on the advertisement. This number, of course, relates to the first broadcast; in the second and third ad publishing, the click rate declines to two percent. In subsequent exposures, the click-through rate decreases to a mere one percent. In this method of advertising pricing, the user not only should observe the ad, but also should actively decide to click on the ad and be involved with the target communication process. This method, however, has problems. Some Internet publishers find this pricing strategy "unfair" because they believe that paying by click merely relates to the user; that is, after exposing the user to the ad, if a blind need or want changes to an active motivation and the user clicks on the ad, the publisher takes an interest in publishing the advertisement. On the contrary, if there is no motivation or desire in the customer, there will be no income for the publisher, but for a certain period, the advertisement occupies a certain space on the site and is exposed to the users. This method, like the previous ones, is not able to cover the issue of interaction, and the only thing that the click-through rate model can do is to become a departure point.

PAY-PER-CLICK

One of the main advertising fee payment models is Pay-Per-Click or PPC. This method first was used by *Goto.com*, which has now merged with Yahoo. In this method, the search engines display the website's or their member companies' links in separate boxes, and usually place those links in the upper part of the screen. The website owner pays a fee to the publisher according to the number of clicks and visits of the users.

This method is designed for advertisers who are concerned about their ad's impression, because the publishers' website is not always in the same position when they the customer's ad is broadcast. In other words, sometimes the website may be in a high-traffic position and sometimes it may be out of traffic; it could even be inactive and in a bad publishing position. Therefore, it is essential

to define a mechanism for these concerns. An important factor in this situation is a "web master," which puts the advertisers' text or graphic links within their sites. When the users click on these links and enter the advertiser's website, the advertiser pays a fee, called a 'bid," to the web master. A bid is defined as the highest per-click price proposed the advertiser is willing to pay.

Pay-Per-Click in Search Engines

Search engines sell their advertising space in online auctions. When the user types a specific keyword, a page consisting of two separate parts is displayed. As explained in Chapter 8, at the upper or paid part of the page, there is a framed area designed for the search engine's advertisement. The results of the search are displayed on the lower part of the page. When the user clicks on the upper links, the advertiser pays a fixed fee per click (the bid) to the search engine. The number of ads that can be advertised is limited. The position offered to the advertisers is graded in different ways, for both advertiser and user according to their interests. Since the ad advertised in the upper part of the screen is more likely to be clicked on than the one in the lower part of the screen, the search engines need a system for allocating advertising positions to their customers.

ONLINE AUCTION

In order to assign a place to an advertiser according to the fee that they are willing to pay per click, an online auction is administered in order to deliver the right position to each advertiser. (Up to the present time, a number of options are also available on this issue which will be discussed within the framework of this book.) In order to find the appropriate position, advertisers must participate in an online auction

English Auction

An English auction is one of the oldest auctions attended by both vendors, and initially, vendors are free to set a base price for their goods; if the prices do not reach the set price, the vendor can end the auction. The buyers offer the highest price they think is appropriate for their business until finally, the item is sold at the maximum price. An English auction is done in two different methods: the first-price and the second-price auction. The first-price auction is conducted confidentially, and buyers are not aware of the price offered by other buyers. Each buyer proposes one price and eventually, the buyer who has proposed the maximum price is the winner of the auction. In 1961, William Vickery, devised the second–price auction, or Vickers, in which, just like the first–price auction, buyers propose their prices; however, the winner buys the item at the second maximum price. In other words, if the winner suggests $200 for an item and the second maximum price is $195, the winner must pay $195-. The important advantage of this method is that participants in the auction are not worried about other competitors' prices; therefore, they determine the value of the item based on their requirements.

Dutch Auction

Unlike the English auction where the prices have an ascending trend, in a Dutch auction, the prices follow a descending process. At the beginning of the auction, the dealer announces the highest base price, and this price keeps decreasing until a buyer accepts that price. This method has two basic disadvantages. First, in this kind of auction, there is no competition among buyers because one of the buyers might be interested in one product and might want to buy it at a higher price. Another disadvantage is that the base price is always much higher than the market price; otherwise, the auction has no interest in selling the item.

EBay Auction

On eBay, there is a special kind of auction known as an EBay auction. On this website, several samples of the same item are up for sale. After being informed about the item and the price, the customer begins the bidding process. The buyer, who has proposed a maximum price, buys the item at the lowest price accepted by the auction. For example, two e-books are for sale, and the base price is 500 dollars for each. Buyer A has offered 550 dollars, and buyer B has offered the same price. In this way, each of them will have one of the books. However, if there is another buyer at 600 dollars, buyer A wins one of the books, since he was the first bidder. The other book is given to buyer C, and buyer B loses the game. Other auctions like American or double auction also exist which are outside the scope of this book. For more information about those auctions, refer to the sources at the end of this chapter. After a brief explanation of an Internet auction, we will discuss the mechanisms used in search engines for selling and pricing the advertisement.

Generalized First-Price Auction

Introduced by *Goto.com*, the generalized first-price auction allows every customer to enter the highest price that they will pay by clicking on the advertisement. In this way, the customer bidding the highest price gains first place. Convenience, low entrance cost and transparency of the process have meant great success for this method to the extent that giant search engines like Yahoo and MSN utilize this method; however, it needs adjustments. The rapid change of proposed prices and the prices-per-click result in some confusion. For example, imagine that there are three customers and two spaces available in the upper part of the search results window. The first space has 200 clicks per hour and the second space has 100. The three customers propose $10, $4, and $2, respectively. The second customer decreases the proposed price to $2.02 in order to achieve first place in the bidding. When the first customer realizes that, an offer of $2.03 is made, and these ups and downs continue constantly, changing the prices per click. It is for this reason that customers buy automated machines or intelligent agents to participate in the auction, resulting in the loss of the search engine's revenue. Since the speed of proposed bids changes rapidly when using intelligent agents, the winning bid is at a minimum. Consider that in the above-mentioned example, an automated machine or other intelligent agent suggests and sets the bid rapidly, while the others set their price manually once a day. In this way, because the third customer has not increased their price-per-click, the highest price for the search engine will be $2.02, following the third customer's bid of $2 and the second one's bid of $2.1. If the second one tries to increase the price and take first place, the automated machine reads that and sets an appropriate price. In this situation, the second customer pays more and is still in second place. This basic problem has motivated researchers to reform the first-price auction process.

Generalized Second-Price Auction

One of the newest pricing and selling mechanisms in advertising is the Generalized Second-Price (GSP) auction. GSP is designed for online advertising and has achieved a lot of success in that field. This is the primary pricing mechanism of Google and Yahoo. Since the first-price auction faced many problems in E-business, the GSP witnessed a rapid growth; in fact, 98 percent of Google's total revenue in 2005, which amounts to $6.14 billion, was achieved by GSP. Similarly, 50 percent of the $5.26 billion revenue of Yahoo was earned based on this pricing model (Expertvoice, 2003). Other interesting statistics show that merchants have invested around $150 billion on this method of pricing (Edelman, et al., 2006). In the GSP method, after registering the maximum price-

per-click in special keywords, the search engine provides sponsoring links and delivers them to the users with search query results. Ranking is still based on the highest bid, and the customer links are listed respectively. If a user clicks on the first customer's link, the customer's payment quota is equal to the second customer's bid in addition to an extra fee. If the search engine displays just one ad to the user, this mechanism would amount to a second standard price that is usually determined by the search engine.

Some important characteristics of this method are important to consider. The first is that all proposed prices-per-click can change at any time. The suggested price for a special keyword works whenever a user types that keyword into the search engine. This enables the advertisers to increase and decrease the prices. The customer whose bid is in second place in the search screen presented to the user is also second. However, the ranking of advertisements the second time a user searches that keyword may be different, because the proposed prices are applied based on this keyword, and a higher price may have been proposed. Second, the search engine often advertises "perishable products" rather than products with a high stability and later expiration date. Third, unlike the other integrated markets in which the measurement and assessment of sold items is usually tangible, there is no unit of measurement in search engine advertising. This is also normal for both parties, because from the advertiser's point of view, this unit is the cost of drawing the customer's attention who makes a purchase. This cost relates directly to the pricing model; when a user completes a transaction, the advertiser pays a fee. From the search engine's point of view, the measurement unit is the sum of the revenues gained from the search.

As the GSP auction develops for online advertising, its rules follow the characteristics of the Internet environment. GSP emphasizes that merchants suggest just one bid for each keyword (unless there is more than one item on sale). This ensures that the base price in each position is equal to the number of clicks for that position. The advantage of being in a higher position for an ad is that it is clicked more. However, when the user clicks on the advertisement in different positions, it is considered that these positions share the same value for the advertiser. According to search engine's approach and the research findings of Brooks in 2004, in a GSP auction, it is supposed that the value of clicking in all positions is the same.

Another issue is that advertisers are different in other aspects regarding the value of each click, especially when they are positioned in the same place. From a technical point of view, these issues are called click-through rate or CTR. Search engines have different stances against these issues. Yahoo does not interfere in the differences in ranking the ads on a screen and rates the ads solely based on the proposed price. However, Google multiples the proposed price by the customer's quality score, which is determined by CTR and other factors in order to determine the customer's rank. Then, according to rank, the position of each ad is determined, so that a higher-ranking customer will pay a little more than a lower-ranking one.

Cost Calculation of GSP Auction

The revenue of the advertiser whose ad is placed in the first position is calculated by the following formula:

$$\text{AR (Advertiser's Revenue)} = (C_i - V_s) - P \tag{1}$$

Where:

- **N:** For every certain keyword, there exist N targets (positions on the screen that are used to display the ad)
- **S:** The price suggested by the customer-per-click (bid)

- **C_i:** Expected clicks for each position
- **V_s:** Value-per-click for advertiser's (S)
- **P:** Sum of total bids, or total money paid to the search engine

Note: the problem makes two assumptions. First, the number of times that one advertising link is clicked on does not depend on the type of the advertisement. Second, the value of each click is not dependant on the position of advertisement.

Positions are set for each i and j. As $i>j$, so $c_i >c_j$ means that clicks expected for position i are more than those of position j. The generalized second-price mechanism follows this model. Suppose that in time t, a user searches a keyword. Prices suggested for this keyword during period t are applied under the title b_s. If no customers (S) have suggested a price for that keyword per click, the b_s would be zero. If some customers have proposed the same price per click, then the ranking of their links in the first page of search results is done randomly. The highest position is awarded to the customer who has the highest price R_1, second place for R_2, and so on until the least prices of [M, S] and the allocation is over. Note that each customer has to propose a single price for each click on their links; the customers should pay the price suggested by the lowerst ranked customer to the search engine as a fee. Furthermore, the sum of customer payments that are in i position or $R^{(i)}$ equals $P^{(i)}$ and is calculated thusly:

$$P^{(i)} = C_i \, b^{(i+1)}, \; i \, [1 \ldots \text{Min} \, [M, S] \tag{2}$$

($i+1$) is the lowest position of customer placed in rank (i), meaning that the number of clicks expected for position i should be multiplied by the price suggested by the customer in the position below i (usually about \$.01 is added to this price according to the search engine's policy). Position i also can take the first to the last rank of search engine slots for advertising. By substituting the second relation into the first one, the customer's revenues can be determined. In addition, if $V_R(i)$ is defined as the value of each click in position i, the equation will be as following, indicating the customer's second revenue formula:

$$AR_2 \text{ (Advertiser's Revenue)} = C_i (V_R(i) - b^{(i+1)}) \tag{3}$$

In the case of some keywords, the number of positions or targets which are represented by M is higher than or equal to the number of customers, $M \geq S$, and the lowest customer price is zero. For example, if the engine has four positions for sale and there are four or less merchants, the fourth one does not pay any fee.

COST PER ACTION

Another type of advertising pricing is Cost Per Action (CPA). When e-business owners use the cost- per-click pricing method to expose their ad to a publisher, they feel secure because in proportion to the money they pay to the publisher, users are attracted to the website. However, there is no guarantee that targeted users are likely to establish a relationship with the site or even least devote some time to checking it out. Thus, the researchers are attempting to find other methods for pricing so that they can make the most of Internet interactivity. In this regard, the idea proposed here is that a supplementary measurement of advertising value and user interaction with target communication should be prepared for the advertiser. The interaction factor can be assessed by the time duration that user is on the website, the number of pages visited, their referrals to the site or some combination of those components.

A mail company first introduced CPA, where advertisers do not pay a fee to the publisher based on the exposure of the ad to the users or the number of clicks. However, the publisher does receive a fee when the user performs an action on the merchant's website, such as selling, e-mail registration, fill-ing out forms, participating in surveys and polls, attending online chats and creating an account. If these actions result in a sale or the delivery of a service, CPA turns into CPS (Cost Per Sale), and the publisher is paid more.

This new method has also been faced with some challenges. Internet ad publishers believe that assessment, paying per click and interaction with the users is out of their realm of responsibility. They do not believe that a publisher should be responsible for user activities on another website where they broadcast their advertising. Internet publishers state that the lack of interaction between users and the site is due to other reasons such as poor web design and unattractive content, which are not under the publishers' control. They believe that they have done their duty in motivating the user to follow-up on the advertising. Some Internet publishers cite the example of printing media. They wonder whether all advertisements in printing media result in sales. Regardless of selling or not selling the product or service advertised in print, a fee is assessed even before the ad is published.

PAY-PER-PERCENTAGE IMPRESSION

Fraud clicks and other fakes in Internet advertising are potential threats for online markets. Some of these frauds are quite complicated. Google considers fake clicks as one of its major concerns, as the money-per-click has to be refunded to the customers. George Reyes, Google's chief executive officer, says "Click frauds and misuses are now the greatest threat for the Internet economy and a big threat for our business model" (Crcomputerrepair.com, 2011). Some solutions have been offered for the problem, including pay-per-impression where the customer is not charged per click on the ad; however, there are still concerns about fraud. Recently, a method called pay-per-percentage impression has been developed which prevents both clicking and publishing frauds. For example, a merchant pays a dollar to the publisher to receive 10 percent of all impressions of their keyword in a week. In other words, one of every 10 users who search the word see the advertisement. If the ad is clicked on, there is no extra payment because someone might conduct a fake search of that word. However, on the assumption that there is no charge per click, it is important to know if all the impressions are the result of real searches. The answer is negative because, for example, there will be Y real impressions and F fake impressions, and in this situation, the advertiser will take 10 percent of Ys and 10 percent of Fs.

The most common fraud is the click fraud. In click frauds, a competitor of a merchant does a fake search for the keyword which relates to the merchant in order to decrease their competitor's ROI and to negatively affect their advertising budget. Unlike the exposure model, in this kind of fraud, the similarity of the keyword is not the source of worry because the competitor easily recognizes the keyword and avoids clicking on it, so do not lose money.

Considering the weaknesses of current paying systems in Internet advertising, researchers are now trying to develop a new and practical strategy. The greatest difference between this system and previous ones is in their processes. Current paying systems emphasize rotational positioning, but in the new paying system, random positioning is advocated because then the fraud possibility greatly decreases. For example, if 10 merchants intend to give their advertisements to a search engine, and the search engine displays the ads consecutively, the first search is devoted to the first merchant, the second search to the second merchant and so on. In the 11th search, the first customer's ad is shown again, and in this way, the competitor who wants to decrease the other customer's budget must know their primary position.

In order to recognize and introduce the right pricing method for any probable situation, Table 1 shows all methods and their distinctive features.

INCOME-BASED PRICING MODEL

Undoubtedly, marketers prefer a positive outcome, and buying is the best reaction to advertising. Advocating this idea, Murphy in 1996 stated that if a website has thousands of visitors, it will reap great profits. However, if a website just has five profitable visitors, it will gain greater profits. All attempts are aimed at motivating website visitors and turning them into profitable ones. Displaying banner advertisements results in the consumer's awareness of the product or service, while user interaction with the target communication process enhances their understanding and comprehension, after which marketing objectives such as attitude changing, intention making and buying will be realized.

The income–based approach in online advertising pricing begins with recognition of the marketing objective for target communication, which results in affecting the consumer's attitude, encouraging the consumer to create a profile or leading the customer to buy. The Internet is a transitional medium for integrated marketing campaigns. One example of this is per-inquiry advertisements that pay an amount of money only for real purchasing with no extra charges. Another example is affiliated programs such as in Amazon.com. In such programs, products that are affiliated to websites are sold by another website whose content is related to the advertising. If a visitor reaches an advertiser via an affiliated website and purchases the product, the affiliating website is paid a referral fee or commission, currently between $.50 and $5.

Although pricing models utilized in online advertising are based on traditional advertising or

Table 1. Comparison between different types of advertising pricing models

Features Methods	Fee Payment	Broadcasting Method	Target Communication	Fraud Possibility	Interactivity
Flat Fee	Periodical and Monthly	Publish without considering traffic	Low measuring potential and navigating non-homogenous user to advertiser website	Medium	Lack of interaction
Cost Per Month	Monthly	Publishing both with and without considering traffic	Inactive	Low	Lack of interaction
Cost Per Mille	Per-thousand of exposure	Publishing both with and without considering traffic	Inactive	Low	Lack of interaction
PPC	Based on click, auction and adaptive bid	Inserting keywords in search engine and web master	Appropriate for search-based advertising. Navigating predicted user to Web.	High	Lack of interaction
Cost per Action	Based on user actions on the advertiser website	Publish with considering website traffic	Pulling targeted users	Very Low	Registration, creating an account, sending e-mail
Pay Per Percentage Impression	Based on random system click	Inserting keywords in search engine	Conveying targeted-search user to site	Very Low	Lack of interaction

mass media when there is a revenue base, these pricing mechanisms may be more related to a direct response pattern. According to a definition by the Direct Marketing Association, direct marketing is direct relationship with a consumer or transaction party who is interested in creating a direct order, a request for supplementary information or lead generation; visiting a store in order to buy a product or service; and traffic generation. Concepts of direct order, lead generation and traffic generation are obviously and directly applicable to the Internet's many–to–many environment. Taking the Internet as a unique communicator and its ability to create and develop the standards and parameters in relation to direct response leads to the creation of a complex model in measuring and pricing.

INTEGRATED EXPOSURE, INTERACTION, AND RESULTS

In creating pricing and measuring models, it is necessary to define and develop a set of integrated

response measures within a period and on the website that provide for exposure and interaction when responding to the target consumer. Yields of interaction and exposure include buying behavior in online stores, and changing the attitude or the number of visitors who want the supplementary information. However, developing these yields requires recognition of the user and the existence of data on the websites involved with integrated marketing. With data in hand, measuring the income effect is possible.

In order to develop the yields mentioned earlier, some psychological and behavioral measures should be taken into account in the assessment of online advertising. These measures include primary navigation patterns by the website, navigation patterns of crossover websites including geographical position, psychographic and behavioral characteristics of the visitors of the website, pages visited by the users, measurement of the cognitive and theoretical elements and user loyalties and repeat visits. Other characteristics of advertisements that should be emphasized are moral and procedural practices. When designing standards for measuring and pricing Internet advertising models, some procedural issues like personal privacy should be particularly emphasized.

PRIVACY

Information exchange networks, the computerized environment, and hardware and software related to the Internet provide unique opportunities to violate people's privacy. In this kind of environment, personal information is collected, combined and manipulated much easier than in the physical world. The way that the Internet gathers such information was impossible in the past; however, finding this information may also be more expensive and time-consuming than in the real world. It has become easier to commit fraud and pass on others' information, and it is not clear as to who is going to misuse personal information.

In assessing the Internet for marketing and advertising targets, the information gathered from consumers has a great deal of importance. There is always a trade-off between the marketers' need to be informed of consumers' personal information in order to conduct target marketing and the consumers' right to privacy. Hoffman and Novak (1999) offered a solution for this trade-off: cooperation with consumers so that the consumers (as the owners of behavioral and geographical data) control the way their information is processed. This solution is based on a many-to-many model of the Internet, letting the users be the directors and act as active partners who play a role in interactive relationships. One website that displays the information of its visitors is Anonymizer.cs.cmu.edu. Depending on which websites the user accesses, information such as the location where the user is connected to the Internet, websites visited, their computer's specifications and the type of Internet browser used can all be saved.

In Hoffman and Novak's study in 1999, it was shown that users assess a great value to their privacy, and this is obvious in surveys and enrollment on some websites. Since the names and information registered on those sites are nicknames, it is obvious that users want to have full control of their personal information. When users realize that visitors use their behavioral and geographical information for business purposes, they want to be guaranteed that their personal information will not be given or sold to others. On the other hand, users are likely to give out that information, knowing that they will be provided with better service, provided they are confident that the use of that information will be in their own favor. Research findings indicate that private strategies in this emerging medium should monitored for interaction, user interest and control to increase efficiency and positive performance.

MORAL PRACTICE

Research has attempted to put an end to consumer rights violation by clarifying some terminologies and mechanisms of the new online medium. One of the most important issues is the disguised advertisement. Suppose that an Internet browser provides a list of keywords searched on the Internet and some links to an advertiser's website. Users should be aware that the links and addresses displayed at the top of the search results are not necessarily the most related topics to their subject, as positioning at the top of the list is actually because those websites pay more fees to the search engine.

CONCLUSION

In this chapter, we focused on different ways paying online advertising fees. From a "flat fee" to "pay-per-percentage of impressions" was discussed. In addition, we scrutinized the auctions by which search engines try to assign a rank to marketers' links. Except for the Vickery auction, which is known as the first auction practiced in the world, other auction methods like the English auction, the Dutch auction, e-Bay auction, generalized first-price auction and generalized second-price auction were mentioned. In addition, we discussed cost calculation in the GSP process, and as a result, we developed a table that presented the similarities and differences of all advertising fee methods. After introducing different ways of paying advertising fees in auctions, we considered consumer privacy concerns and pointed out consumer-related words. At the end, moral practices were addressed. Chapter 6 consisted of practices that marketers need to be effective in online advertising. The answer to the question of how to pay an advertising fee can be found in this chapter. The discussion offers readers and marketers the opportunity of having a user-friendly text to explain real-world problems.

REFERENCES

Aggarwal, G., & Hartline, J. D. (2005). Knapsack auctions. In *Proceedings of the First Workshop on Sponsored Search Auctions*. ACM Press.

Akamine. (2009). *Generalized second-price auctions (GSP)*. Retrieved September 18, 2009, from http://expertvoices.nsdl.org /cornell-info204/2009/02/25/ generalized-second-price-auctions-gsp/.

Asdemir, K. (2006). Bidding patterns in search engine auctions. In *Proceedings of the Second Workshop on Sponsored Search Auctions*. ACM Press.

Auction Papers. (2011). *Website*. Retrieved from http://www.cramton.umd.edu /auction-papers. htm.

Balachander, S., & Kannan, K. (2006). *Pricing of advertisements on the internet*. Purdue CIBER Working Papers. Retrieved from http://docs.lib. purdue.edu /ciberwp/47/.

Brooks, N. (2004). *The atlas rank report, part 2: How search engine rank impacts conversion. Technical Report*. New York, NY: Atlas Institute.

Clarke, E. (1971). Multiparty pricing of public goods. *Public Choice, 11*, 17–33. doi:10.1007/ BF01726210

Crcomputerrepair.com. (2011). Click fraud - Threatening the internet economy. Retrieved 9 September from http://www.crcomputerrepair. com /articles/ppc-advertising/46010.php.

Edelman, B., Ostrovsky, M., & Schwarz, M. (2006). Internet advertising and the generalized second price auction: Selling billions of dollars worth of keywords. In *Proceedings of the Second Workshop on Sponsored Search Auctions*. ACM Press.

Goodman, J. (2005). Pay-per-percentage of impressions: An advertising method that is highly robust to fraud. In *Proceedings of the Workshop on Sponsored Search Auctions*. Vancouver, Canada: ACM Press.

Groves, T. (1973). Incentives in teams. *Econometrica: Journal of the Econometric Society, 41*, 617–631. doi:10.2307/1914085

Hoffmann, N., & Novak, T. P. (1995). Marketing in hypermedia computer-mediated environments: Conceptual foundations, project 2000. Retrieved from http://www2000.ogsm.vanderbilt.edul.

Hurley, K. B., & Varian, H. (1998). *Internet publishing and beyond*. Cambridge, MA: MIT Press. Retrieved from http://www.elabresearch.ucr.edu /blog/.../vita.novak.March%2010%202009.pdf.

IAB.net. (2011). *23% year-over-year increase demonstrates growing importance of digital marketing & advertising.* Retrieved 26 May 2011 from http://www.iab.ne t/about_the_iab/ recent_press_releases/ press_release_archive/ press_release/pr-052611.

Kannan, P. K., & Kopalle, P. K. (2001). Dynamic pricing on the internet: Importance and implication for consumer behavior. *International Journal of Electronic Commerce, 5*(3), 63–83.

Kevin, J. D. (2005, May 3). Internet ads click with firms: Some shift budgets. *Wall Street Journal,* p. B8. Retrieved from http://proquest.umi.com /pqd web?did=831167291&sid=9&Fmt=3&clientId= 9269&RQT=309&VName=PQD.

Lan, Z., & Nagurney, A. (2007). A network equilibrium framework for internet advertising: Models, qualitative analysis, and algorithms. *European Journal of Operational Research.* Retrieved from http://www.elsevier.com /locate/ejor,2007.

Murphy, I. P. (1996). On-line ads effective? Who knows for sure? *Marketing News, 30*(20), 38.

Novak, T. P., & Hoffman, D. L. (2000). Advertising and pricing models for the web. In Hurley, B. K., & Varian, H. (Eds.), *Internet Publishing and Beyond: The Economics of Digital Information and Intellectual Property.* Cambridge, MA: MIT Press.

Shipley, D., & Jobber, D. (2001). Integrative pricing via the pricing wheel. *Industrial Marketing Management, 30,* 301–314. doi:10.1016/S0019-8501(99)00098-X

Vickrey, W. (1961). Counter speculation, auctions and competitive sealed tenders. *The Journal of Finance, 16,* 8–37. doi:10.2307/2977633

Weisman, R. (2006, February 12). Virtual ads pose real threat to traditional media. *Boston Globe.*

Zenithoptimedia. (2009). *Internet advertising expenditure report.* Press Release. Retrieved from http://zenithoptimedia.com.

Chapter 7
How Online Advertising Affects Buyer Behavior

ABSTRACT

Why don't consumers demonstrate the same behavior when confronted with identical advertisements? What is the reason for these different perceptions of the same stimuli? How can we shape the right perception in the target audiences? How will advertisers be able to create a common concept which will result in a common behavior?

Being informed about customer reactions, especially when they are exposed to online advertising, requires comprehensive knowledge of consumer motives. Reacting and displaying a given behavior is based on the reasons or motives that led a customer to the Web. In this chapter, the authors will discuss online buyer behavior when faced with an online advertisement. In this regard, the terminology, methods, and models will be introduced in detail, and they will identify the key concepts that form customer behavior, and distinguish between tangible and intangible features that affect online user behavior.

USES AND GRATIFICATIONS

The Internet consists of people and sources, which have developed networks to be used anywhere and anytime (Hoffman & Novak, 1996). These networks have involved more than two billion people all over the world by 2011, i.e. one out of every three people has access to the Internet (Internetworldstats.com, 2011). Many studies have investigated the online medium and considered its features; for example, Berthon *et al.* (1996) indicated that the online medium has exclusive features such as interactivity, excluding distances, low cost of implementing ad campaigns, target-oriented ability and easy access (Berthon, et al., 1996).

The Internet has improved interactive tools and created strong relationships with its customers (Ko, et al., 2005). In spite of the many theories that have been raised, the critical questions for all of

DOI: 10.4018/978-1-4666-0885-6.ch007

them are how do users interact with the Internet and how do they behave? One popular theory is the "Uses and Gratification" theory. This is an important theory because it presents a comprehensive framework for analyzing psychological, behavioral and communicational aspects (Ruggiero, 2000). The uses and gratification theory is a communicational approach based on psychology, which focuses on individual use and choice by asserting that different people can use mass media for very different purposes (Severin & Tankard, 1997). A lot of studies have examined users via the uses and gratification theory, examining the psychological needs which motivate people to use the medium. There are four concepts in the uses and gratification theory: motives, use, gratification and active user (Lin, 1999). This theory is based on the assumption that all users behave objectively and are active users of the medium. In addition, they are aware of their needs and choose an appropriate medium by which to fulfill them. This theory is a clear approach, and its principles have been examined by many researchers and are applicable to all aspects of media communication.

Applying the Uses and Gratifications Theory to the Internet

The rapid growth of the Internet necessitates the application of the uses and gratifications theory, as this media requires a higher degree of interaction with its users in comparison with other media (Ruggiero, 2000). Since the Internet is a "consumer media" and its users choose and visit their favorite websites, knowing the variables affecting the users' preferences is important. Many studies have been conducted on users' behavioral and psychological indicators in order to identify a set of common variables of user motivation that encourage them to use the Internet (Larosa, et al., 2001). As an example, Korgaonkar and Wolin (1999) recognized 45 motivational observer variables for using the Internet and classified them into seven groups: social escapism, transactional

security and privacy, interactive control, socialization, non-transactional privacy and economic motivation. They also reported that people use the Internet based on one of three motives: searching information, entertainment and spending leisure time. Before Korgaonkar and Wolin's study, Papacharissi and Rubin (2000) recognized the motivations for using the Internet, classifying these primary motives into five categories: interpersonal utility, pastime, information seeking, convenience and entertainment. Results show that the uses and gratification theory is one of the most cited methods for identifying motives and a prerequisite for advertising on the Internet. To discover how the uses and gratification theory is applied to online advertising, we need to define some critical concepts.

INTERACTIVITY

Interactivity is one of the most sensible characteristics of modern media. Interaction allows users to participate in the process of persuasion by controlling the advertisements they see, accessing needed information and ordering at any time according to their personal needs and preferences (Hoffman & Novak, 1996). Reciprocal actions or interaction is a complicated and multi-dimensional concept. It is difficult to find a general framework in which interaction can be defined (McMillan & Hwang, 2002).

Internet interaction takes place either by "Human-human" and "Human-message" interaction. For example, human-message interaction involves choosing, manipulating, tracing, directing, editing a form, speed and content. Human-human interaction involves two-way communication like mutual discourse, interpersonal interaction, role exchange, connectedness, responsiveness and reciprocal communication (Ko, et al., 2005).

One model based on the uses and gratifications theory developed to identify the effective factors in an online audience's behavior is the Structural

Equation Model of Interactive Advertising, which was introduced by Ko *et al.* (2005). In this section, we will focus on Ko's model and will explain consumer behavior in the online environment.

Modeling of Interactive Advertising

Studying consumer behavior on the Web must have its roots in the traditional body of knowledge as reported by Ko *et al.* (2005). Based on previous studies of the uses and gratifications theory and Internet interaction, their model demonstrates the relationships between motivation for using the Internet, duration of time at a website, interactivity, attitudes and purchase intention of online customers in a structural framework. This model has four basic sections based on the uses and gratifications theory: 1) primary motives: the first motivating force before visiting a website; 2) duration of time at a website; 3) interactivity; and 4) attitudes and purchase intention after visiting the website.

The duration of time spent at a website and interaction can originate from the objectives and permanent decisions of the user. These decisions are dependent on antecedent (motivations) and consequent (gratification) conditions. Gratification is an internal reaction to the medium by the user, revealing the user's satisfaction with the medium (Blumler, 1979). According to variables like attitude toward the brand, attitude toward the website and purchase intention, the three following effects are discussed in this model:

- The effects of using Internet motives based on the extent of website exposure and the extent of interactivity on the website;
- The effects of interactivity on the effectiveness of the advertising;
- The casual relationship among advertising products.

Based on previous findings, the focus of the model is on the four primary motives of enter-

tainment, convenience, information and social interaction. This model indicates t how people with different motives use the Internet. It also shows how people with different motivations react to online ads. For instance, users with high entertainment motives expose themselves more to programs and advertisements than those with low entertainment motives. Thus, it is expected that a person with high motivation is more likely to visit the site (Alwitt & Prabhaker, 1992) and will also spend more time at the website. It can be concluded that motivation for using the Internet has a substantial effect on users' attendance at a website (see Figure 1).

Motivations for using a specific medium vary (Flanagin & Metzger, 2001). When people have high motivation, they try to find the websites and ads which fulfill their information needs, and they may perform the search repeatedly (Madox, 1998). Finding information will unconsciously increase their motivation to interact with anything that helps them find the information they seek. During their search, they may participate in online discussions on websites. It is expected that these customers with high motivation will increasingly interact with messages and advertisers. As a result, the online customers' primary motives redirect the kinds of interactions that they have with a website; that is, message (Human-message) and advertiser (Human-human). When customers interact with tahe message and advertiser, there is an opportunity to process extra information about the organization's website and product. Most probably, this opportunity evokes a positive assessment of the ad and brand by the customer (Li, 2002). The attitude toward the website and ad directly affects the attitude toward the brand. Briefly, attitude toward a website directly affects the brand and attitude toward brand affects the customer's buying intention accordingly (Ko, et al., 2005).

Ko *et al.* (2005) examined 10 variables where duration of time is affected by the first four motives of information, convenience, entertainment, and social interaction. As mentioned earlier, us-

Figure 1. Sample of rational and emotional advertisements

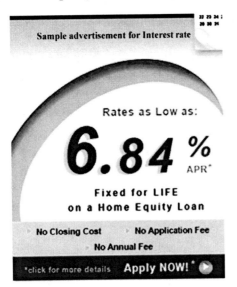

ers' duration of time spent on a website varies because they connect to and use the Internet based on different motives. The attendance of online customers on a website, originating from their primary motivations for the search, is affected by human-message and human-human interaction. The extent to which the interaction continues is in accordance with the customer's primary motives and whether a more positive attitude will form in the customer's mind. Users with a high motivation for seeking information are likely to interact with the message rather than with people, and those who enter the site with high social interaction are more motivated to interact with people and show a negative reaction to interaction with messages. A key variable which is reported by the Ko *et al.* (2005) model is attitude toward a website.

Attitude toward a website is related to both human-message and human-human interaction. Human-human interaction has, of course, more influence upon a customer's attitude. If a website can interact with its users, and the users can interact with other users of a product or service, the advertiser can enjoy a more positive outcome.

In this situation, interaction is the cause of the customer's entrance into the Web, and it offers a prime situation for advertising. Attracting customers to an interactive website forms their attitude toward the website, and consequently forms their attitude toward the brand. The extent to which the website has formed a more positive attitude in customers, the purchase intention will be increased as well. Most importantly, customers with a positive attitude gradually become loyal online customers; this is the utmost objective of an advertisement. When a brand has a positive image in customers' minds, in subsequent ads draw more attention. This is a big step in creating loyal customers who will continue to visit the website bringing a lot of income opportunities. This motivates other advertisers to want to place their ads this website.

When advertisers broadcast online advertisements, whether shown on their own websites or on other organizations' websites, they should consider the customer motivation of the product or service. Advertisers must examine which is the main motive for bringing customers to the Web.

Once these motives are identified, advertisers must design appropriate interactive elements for the website. Customers who enter a website with a high motivation for entertainment or are attracted by emotional appeal will definitely have different behaviors than those who visit the site seeking information. Users who enter a website seeking information avoid all enhancing and appealing features which are designed to increase traffic, and they only react to those informational signs or links which are related to their subject. In other words, they are not attracted by website design. If the organization has invested emotional appeal into an ad, the investment will be in vain for these users, because the customers' primary motivation is not to engage with ads. On the other hand, users who have entered the website with entertainment goals or have clicked on an advertisement have different motivations. For these users, advertisers should pay more attention to aspects with emotional appeal and entertainment value. Users who search this way are called Internet surfers, and they react more to advertisements that stand out among other components on a website and are usually able to encourage customers to visit the website.

Rules of Netiquette in Internet Advertising

Netiquette is etiquette for the Internet, and it means being polite to others on the Web. As we know, there are no facial clues or body language to help us understand another person on the Web as there are in face-to-face meetings. When users surf, they may be sensitive to impolite or offensive behavior. According to Thomsen (1996), "Since there is no central authority, the users themselves have taken to policing the Internet. The advertiser has to live by these rules. Otherwise, they may be 'flamed,' which is a nasty note containing threats and curses or in the worst case be boycotted" (p. 20).

Netiquette: A Prerequisite for Online Advertisements

In order to address the netiquette issue in the online advertising context, we are faced with two conditions.

Objectionable products (Heidarzadeh, et al., 2011) are those goods that might cause embarrassment or shame in purchasing or selling (for example, some kinds of cosmetics and toiletry products). It is difficult to behave in a netiquette manner when advertisers are placing banners for these kinds of products on the Web. Although objectionable products are intrinsically bothersome, users are more likely to react to online advertisements that use off-putting clues and appeals (Heidarzadeh, et al., 2011). We know that the Internet enhances cross-cultural communication and hence lowers the barriers between cultures. In addition, it allows marketers to trace and analyze the depth of word-of-mouth in social networks, and offers the chance to target opinion leaders directly. Considering these issues, we know that advertising in a netiquette manner may result in different outcomes. For those users who connected to the Internet in religious countries, advertisements may evoke negative reactions, especially if we do not consider governmental filters norms). Non-netiquette advertising is more affordable for objectionable product advertisers, and negative reactions may occur when a user is not in an entertaining mood and is strictly goal-oriented. When a user is in a goal-oriented mood, wanting nothing more than to search the Internet for information, publishing an advertisement without paying attention to netiquette considerations not only does not persuade the user, it also may be viewed as loathsome. Netiquette is veritable life-and-death for branded products, because a loathsome image in social networks and forums will affect other products of the advertiser.

Pleasant products are those which create no shame for either purchaser or seller. There is no doubt that pleasant product advertisers find it easier to employ netiquette. Intrinsically, pleasant products are advertised by using positive and ethically oriented appeal. Developing netiquette advertising in this situation will definitely work better in persuading consumers to follow an advertisement or make a purchase.

To examine the netiquette issue in detail, we have developed a framework. As shown in Figure 2, the vertical axis shows the degree to which a market uses the Internet in its business, and the horizontal axis represents the degree to which marketers have no choice but to use completely non-netiquette practices for selling their products. In this figure, we can see four areas and four inclined axes (advertising strategy, branding strategy, appeal type, and selling strategy). When advertisers do business in an Internet-only market that is filled with non-netiquette practices for selling a product (area four), they must try to use a personalized advertising strategy. In the opposite position (area two), when advertisers are in a clicks-and-bricks market, which consists of netiquette practices, they must employ a mass-advertising strategy.

In a branding strategy, when advertising is in a clicks-and-bricks market that has little netiquette practices (area one), they can use companies' physical facilities and prior performance to develop a corporate branding strategy. On the opposing side (area three), which is an Internet-only market filled with netiquette practices, advertisers can develop a single branding strategy. Each brand has its own advertising message, and whenever it faces any crises, the other brands would not suffer. In regards to type of appeal, an Internet-only market filled with non-netiquette practices (area four) ties marketers' hands, and they have no choice but to employ non-principled appeals to sell their products. Conversely, in area two, which is formed in a clicks-and-bricks market with netiquette practices, advertisers must use principled appeals. As a selling strategy, when marketers are doing business in an Internet-only market that is somewhat netiquette, they must use a direct selling strategy. When faced with a situation where they must use semi-direct selling, marketers choose an online ordering process and an offline delivery system.

GENDER DIFFERENCES IN BEHAVIOR, ATTITUDE, AND BELIEF

One of the effective variables in forming a behavior is human nature. Any behavior of a human being is affected by rational and emotional factors like gender. Depending on their gender, human beings have different reactions toward most natural or unnatural phenomena. The Internet is not exempt from this rule. Consumers use the Internet differently depending on whether they are male or female, and these differences are observed in Internet ads as well. The users' perception based on gender has three dimensions in advertising:

- Use patterns
- Online privacy concerns
- Behaviors (Wolin & Korgaonkar, 2003)

If users are different in their attitude, communication and behavior pattern due to their gender, it is important to consider the processes that should be utilized to assess the effectiveness of the advertising. Since appropriate evaluation of advertising effectiveness regarding gender allows the advertiser to achieve the target group with a lower cost, many studies have been published on the effectiveness of advertising with gender consideration; these show that gender differences are effective when paying attention to an advertisement. Gender is a key variable in classifying the market, and. there are some factors which should be taken into account when advertising as these factors are different for males and females:

Figure 2. Netiquette and advertising: selecting areas for making right decisions

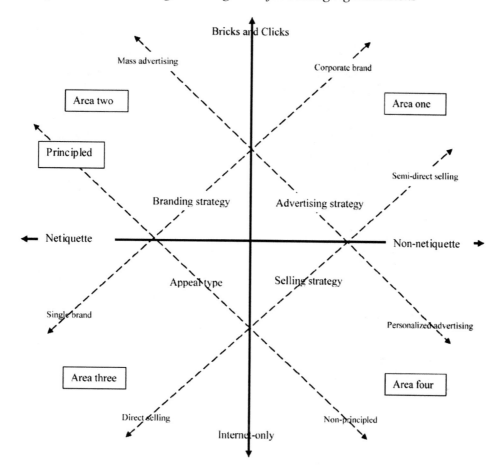

- Identifiability
- Accessibility
- Measurability
- Responding to marketing mix factors
- Profitability (Darly & Smith, 1995)

Advertisers must recognize the beliefs, attitudes and behavioral patterns based on gender and apply them in advertising design. To understand users' beliefs, attitudes and behaviors, advertisers should focus on message content, because forming the primary framework of these behavioral characteristics depends on the effectiveness of the advertisement on user perception. In analyzing the different factors, which can result in an effective ad, some characteristics should be considered as advertising topics (see Figure 3):

- The current stereotyping about differences between the perceptions of men and women.
- The way in which information is analyzed by men and women. (For example, consider the clues and cues that persuade female users to follow ads and apply them in designing an objective and effective advertisement.)
- Positioning gender-based brands. (This is critical in order for the organization to be aware that its brand is popular among men or women.)

According to gender, in what dimensions are customers' perceptions different? Studies show that men in general have a more positive attitude

Figure 3. Sample of emotional and gender-based advertisements

toward online ads than women. Men usually search the Internet for entertainment, searching for information and shopping in particular, while women usually use it for communication purposes. Wolin and Korgankar (2003) showed that men perceived online advertisements as either profitable, enjoyable, or informative.

- Men find Internet ads more enjoyable than magazine and newspaper ads.
- Men find Internet ads more useful than magazine, newspaper and radio ads.
- Men find Internet ads more informative than magazine, newspaper and radio ads.

The study also focused on aggressiveness, deceptiveness and usefulness, and concluded that women believe that online ads are:

- More annoying than magazine and news-paper ads.
- More annoying than radio and TV ads.
- More deceptive than TV ads.
- More useful than TV ads.

Due to this report, we can conclude that men have more positive impressions of online advertisements than women and prefer them to traditional advertising.

BEHAVIORAL DIFFERENCES IN TERMS OF INTERNET USAGE

Internet usage has influenced customer motivation to peruse online advertising and to purchase. A customer's reaction to an online advertisement stems from his own beliefs and attitudes toward the Internet. One factor that helps form customers' beliefs and attitudes is the amount of time a customer spends on the Internet. According to Wolin and Korgankar (2001), customers are classified as either heavy or light users. Users from the heavy group have some or all of the following characteristics:

- Higher education
- Higher revenue
- Young age group
- Professional business owners

Heavy users usually have more positive attitudes toward Internet ads. Compared to light users, heavy users believe that Internet ads are more enjoyable, entertaining, useful and less boring or annoying than traditional ads. Consequently, creating a common ad for all users may not result in reaching the target audience. When advertisers design a ads for heavy Internet users, one point should be considered; since these visitors have used the Internet for a long time, they may find that some Internet advertisements promote objectionable products. When advertisers broadcast objectionable or unpleasant products, they usually use unethical cues and materials to appeal to customers. Therefore, in designing ads for heavy Internet users, advertisers must take ethical issues into consideration. When designing advertisements for light users, it should be noted that whereas users assess product features on the basis of their own beliefs and use the Internet to satisfy their needs, they do not think that the Internet is as much of a powerful device for business as do heavy users. Thus, the security aspect of Internet advertising and buying should be emphasized for light users. Also, to persuade light users to follow an advertisement, marketers must stress the informative and enjoyable nature of online advertising (Wolin & Korgankar, 2001).

Heavy users believe that Internet advertising and buying will decrease customer costs and that Internet advertising is necessary. In order for adver-

tisers to have more influence on heavy users, they must focus their designs on comparative prices and show comparisons with their competitors.

For light users who are less familiar with online advertising and buying advantages, marketers should highlight the comparisons between online and traditional purchasing.

INTERACTIVE ADVERTISING MODEL (IAM)

The second model that examines customer behavior toward online ads is Rodgers and Thorson's Interactive Advertising Model, which was introduced in 2000. There are some differences between IAM and other models in integrating patterns and attitudes. The patterns that are presented in the IAM include the functional concept of how the users enter the Internet and a processing concept of what the users do when confronted with online advertising. Both operate on the basis of the online advertising motives structure.

General assumptions are based on the understanding that information processing is done in an interactive environment and is related to a functional structure. This model tries to classify the different types of online advertising and recognize their features. It also attempts to find the effective variables which shape and influence the user's attention, memory and attitude.

Rodgers and Thorson believed that an integrated medium requires an integrated processing model and that information processing is exactly related to usage and the structure of advertising. The key items of the IAM model include customer-controlled and advertiser-controlled aspects with the customer-controlled aspect consisting of functions and the information process.

The advertiser-controlled aspect consists of online advertising structures, ad formats and ad features. Considering this, customer response is formed based on the type of format and customer processing in the customer's mind. So in the customer-controlled aspect, the general assumptions of the IAM are based on three features:

1. Information processing takes place in an interactive environment.
2. Users try to put themselves in a position in accordance with the environment and are considered experienced uses.
3. The model answers the questions of how and why to use the Internet, because human behavior reason is related to their cognitive attempts to solve problems.

Customer-Controlled Aspect

One of the rational methods for studying how users process online ads is to assess the domain under the control of both customer and advertiser, because the advertisers always study customer behavior to see how and when they process and visit the ads. With the emergence of the Internet, this issue has become more complicated, since control of ads has moved from the advertiser to the customer. The customer actually has more control over the advertising than either the marketer or the advertiser. The interactive advertising model represents a general framework of how customer response is the outcome of both aspects. Therefore, we will analyze all components of the interactive advertising model.

Function

Before analyzing how users process Internet advertising, it should first be made clear why they use the Internet. In this regard, there is a functionalist approach that states how people are motivated. Functionalist patterns provide an integrated understanding of the information process and also allow the model to form conclusions about why and how customers use the Internet. In this way, the approach introduces the programs and actions which are necessary to recognize the primary motivations to use the Internet.

Using the Internet does not begin by reacting to an advertising message; it begins by responding to drives like the need for buying. When this need appears, customers will visit the Internet, seeking an ad which fulfills their needs. The IAM starts with motives and continues with information processing. This means that motives fill the user's mind through the information process. Customers' knowledge about how and why they use the Internet results in identifying the factors which attract the users to the Web and encourage them to use it again. In this way, the analyzers of customer behavior can form a complicated pattern of behavior and attitude of the users. First, we should deal with the mechanisms that pull people to Internet.

Internet Motives

Motive is an internal desire to satisfy a need (Papacharaissi & Rubin, 2000). An Internet motive can be viewed as an internal motivation to perform any kind of online action. The motive in using the Internet focuses on the customer-controlled aspect, since the Internet requires at least a little related knowledge. Nearly 12 researchers have studied Internet motives, and the results of their studies classified the motives into the following categories: shopping, information-seeking, Internet surfing, communication, social escapism and convenience (Rogers & Thorson, 2000). There was also a study in 1999 by Rodgers and Sheldon which classified 100 motives of using the Internet into four similar categories including searching, shopping, entertainment and communication. According to this model, to fulfill a need on the Internet, motives should affect attention, mind and attitude toward the Internet. The important supposition of the model is that there is a kind of switch among user's motives, .i.e. it is possible for a user who accesses websites with an information-seeking motive to become tired or disappointed. In this situation, the first motive may be forgotten, and the user will continue to surf based on new motives like entertainment. In addition, other elements may awaken hidden motives. Motive switching is an important factor which is not easily understood. This issue is derived from the complicated nature of the interactive environment. For example, a user enters with the initial motive of shopping, but becomes disappointed because the search engine cannot find the desired results. At this point, the customer may show a willingness to explore shopping-oriented advertising. One way to conceptualize this motive-switching process is to think about the broader concept of user mode. A mode, as represented in the second component of the IAM, is defined as the extent to which Internet activities are goal-directed. There are two types of modes: serious and playful.

The enjoyment-based mode is inclined to entertainment and is more related to the present time, while the object-oriented mode is related to fulfilling and following the action for which the user has connected to the Internet and is related to the future. It can be stated that researchers are among Internet surfers who follow an object-based mode. Object-based modes direct the Internet experience to finding a target rather than entertainment. Thus, cognitive attempts are based on goal-oriented purposes and are less related to marginal cognitive attempts like attention. On the other hand, Internet surfers are mostly present-oriented and are most probably curious users who enjoy exploring the Internet. It is expected that they click on the ads in their cyber journey even more than researchers. Their mode is affected by their initial motivation. Two-way arrows show that the mode may be changed at any time, meaning that the user may be using the Internet for enjoyment-based and objective-based reasons at different times. This psychological reversal (Walters, et al., 1982) causes the user to switch his final goal to an ordinary one within a day, even within a few minutes! A switch in a user's motivation

has a great effect on information processing of interactive advertising.

Information Processing

Information processing, a function-based issue based on psychology, is an old concept that assumes that everyone has inputs and outputs, and information processing occurs in between. In this model, the cognitive psychology approach has been utilized to process information. Cognitive psychology is much more compatible with behavior-based patterns and complicated mind applications like attention, attitude, mind and decision-making. Cognitive psychology acts hierarchically; customers first gather information by paying attention to advertising, then they process that information and put the new information together with their existing knowledge and form attitude and buying decisions about the product. However, as the model expands, it becomes more complicated. With the emergence of product involvement and customer preference, predicting customer behavior gets more and more difficult. McIlnnis and Jaworski (1989) studied the variables in processing advertising information and classified them as follows: (Since all variables deal only with human reactions, they are compatible in any environment.)

- Need
- Motivation
- Ability
- Attention
- Cognitive and emotional processing
- Attitude formation

Advertiser-Controlled Aspect

After investigating customer-controlled variables, the different variables under the advertiser's control are discussed. Advertiser-controlled aspect does not mean that the customer has no control since there are some websites that allow their users to manipulate the constructive elements of the website and create their own private website (see *McDonald.com* for more information). The most important variables under the advertiser's control are structural elements like advertising types, advertising formats and advertising features. To describe the customer's information processing, advertisers should first know two key concepts: 1) the motivation features which were discussed earlier; and second, the advertising message stimuli features to understand how these motives work together in order to guide information processing. In fact, when advertisers are informed about the environment in which stimuli are broadcast, they are able to more narrowly predict customer reactions. There has been a massive attempt to describe a stimulus environment in which people interact with one another. The environment is important because it substantially affects customer response; the Internet is a more complicated environment, because the customer has control over advertisements the same as the advertiser.

The IAM structural elements include advertising type, advertising format and advertising feature. In this model, information processing, as well as consumer responses, will hinge on the presentation of the interactive ad itself. This presentation, it is believed, also interacts with the individual's motive for using the Internet, as well as the mode in which the motive is carried out. The three elements cooperate with each other to affect the user's attitude and behavior. The first element, advertising type, is the first feature by which an ad can be rated. All ads in every media can be separated into five categories:

- Products/services advertisement
- Public Service Announcement (PSA)
- Issue advertisement
- Corporate advertisement
- Political advertisement

Any one of these kinds of ads has a special structure in which the ad is clearly perceived. Each category into which advertising is placed will fulfill the customer's possible needs. For instance, when an ad is developed for a political group, it is expected that the advertised candidate will win a lot of votes if the ad is successful. However, there is no expectation to increase the shopping intention of a customer with this type of ad, because shopping intention increases for service or product ads. The other reason for the existence of the advertising type in the processing model is that advertising type determines cognitive tools. For example, when an advertisement is broadcast in the political field, the user's attention may be drawn by an ad which promotes a common belief between the candidate and voters. On the other hand, it is possible that an advertising issue such as health or hygiene may be ignored by the user because there is no appropriate interest about these types of ads. Regardless of pleasant or unpleasant views about advertising, there are many responses to different ads. According to studies, a PSA is more appropriate when based on reputation and the understanding of social responsibility (Halley & Wilkson, 1994). Therefore, the type of advertisement reveals how much cognitive effort should be devoted to processing online ads. Also, the ad type interacts with the customer's motives to affect decision and response. It is obvious that the advertising type is not enough to predict information processing on its own. Thus, the subject of advertising format will be emphasized. As you see in the model (and will be discussed in chapter 11), some Internet advertising formats include banners, pop-ups, sponsorships, interstitials and websites. There have been a lot of studies on the relationship between advertising format and information processing. For example, banners cause increasing customer awareness. As a banner broadcasts in larger formats, it earns a higher click rate (Briggs & Hollis, 1997). Obviously, clicks on a banner means that there is a positive attitude toward it (Brill, 1999). This means that the ad could transfer the advertiser's message in a positive way or attract the customer to its message and him to click the banner for more information. Pop-ups and interstitials, which are really similar, are different in many aspects, and these differences have put them in different categories from the customer's point of view. Interstitials have a more negative connotation for customers, since they occupy the entire screen and do not have options for exit, while pop-ups are displayed on only 10% of the screen and, unlike the interstitials, do not stop or prevent the user's search and surfing. They also provide options for users to delete the ad if they do not like it. An ad which stops the user's surfing is considered unfavorable. In relation to the user's intention, it can be said that when users enter a website for research, they can easily ignores such ads in the pursuit of their main goal. However, when customers are in the enjoyment-based mode or have an entertainment-based goal, these types of advertising are considered as a form of entertainment, and users try to follow them. In fact, pop-ups and interstitials are attractive for a user who has an entertainment as a primary motive intention. Also, in sponsorship advertising, it seems that a user's response depends on the motivation and the time of exposure to an online advertisement. When the ads are directly advertised through a company's website, involvement of information processing and customer behavior is likely to be different and more complicated than with other methods, because the customers visit the website with a wider range of motivations. In this case, all users have special desires. Some want Internet games; some want online chats and others need a fast and clear move through a website to find information. Therefore, the time spent at the website for these users is longer than for other forms. The complicated nature of a website results in the expectation of a wide range of responses by the users. This complexity is more obvious when we consider users with an insufficient ability to use the computer and the Internet, the frustration of not finding favorites and the high motivation

for involvement with the website. Briefly, online advertising formats are constantly interacting with a user's primary motives, and the target-based or enjoyment-based modes which results in different processing of advertising messages.

Advertising Features

Many attempts have been made to describe advertising features. Thorson and Leavitt, (1986) divided features into objective and subjective. In objective features, advertisement assessment is based on a customer's response; while in subjective features, assessment is based on advertising motive. These features are classified for print, broadcast and Internet media. Moving from print media toward the Internet, the structural features become more complex, as Internet advertising features include broadcast and print media. In print media, subjective features have clear variables like color, size, typeface, product class and appeal; in the objective structure for broadcast and print media, customers receive a direct assessment of the commercial messages. A variety of studies have been conducted to identify the effective factors in these assessments. For example, Leavitt and McConville (1970) have classified these factors into four groups: stimulating, relevant, gratifying and familiar. However, in the adjective checklist, the studies recognize seven factors: entertainment, confusion, relevant news, brand reinforcement, empathy, familiarity and alienation (Schliger, 1974).

According to a study developed by Rodgers and Thorson (2000), in traditional advertising, research outcomes have the potential to work accurately on the Internet. Therefore, the method of describing the message structure can often be the same at different times. For instance, the adjective check list can be the same for online advertising as it is for traditional advertising; this is also supported by other studies. For example, Bucy (1998) conducted a study of 496 well-known websites and recognized some common features of their online ads including animation, color and graphics. The issue of an advertising request is related to the rational or emotional appeal of the ad and the percentage of customer involvement with the product. For example, interaction is a feature which was added due to the emergence of the Internet. It is a new feature which, as discussed before, distinguishes the Internet among other media.

In relation to objective advertising structure on the Web, some t factors have been recognized which are useful for increasing user response rate.

- **Entertaining features**: The extent to which a website is attractive and the percentage of emotional appeal which it utilizes to influence and pull users to the Web and hold their interest.
- **Content quality**: The extent to which the website has an appropriate compatibility of content with customer need in a designated target audience. The more the website's compatibility is aligned with customer needs and the faster the content is updated, the more the website will have a loyal customer group.
- **Website navigators**: The extent to which the website is found easily in search engines and uses a reliable site map. Navigators or intelligent agents are designed to guide users to reaching their goals easily.

The initial attempts to recognize objective and subjective ad features allow advertisers to predict the responses of prospects to these features. For example, when customers visit a website with the initial motivation of searching and researching, they can also be attracted to animation and movement (Rodgers & Thorson 2000).

LIFESTYLE

The partitioning approach categorizes users' lifestyles in different formats, so that identifiable features can be stated for each category (Kamakura & Wedel, 1995). This sectioning method is a useful tool for planning advertising (Kaynak & Kara, 1996). Numerous studies indicate that lifestyle is an important variable that influences the way users use the Internet for various activities (Schiffman, et al., 2003; Kim, et al., 2001). The particulars of lifestyles provide correct and practical information about users so that advertisers can meet user needs in competitive and complex markets (Kamakura & Wedel, 1995). This point gains more importance as the Internet increasingly penetrates different levels of society and encounters more lifestyles (Weiss, 2001; Schiffman, et al., 2003). The partitioning approach to lifestyle is capable of identifying useful and important sectors so that advertisers can target appropriate users and create more efficient Internet advertisements. In addition, by studying lifestyles, advertisers can identify differences among the views of users (Yang, 2004). In addition, advertisers must acquire knowledge about the differences in users' views about Internet advertisements, which are created based on a variety of lifestyles in order to offer more purposeful advertisements (Yang, 2004). Two papers will be addressed here. First, Kim *et al.* (2001) investigated the lifestyles of Internet users and concluded that there are six general lifestyles that should be considered: innovative/leader, imitator/flatterer, serious buyer, sociable person, conservative/polite person and family-oriented person. This study also showed that there is a strong relationship between the lifestyles of users and their views about Internet advertisements. For instance, the leader/innovative lifestyle user believes that the Internet contains useful and special information (Kim, et al., 2001). The second study, conducted by Yang (2004), identified three different lifestyles among Internet users: experienced, traditional and extremists. Individuals in each group have unique characteristics and exhibit different behaviors compared to those in the other groups. Among these three types of lifestyles identified by Yang (2004), the traditional are less inclined to engage in Web and Internet shopping, and more importantly, they have the most negative view of Internet advertisements. We can see that lifestyle is a variable which, when taken into account, can increase the efficiency of Internet advertisements. The more the designed advertisement is in accordance with the lifestyle of the target user, the more it will result in a higher click rate; at the least, it does not lead to the user's avoidance of the advertisement.

CONCLUSION

This chapter discussed the online environment and its requirements for developing an online advertising campaign. The chapter has illustrated how gratifications and uses are applied to interpret online user behavior. Also, the role of interactivity and its effects on the duration of consumer presence were discussed. Human-human and human-machine were the two features that relate to customer surfing time. Rules of netiquette were examined in this chapter as well, and an exclusive framework was presented. Then, gender preferences in the online environment were discussed, and it was stated that in sum, men have a more positive image of Web advertising in comparison to women. In addition, two types of online advertising models were investigated which are developed on the basis of customer behavior.

All advertisers and marketers need to be aware of the effects of customers' beliefs, primary motives and attitudes about the purchasing decision. Before developing their online advertising plans, marketers need to use online surveys to recognize consumer surfing motives, such as whether they are online to research, shop, be entertained or communicate. Furthermore, advertisers need to know when and why a customer switches to another motive. In this regard, marketers must diligently search for the core need which customers are trying to satisfy, remembering that their advertising will be successful only if they broadcast the right

clues and appeals to pull in the online consumer. Additionally, they must conduct research into all of these features to find clues as to how to reach and serve consumers more effectively. To comprehend how online users actually make their purchasing decisions, marketers must identify what cognitive tools influence their buying decision, attention, memory and attitude. Advertisers must develop ad features, ad types and ad formats according to the most cognitive tools. If they can develop an appropriate advertising campaign, users will make the decision to click on an ad, search to find the website, email the advertiser, change attitude and/or make a purchase.

REFERENCES

Alwitt, L. F., & Prabhaker, R. P. (1992). Functional and belief dimensions attitudes to television. *Journal of Advertising Research, 32*(5), 30–42.

Berthon, P., Leyland, F. P., & Watson, R. T. (1996). The world wide web as an advertising medium: Toward an understanding of conversion efficiency. *Journal of Advertising Research, 36*(1), 43–54.

Blumler, J. G. (1979). The role of theory in uses and gratification studies. *Communication Research, 6*(1), 9–36. doi:10.1177/009365027900600102

Briggs, R., & Hollis, N. (1997). Advertising on the web: Is there response before click-through? *Journal of Advertising Research, 37*(2), 33–45.

Bucy, E. P., Lang, A., Potter, R. F., & Grabe, M. E. (1998). *Structural features of cyberspace: A content analysis of the world wide web.* Paper presented at the 1998 Conference of the Association for Education in Journalism and Mass Communication, Theory and Methodology Division. Baltimore, MD.

Darly, W. K., & Smith, R. F. (1995). Gender differences in information-processing strategies: An empirical test of selectivity model in advertising response. *Journal of Advertising, 24*(1), 41–56.

Haley, E., & Wilkinson, J. (1994). And now a word from our sponsor: An exploratory concept test of PSAs vs. advocacy ads. In *Proceedings of the 1994 conference of the American Academy of Advertising*, (pp. 79-87). American Academy of Advertising.

Hoffman, D., & Novak, P. (1996). Marketing in computer-mediated environments: Conceptual foundations. *Journal of Marketing, 60*, 50–60. doi:10.2307/1251841

Internetworldstats.com. (2011). *Internet usage statistics, the internet big picture, world internet users and population stats*. Retrieved July 18, 2011, from http://www.internetworldstats.com / stats.htm.

Kamakura, W. A., & Wedel, M. (1995). Life-style segmentation with tailored interviewing. *JMR, Journal of Marketing Research, 32*(3), 308–317. doi:10.2307/3151983

Kaynak, E., & Kara, A. (1996). Consumer lifestyle and ethnocentrism: A comparative study in Kyrgyzstan and Azarbaijan. In U. Schoeneberg (Ed.), *49th Esomar Congress Proceedings*, (pp. 577-596). Amsterdam, The Netherlands: ESOMAR.

Kim, K. H., Park, J. Y., Ki, D. Y., & Moon, H. I. (2001). Internet user lifestyle: Its impact on effectiveness and attitude toward Internet advertising in Korea. In C. Ray (Ed.), *Proceedings of the 2001 Annual Conference of the American Academy of Advertising*, (pp. 19-23). Salt Lake City, UT: American Academy of Advertising.

Ko, H., Cho, C. H., & Roberts, M. S. (2005). Internet uses and gratifications structural equation model of interactive advertising. *Journal of Advertising, 34*(2), 57–70.

Korgaonkar, P. K., & Wolin, D. L. (1999). A multivariate analysis of web usage. *Journal of Advertising Research, 39*(2), 53–68.

Korgaonkar, P. K., & Wolin, D. L. (2001). Web usage, advertising, and shopping: Relationship patterns. *Internet Research: Electronic Networking Applications and Policy, 12*(2), 191–204.

Kowalczykowski, M. (2002). Disconnected continent. *Hayward International Review, 24*(2), 40–43.

Larose, R., Dana, M., & Estian, S. M. (2001). Understanding internet usage: A social cognitive approach to uses and gratification. *Social Science Computer Review, 19*(4), 395–413. doi:10.1177/089443930101900401

Li, H., & Bukovac, J. L. (1999). Cognitive impact of banner ad characteristics: An experimental study. *Journalism & Mass Communication Quarterly, 76*(2), 341–353. doi:10.1177/107769909907600211

Lin, C. A. (1999). Online-service adaption likelihood. *Journal of Advertising Research, 39*(2), 79–89.

Maddox, K. (1998). E-commerce becoming reality. *Advertising Age*. Retrieved October 26, 2010, from http://www.adage.com.

McMillan, & Hwang, S. J. (2002). Measure of perceived interactivity: An exploration of the role direction of communication, user control, and time in shopping perceptions of interactivity. *Journal of Advertising, 31*(3), 29–42.

Morris, M., & Ogan, C. (1996). The internet as mass medium. *The Journal of Communication, 46*(1), 39–50. doi:10.1111/j.1460-2466.1996.tb01460.x

Papacharissi, Z., & Rubin, M. A. (2000). Predictors of internet use. *Journal of Broadcasting & Electronic Media, 44*(2), 175–196. doi:10.1207/s15506878jobem4402_2

Rodgers, S., & Thorson, E. (2000). The interactive advertising model: How users perceive and process online ads. *Journal of Interactive Advertising, 1*(1), 26–50. Retrieved from http://jiad.org/vo1/no1/rodgers/

Ruggiero, T. E. (2000). Uses and gratifications theory in the 21st century. *Mass Communication & Society, 3*(1), 3–37. doi:10.1207/S15327825MCS0301_02

Schiffman, L. G., Sherman, E., & Long, M. M. (2003). Toward a better understanding of the interplay of personal values and the Internet. *Psychology and Marketing, 20*(2), 169–186. doi:10.1002/mar.10066

Severin, W. J., & Tankard, J. W. (1997). *Communication theory: Origins, methods, and use in mass media* (4th ed.). White Plains, NY: Longman.

Thorson, E. (1996). Advertising. In Salwen, M. B., & Stacks, D. W. (Eds.), *An Integrated Approach to Communication Theory and Research* (pp. 211–230). Mahwah, NJ: Lawrence Erlbaum.

Weiss, M. J. (2001). Online America. *American Demographics, 23*(3), 53–60.

Yang, K. C. C. (2004). A comparison of attitudes towards Internet advertising among lifestyle segments in Taiwan. *Journal of Marketing Communications, 10*, 195–212. doi:10.1080/13527260042000181657

Chapter 8
Internet Advertising Strategies

ABSTRACT

At present, the advertising business is concerned with several issues regarding online marketing including: the emergence of new advertising strategies, changes in the consumer market, growing competition due to globalization, limited human and financial resources, lack of technological skills, and time limitations. Identifying these changes and deciding how to use them to achieve a better response rate is crucial for success. Creating advertising strategies in harmony with the Internet is just as important.

Advertising is a broad concept; in this book, the authors have presented a precise look at its practical domains. Modern advertising has become low-cost with fast access to target users, transferring a persuasive concept to customers and getting a positive behavioral reaction. The last part of their definition is indicative of a new method of advertising, which goes a step further than other methods. A positive reaction embedded in an advertising function comes from advertisers' use of new communicational practices to transfer and receive messages. The emergence and application of new technology necessitates using the appropriate tools. In this chapter, the authors first define these new tools (strategies). Then, they discuss the differences between online and traditional advertising strategies, and offer an integrated model of Internet advertising strategies. Finally, the authors introduce different kinds of appropriate Internet advertising strategies. The purpose of this chapter is to focus on online advertising strategies and provide a fundamental understanding of their relationship to marketing practices. They examine why firms must use online advertising strategies and give some examples of how online advertising strategies can help companies make sound marketing decisions.

ADVERTISING STRATEGY

Strategy is a term usually applied to qualitative concepts rather than quantitative ones. Strategy is mentioned with words like tools and practice in strategic management literature (Kaplan & Norton, 2001, p. 34). The strategy or main solution is

defined on the basis of an organization's limited resources and environment analysis to achieve a predicted organizational goal. In the advertising context, strategy is developed for broadcasting methods which try to deliver a promotional message to a target audience. Therefore, we define advertising strategy as follows: the tools and practices that are designed to promote business

DOI: 10.4018/978-1-4666-0885-6.ch008

dissemination actions and promotional campaigns whereby a company can reach their advertising goals and outperform its competitors.

According to Schwartz (1998), the Web as it relates to the advertising industry is an enormous challenge and the greatest opportunity for long-term success. There are questions that advertising researchers must answer before launching a Web strategy. For example, is Web advertising different from traditional advertising? Does it require any new promotional strategies? (Godin, 1999; Hoffman & Novak, 1995; Zeff & Aronson 1999). Different responses have been presented by different scholars. From a comparative point of view, there are some common features in both advertising practices because the primary goal of all advertising campaigns is "information dissemination" in order to reach more members of a target audience. There is also the viewpoint that forms a new role for consumers in the information dissemination process that we know it as interaction.

Compared to traditional media, Web advertising has reformed the main operational bases like gathering information, cooperation, communication, interaction and transaction (Gretzel, Yuan, & Fesenmaier, 2000), and has provided new definitions for some of them. As discussed in Chapter 2, the concept of communication has changed from one-way to two-way communication.

The concept of a transaction and buyer decision-making model eliminates the need for previous information gathering tools like reference groups, and transactions and decisions are now based on comparison tools presented in online media. Therefore, in the new media, the opportunity is not that of performing things faster than the competition, but in reengineering business models to achieve more profit by both creating long-term relationships with customers and delivering value to them (Hagel, 1999).

In traditional media, branding gives customers a strong image of the product so that they will spend less time in the decision-making process.

Broadcasting a remarkable trademark, logo, icon or other commercial signs of a company on the Web is actually cheaper than doing it through other marketing channels. However, there are some concerns about strategy development in Web advertising. For example, what is the right online advertising strategy? What is the best practice for developing a Web-based advertising campaign? How are marketers able to create an innovative advertising strategy in an organizational framework? Levinson and Rubin (1995) stated that in developing an advertising program for any online business, marketers should consider these six stages:

1. A mission statement which defines or redefines the business in particular.
2. Setting the main objectives which are expected to be accomplished by advertising campaign.
3. A comprehensive list of resources which are necessary for implementing the effort.
4. Setting a list of objectives which need to be attacked.
5. Setting a list of the needed tools and tactics which are necessary to attack the objectives and accomplish them.
6. Determining a schedule which controls the whole process.

Scholars have added more items to this list; for instance, Sterne (1997) has emphasized management support and the creation of a setting-up procedure. However, with regard to Levinson and Rubin (1995) and Kotler's (2001) five Ms of advertising, it seems that an online advertising strategy needs two other basic requirements:

1. Utilizing intelligent technologies and behavioral targeting, and identifying the new target audience at the earliest possible opportunity.
2. Establishing a constant relationship with affiliated advertising networks for the purpose of receiving leads from the companies

that monitor online communities and record customer preferences. In this situation, a marketer will be able to redirect the right advertising toward the targeted customers.

Using these two approaches, main texture or substantial material of media will be aggregated and result in the prosperity. However, the important point is that each online strategy should not be neglected and should be revised periodically since the environment in which advertising is broadcast has a dynamic nature and is constantly open to new changes and technologies. Therefore, if marketers do not revise their strategies, even the best strategies will wane. Another important question is whether applying a new technology leads to a successful advertising strategy. The answer is surely "No" because success in the online environment is not just related to technology! Other factors, like analyzing traditional models, reengineering and reforming the organizational structure have become equally important (Forroster Research, 1999). Integrating new and innovative technologies permits the company to differentiate itself from old and inefficient practices, and positions it with a differentiated comparative advantage in a global market (Gretzel, Yuan, & Fesenmaier, 2000). Making changes in an organization is necessary for a successful strategy.

Changes can be considered as new thoughts or operating differently (Hultmen, 1998), or some other innovative method. The adoption of new technologies without changes in organizational culture and structure will not work. That is why simply implementing new technologies fails. When marketers design and conduct a new online advertising strategy, in most situations they are faced with problems stemmed from a lack of harmony between the organization's structure and the requirements of the new technology. Organization managers develop new technological-based strategies for a company's current structure and business models, and outstanding marketing or-

ganizations redefine the firm's nature, business model, main process and basic goals.

IDENTIFYING THE OBJECTIVES

For determining appropriate and timely goals, a marketer must recognize the needs, which are required for information broadcasting to a targeted public. In fact, business owners must decide why and how they want to get a response from advertising. Answering this question correctly will determine the main criterion in the company's advertising orientation. By finding the appropriate answer to the above question, an organization must choose the right advertising strategy to fill the gaps between organizational needs and objectives. For example, a company has recognized that its brand has less penetration in a target market. To fix the problem, the company will adopt a strategy called "increasing brand awareness." In this situation, marketers use online promotional tools to attract customers and to push them to a website where they are able to complete a brand awareness strategy. There is an applicable quotation of Cornin by King (2000): "Since each Internet advertising and selling strategy is tailored to fit a special set of objectives and opportunities, there is no universal blue print for implementation" (Cornin, 1996). He introduced nine strategies and emphasized the importance of each in a company's prosperity:

1. Well-organized site
2. Visually appealing site
3. Capturing visitors to the site
4. Using traditional media
5. Targeting
6. Interacting with customers
7. Giving something for free
8. Generating repeat visits
9. Multi-language sites

To identify advertising goals, there are three main orientations for an advertising campaign:

1. **Informative objective:** The function of advertising is to offer information about a firm's products and services. With an informative objective, advertisers introduce their competitive advantages to potential customers and to illustrate a new competency to current customers. An informative objective of advertising is delivering a kind of purchasing reason to the customer, because in the purchasing decision-making process, the customer attempts to find reasons for buying.

2. **Protective objective:** Advertising plays the role of promoter/defender in order to support the customer. By following protective objectives, advertisers minimize or eliminate the customer's ambiguities and anxieties which may happen after buying the product or service. With this objective, advertisers can use different methods, such as online interaction, sending a congratulatory email, illustrating product features, giving away some kind of promotional item such as a free magazine subscription or offering a membership card for online communities. For this objective, advertisers should present integrated and comprehensive information to a customer so that this kind of advertising plays a synergic role. In this regard, a protective objective of advertising changes to a **comparative objective** so that the company is able to protect its market share.

3. **Influencing objective:** With an influencing or motivating objective, advertising plays a major role among the other aggressive promotional tools of a company in order to add more value to its market share. In this strategy, the firm broadcasts its brands and products to customers by developing forced and intrusive strategies like pop-ups. An influencing objective is a good strategy when entering a market to quickly expand market share.

Being aligned with the firm's market position is a core factor in setting advertising objectives. If the firm is a leader in a specific market, the advertising objective should be designed to protect the firm's brand image. In this situation, marketers must develop an advertising campaign with rational appeal that shows the company has well-designed products, is a knowledgeable specialist and is competent in process engineering. Market leaders are easily recognized in a market, and an advertising campaign just needs to emphasize the company's core competencies. There is no need to develop an advertising campaign with emotional appeal; it is enough that advertisers remind customers of new advantages of the brand in order to sustain a good company image.

Other challengers in a specific market must be met regarding the influencing objective of advertising. Decreasing the market share of a competitor and grabbing that share while preserving current market share are the reasons why a company has to spend money for advertising. In applying advertising campaigns to the Internet, the key point is that marketers must be informed about various advertising strategies for this environment. Marketers should compare their advertising objectives with the requirements of online strategies and make a decision as to which strategy is better for their goals.

Companies must decide which online advertising strategy is the best for them. In other words, which online advertising tools are suitable to achieve the company goals? To answer these questions, we will examine different kinds of strategies as different situations call for different strategies. Therefore, in this section, we will focus on different types of online advertising strategies.

PUSH-INTERACTIVE-PULL STRATEGY

Conventional advertising practices in traditional media are based on two well-known strategies: push and pull. In the push strategy, manufacturers develop promotional messages to influence dealers, intermediates and wholesalers. Intermediates will also encourage customers and create a demand for manufacturers' products. In this advertising strategy, demand management is based on customer background and awareness of the product. The push strategy assigns some functions of advertising to intermediates in order for them to do sales promotion to improve sales. In the pull strategy, the target of advertising messages is consumers. Unfamiliarity with the brand, unattractiveness of the products and being new in the market are some reasons for manufacturers to use the pull strategy. In implementing a pull advertising strategy, it is important that advertisers remember two issues: vast advertising and broader distribution.

In traditional media, consumers can remove themselves from the advertising message. When advertising creates a gap in an audience's favorite program, consumers want to fill the gap; for example, they may change TV channels. This is a weak point which leads us toward other communication channels which allow the consumers to take more positive action in their gap-filler mode.

Unlike traditional media, however, the Web is not a push or unconnected media; it is a dynamic or pull media where consumers actively follow the information. This means that consumers are in a lean-forward than a lean-backward mode (Cleary, 1999). As the Internet can be controlled by users, they are more empowered in comparison with other media (Schlosser, Shavitt, & Kanfer, 1999). Also, the Web may sometimes adopt a push strategy. For example, there is some software that permits users to restore their data from the Web and shows them how. In this case, intelligent and technological factors save the customer profiles on their client's browser to be available for the user when entering the site. The profile is also shared among other members of the network. Therefore, the new technology and suitable advertising, along with consumer needs, push consumers toward the website. Other advantages of advertising on the Web are its interactive nature new technologies which allow customers to take an inverse advertising stance to offer their wants in the form of an advertising format. In this regard, customers are able to advertise what they need and want instead of searching for the advertisements of a desired product. Thus, the general model of online advertising strategy changes from a push-pull strategy to a comprehensive model of a push-interactive-pull strategy (see Figure 1).

In online advertising, a manufacturer places his advertising on the Web (push), and then users choose to view it (pull). If the advertisement grabbed the users' interests, they demonstrate a reaction such as clicking, sending email or creating an interactive relationship. Therefore, online advertising involves a push-interactive-pull strategy. As shown in the interactive part of the model, consumer can attend to an ad campaign and make demands simultaneously. First, the user searches for an appropriate manufacturer for a desired product, acting in an advertiser role and developing some informative messages. On the other hand, he is also a simple consumer who is exposed to manufacturer advertising, branding and sales promotion. In, the user is motivated to follow up on the advertising and essentially is in a pull mode.

Inverse advertising presents a new opportunity for manufacturers to adopt navigation and tracking tools that recognize consumer interests. Tracking consumers' former behaviors will somewhat reveal wants and will let marketers uncover their real demands. In this case, marketers are able to identify a framework of consumer wants. In inverse advertising, consumers have a chance to describe their desired physical products. The push-interactive-pull strategy will bring about a

Figure 1. The push-interactive-pull online advertising strategy

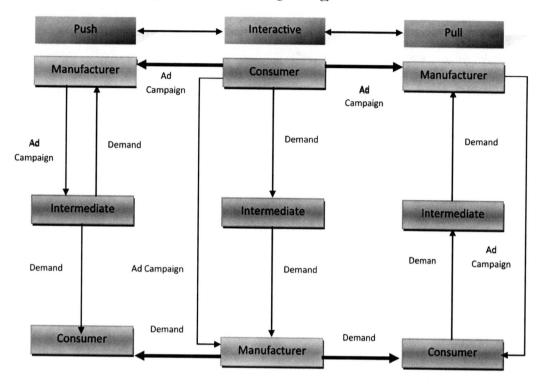

marketing offer (a common accepted concept) which is developed from consumer behavioral tracking and is also the desired product. In other words, advertiser and consumer shape a joint intangible cooperation for satisfying the two-fold goal of marketing: promising superior value and delivering satisfaction.

SEARCH ENGINE ADVERTISING (SEA)

The best method for finding a product or service on the Internet is via search engines. Users employ different search engines to find their needed products or services. Search Engine Advertising is a strategy where advertisers register their products on a search engine, and when users search for words similar to registered products, the search engine displays the registered links. The search engine fee is based on Pay-Per-Click (PPC). PPC

is the one of the best payment methods because it is a goal-oriented method, has more effectiveness and also offers a high return on investment. Keywords are the basic elements of SEA. According to Abhishek (2007), the number of keywords used amounts to more than one billion. Some are presented by advertisers and others are suggested by the search engines. Frequently used keywords indicate that advertisers have a tendency to use these keywords; however, less frequently used keywords should be considered by advertisers to avoid negative traffic. A frequently used keyword is much more expensive compared to a less frequently used keyword that is sometimes free. Purchase of frequently used keywords is usually performed through an online auction. The prices range from one cent for a less frequently used keyword to several dollars for a frequently used keyword.

Another noteworthy issue in SEA is the rank of advertisers' links and how they are positioned on search engine pages. Being on the first page of the search engine results means there is more of a chance of pushing users to those websites. On the results page, there are two main parts: the upper part called a query-leg or the top slot (paid results), and the lower part which is known as lomilomi or organic results. Each part has a different cost. For example, if a user is looking for a laptop, he may view this page in his screen server (see Figure 2).

Advertisers are willing to pay a fee to a search engine in order to position their links in the upper part of the results page and compete in the online auctions. There are many advantages for placing an advertiser's link in the top slot. Those links are introduced to customers separately so there is more of a chance they will be clicked by users. The top slot also has a psychological impact on users, because when a company's link is placed

in that region, it shapes a positive attitude in the users since they assume that upper links belong to outstanding firms.

According to Bartz (2006), there is a relationship between searching and the percentage of user clicks so that by increasing the number of searches, clicking on lower parts will increase. For that reason, marketers must develop a practice for finding the right keywords for improving their advertising links on the results pages of search engines. Figure 3 introduces a framework that shows all the stages in providing the right keywords for a company's products

As shown in Figure 3, there are three main stages in identifying website keywords. In the first stage, the company begins to gather likely keywords and stores them in a database. Then it performs the primary assessment, recognizes appropriate keywords and conveys them to word-

Figure 2. A sample of search engine advertising

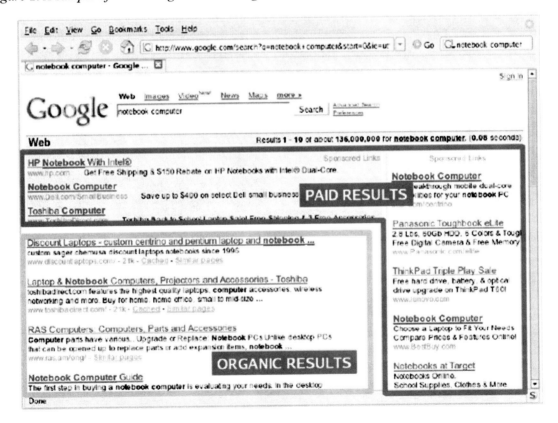

Figure 3. The process of gathering and selecting keywords for website

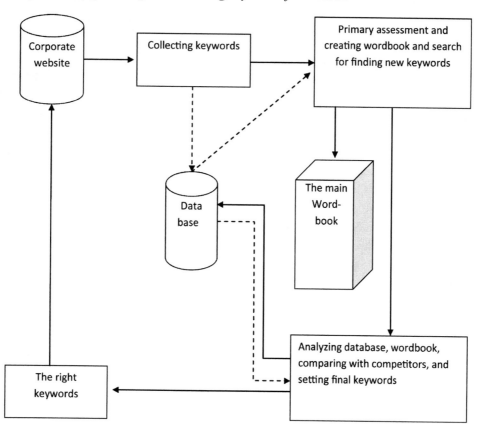

book. At the end, the website does the ultimate revising and identifying of the final keywords. To ensure they have the right keywords, marketers must search websites which are well-matched with their own websites and their business models. One of the best ways for finding appropriate keywords is scrutinizing those websites which are on the first results page of search engines, especially those that are positioned at the top.

Marketers must find out why these links are placed on first page. To answer that question, marketers should develop information retrieved from HTML pages and identify which words or phrases are the reason for placing a website link in the lower part of the results page of the search engine.

As a starting point, new players in the market can use established devices introduced by search engines. For example, Google offers a unique tool in the frame of its Adwords program. Google constantly searches the keywords that are used more than other words and saves them in its database. Moreover, Google periodically scrutinizes its registered and indexed websites to determine what words from which website are searched continuously. Hence, Google could develop a strong database that has more applicable keywords. Google presents these applicable keywords to indexed websites and asks them to introduce their keywords to Google in return.

The Seven Right Steps in SEA Strategy

To improve SEA strategy, it is necessary that marketers pay attention to some key points. Our seven-step is able to conduct a reliable SEA strategy for marketers (see Figure 4).

- **The right segments:** Segmenting the users and differentiating the target audience are good ways to offer customized service. As we will discuss in Chapter 12, the Internet provides an venue for advertisers to recognize and organize their online customers. By organizing the users, marketers will understand what kind of audiences search and view their websites, and what kind of similarities consumers share.

- **Identifying the right keywords:** From the consumer point of view, each product has an individual name/word. This may be the real name of the product or it can be a brand name which is a market leader embedded in the consumer's mind. For instance, "Tide" is P&G's laundry powder brand; it is not unusual for people who are looking for detergent or cleaner to use the word "Tide" when they mean washing powder. Hence, keyword identifications are a process by which marketers are able to determine the words that are used frequently by users in their routine, everyday discussions and interactions.

- **The right search engine:** Good execution of a SEA strategy is related to a company's attempt to find the right search engine, not the best search engine. The best search engine undoubtedly is Google, but that does not mean that it is right case for any situation. According to Searchenginewatch.com (2007), there are five giant search engines (Google, Yahoo, MSN, AOL, and Ask Jeeves) that own more than 85 percent of customer search traffic (see

Figure 5). The question is, which one is the right search engine for a company? Choosing a search engine is a challenging issue. On the base of user type, there are two approaches: **goal-oriented users** and **surfing-oriented users**. The goal-oriented users are the Internet visitors who are just looking for their own target and for this reason, choosing Google. The surfing-oriented users, however, are Internet visitors who are not on the Web to find a solution for their problems, but are there for leisure and entertainment. Hence, they will choose Yahoo, because Yahoo is a vertical portal (see Chapter 9) that provides information in different contexts for this type of user. Surfing-oriented users are usually light and medium younger users who are motivated by emotional appeal. As a result, marketers must identify which kinds of users (goal-oriented or surfing-oriented) are searching for their products in order to find the right search engine for their SEA strategy.

- **Setting the right link:** In order to identify the right link to a website, previously identified keywords must be placed where they can easily be seen and read by search engines. In determining the right link, marketers should use distinct phrases for Google and Yahoo because we know that they have different types of users. Marketers must also design the links so that they can entice users to click on them, possibly using some facilitators such as sales promotion and certificates. Designing the right landing page: The landing page is directly linked to the keywords and phrases that are displayed by search engines. When users see a link in the results page of a search engine and click on it, they are immediately sent to a website landing page. In designing the right landing page, marketers and website technical personnel must include information that has a positive connection with the

Figure 4. Seven steps in the implementation of SEA strategy

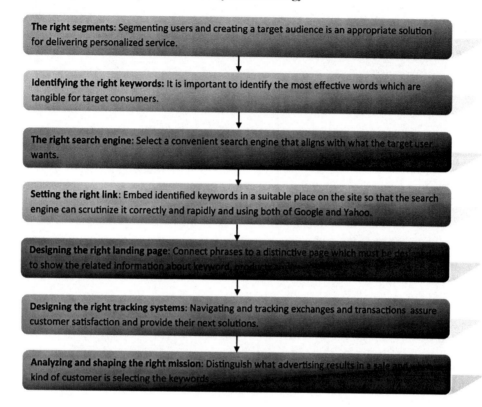

website's link. Having the right landing page will increase the effectiveness of the SEA strategy because users do not enter a website's home page and then begin to seek information. Reaching an intended solution without any problems will build up loyalty and satisfaction in customers. Whether customers find a product or not, creating and delivering satisfaction will result in continuous interaction with the website. Moreover, a well-designed website is able to assist them in finding their favorite products. The well-designed website could even result in an online purchase. When designing a proper website, marketers should study a standard—one that has a navigation section to direct its users. Navigation tools, which usually are placed at the left side of the web page, redirect online customer to the transaction stage.

- **Designing the right tracking systems:** As we will discuss in Chapter 12, when users subscribe to an online newsletter or register in an online community, the website is able to trace their activities. Google and Yahoo have introduced their own analytic website where services for marketers is complimentary (see Figure 5).

- **Analyzing and shaping the right mission:** By analyzing its advertising and entrance portals, a marketer is able to understand which advertising has resulted in selling, which keywords are chosen more than others, what landing page is effective and what kinds of users have visited the website. Then marketers make necessary revisions in their process, placement,

Figure 5. A sample of Google analysis

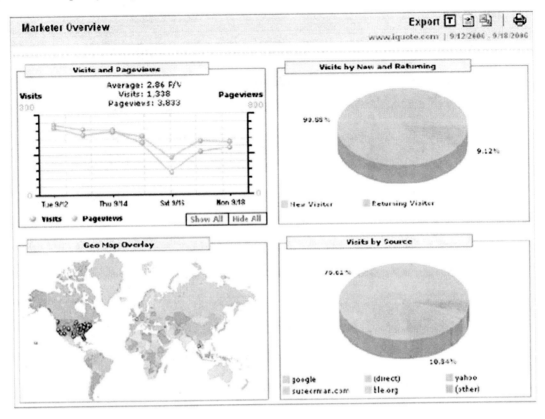

search engine and keywords in order to shape the right mission to reach company goals.

INFORMATIVE STRATEGY

When customers have a high involvement with one product, they will tend to gather more information about it. In other words, they will have high motivation and easily be persuaded to search for this product, so advertisers must be ready with an informative strategy. Informative strategy is an online advertising strategy whereby advertisers try to disseminate targeted information that will eliminate customers' confusion and concerns. In executing an informative strategy, marketers must reach two goals within the publishing banner format: 1) create appropriate ports for pushing

customers to the Web; and raise customer awareness about the company's brands. A banner is an effective solution for an informative strategy because the banner can increase brand awareness and customer loyalty even if there was no click (Brigges & Hoils, 1997).

An informative strategy is well-suited for those marketers who need high interaction and participation in selling its products. Hence, in implementing an informative strategy, advertising content and design should of high quality. Whereas some advertising messages offer little information about a product, the concept of content quality involves another dimension—website quality. When customers are attracted to and enter a website, the website must try to satisfy their needs. The website is the main element in an informative strategy because customers who purchase products with high involvement receive their information from complementary sources like the website. The website's design is the winning point in this strategy. In this regard, marketers must recognize what kind of high involvement has directed customers to the website, and whether that customer involvement is rational or emotional. To answer this question a simple method is tracking customers' previous click streams which will reveal their interests and also whether they have acted in response to emotional or rational stimuli.

After considering customer involvement, website owners should design the main structure of website accordingly. If the marketers find that their users are involved emotionally, they should create a website incorporating animation, images and flash technology in order to be aligned with user involvement. However, if the marketers discover that the users are sensitive to rational features, they must design a statistical and specialized website to advertise the company's message. This does not mean that a rational-based website should ignore images or graphics; rather, their main focus should be rational factors with images and graphics applied appropriately.

To implement an informative strategy, we have developed a practical study in the crane context. In this study conducted in *Hadef.ir*, we first focused on the crane industry and recognized influencing features in customer preferences and behaviors. Whereas the crane industry is a specialized industry with high-dollar, specialty products like cranes, winches and hoists, this industry is positioned in the high involvement and rational buying group. When a product is positioned as the rational buying group, the role of informing and confidence building will increase so that the website can respond to customer motives for information processing.

When responding to customers with high motivation, the designers of a website should focus on two major considerations. The first is the informing aspect that is responsible for answering the informational needs of customers. It

also has the task of publishing some requirements like the firm's core competencies, competitive advantages and technical points, and explaining how this brand works in different environments. The second consideration is confidence building where the customer's brand awareness is increased via illustrations and digital videos of other large projects. To address this, we designed an online resume to highlight photos and information about companies where *Hadef* has implemented a hoist and winch. To further increase customer confidence, we displayed *Hadef's* credited certificates that *Hadef* from an outstanding institute in the large banner-poster. Then, a direct link to the awarding institute was placed under the banner so that customers could see the original certificate (see Figure 6.

Results were positive, because after implementing the informative strategy, online as well as offline orders increased. One of the remarkable outcomes in applying the informative strategy was the decline in negotiation time. Personal selling and negotiation are two noteworthy tools of marketers, particularly in promoting specialty products. Ambiguity and improper information results in lengthy negotiation time. In that situation, it is best for the customers to decide while marketers show them links to informational resources that will build confidence. Hence, we developed some entrance portals for customers that redirects them to websites (see Figure 7). The use of promotional banners helps persuade users to visit a website. Providing detailed website information to potential customers and executing a parallel advertising strategy along with an informative strategy (see image-making strategy) results in a considerable decline in customer uncertainty. Finally, our study showed that applying an online informative strategy helps avoid lengthy negotiation and raises customer confidence for doing business with a company.

In developing an informative strategy, marketers can provide some facilities on their websites.

Figure 6. Hadef.ir

For instance, marketers can create icon options, which involve some titles like *History, Help, Products* and especially Frequently Asked Questions or *FAQ*. Having FAQ is necessary because the same motives and involvement usually lead to similar questions from users. When customers have unusual questions which are not addressed in FAQ, marketers should answer those questions via email in less than 12 hours. To improve customer information about a company, a website must also have titles such as *About us* or *Our time*. It is essential that a *User Forum* area is designed into website so that customers can share their experiences about products with other customers and website owners. According to Thomsen (1996), online customers are interested in such discussions with website owners.

IMAGE-MAKING STRATEGY

Image-making is more related to customers' emotional rather than rational senses. There are two major types of image-making strategies: image-making using online advertising formats and image-making for a company's brand. In regard to the second type of image-making, developing a strong brand image, especially for high involvement products, is a reliable method for increasing a firm's market share. With low involvement products, there is no substantial effort to recognize one specific brand or company. Hence, marketers who have a high involvement product must use an image-making strategy for their brand. How do marketers create a successful brand among their customers?

There are a variety of methods a company can use to develop a successful image-making strategy for brand. In our *Hadef.ir* practical study, we executed such a strategy. Whereas Hadef is

Figure 7. Hadef promotional banners used as enter ports (Hadef.ir, 2010)

a well-known brand in the lifting and material-handling market and its subsidiary (*Aseman Asa Sanat*) in Iran was an unknown brand, we focused on an image-making strategy. In this case, the core concentration was on the website and its operational capacity. The goal was creating a positive image for *Asman Asa Sanat*. The analysis shows that if the *Hadef* logo was positioned next to the *Asman Asa Sanat* logo, customers would associate the two logos and have a positive image of both companies. Assisting this effort was the fact that *Hadef* already had a positive image with international customers and enjoyed customer preferences. In website designing, we identified the best position for the two companies' logos. As shown in Figure 6, the *Hadef* logo was placed on the left and the *Aseman Asa Sanat* logo was placed on the right side of the web page. Also, the website ID was changed from asmanasasanat.ir to hadef. ir in order to create harmony between the original *Hadef* and its subsidiary. Moreover, changing the ID resulted in getting a better position on the results page in Google. The enthusiastic results were manifested in more orders, the number of inquiries also sharply increased. Now, the *Aseman*

Asa Sanat logo is perceived as an internationally accepted logo among other lifting competitors.

The image-making strategy is suitable for those marketers who are introducing a product or service or attempting to increase a product's life cycle. In that scenario, image-making helps marketers to influence a customer's emotions by publishing figurative advertising. Figurative advertising is a picture-based advertising strategy where marketers target emotional or surf-oriented customers. These advertisers operate a kind of image internalizing for their products so that their product can be easily distinguished from other products. When this strategy is implemented correctly, companies can improve their brand image by exaggerating their products' features. There is a direct connection between a website and the advertising formats on it so that when interested customers are redirected to the website, they have a positive attitude toward finding figurative information. Moreover, emotional-based customers tend to seek additional information based on figurative data. Advertising designers must consider this fact so that they can produce captivating advertising in order to create an expectation in customers that they can gather more figurative data on the advertiser's website. Therefore, marketers must develop an image-making strategy that focuses on the Internet surfer because Kongankar and Wolin (2001) showed that this type of online user is probably going to click on an emotionally based advertisement.

ONLINE DIRECT SELLING STRATEGY

Having a prodigy as an Internet provider enables a company to introduce its advertising properly and to deal with customers who enthusiastically have chosen the company website and want to investigate its products or services. This presents an incredible selling opportunity. If customers invite advertisers to negotiate, that is a signal that they are ready to buy. As stated by Belch and Belch (2006), "Direct marketing is in itself a form of advertising. Whether through mail, print, or TV, the direct response offer is an ad" (p. 465) where the customers announce their needs and wants, and ask the advertiser to satisfy their demands. A direct selling strategy is well-executed by a variety of tools such as online catalogues.

Sending a catalogue is a marketing practice where companies like Pottery Barn and JCPenney have been extremely successful. New concepts like Internet direct marketing or Internet direct selling in a marketing context have developed as a novelty section in the form of an online catalogue. An online catalogue is a digital type of product brochure that has slightly changed the interactive structure in that catalogue sending in the form of a package mailed to a customer is no longer customary; instead, the customer visits the catalogue's address! First the customer observes the marketer's catalogue on the website, and the downloaded catalogue could result in a buying intention where the customer will send a transactional solution. A transactional solution is a specific offer in order for consumers to meet

their needs and wants, not for marketers to satisfy those needs.

If online catalogue is considered from a comprehensive point of view, it is clear that all websites' leads and pictures are an online catalogue. This new marketing concept could greatly decrease the cost of providing and printing catalogues. In the developed form of an online catalogue, marketers are able to use video-based catalogues to promote their products. What kinds of businesses should use this online direct selling strategy?

The online direct selling strategy is appropriate for those industries that need to take customer requirements into consideration in the production process. These industries usually have one standard product that cannot be suitable for all markets, and product design is naturally related to customer orders. For example, the manufacturers of production lines or workshop materials need some basic information of a customer's condition such as production capacity, considered deployment place, square footage and al temperature. After compiling this information, marketers can offer a customized catalogue to customers; the customer offers feedback and eventually places the order. Hadef.com is good case for understanding the online direct selling strategy (see its customized catalogue in Figure 8).

VIRAL ADVERTISING STRATEGY

Have you ever advertised in any media for free? Indeed, where can marketers find free media to advertise their promotional messages? Marketers answered these questions by developing a new concept: viral advertising. Viral advertising is a marketing technique that uses pre-existing social networks to increase brand awareness or to achieve other marketing objectives (such as product sales) through a self-replicating viral process, similar to the spread of pathological and computer viruses. It can be delivered by word-of-mouth or enhanced by the network effects of the Internet.

Viral advertising is a marketing phenomenon that encourages people to pass along a marketing message voluntarily. Viral promotions may take the form of video clips, interactive flash games, advergames, eBooks, images or even text messages (Besla.org, 2010).

The viral campaign creates a message like a short video clip that is so compelling that much of the advertiser's work is done for them when their prospective customers forward the message to their contacts, quickly building up an audience of millions. An entire industry has sprung up dedicated to unraveling what makes viral ads infectious. GoViral, for instance, specializes in launching viral campaigns—in part by "seeding" clips on the Web in places where they are picked up by the online populace (Timesonline, 2010).

The viral advertising strategy is developed on the basis of an advertisement's extraordinary attractiveness. When an advertisement is designed and publicized so that it is able to fascinate and influence its audiences, those users convey the excitement of the ad to others, and the result is a new media for broadcasting. Message transfer can be affected in chat rooms, by sending email or by announcements in online communities. Penetrating the Internet via cell phones has helped develop this marketing practice. By equipping mobile phones with Bluetooth technology, the trend of utilizing the viral strategy is moving swiftly. The new software allows people to send any messages to customer cell phones or laptops (see *Bluetooth-advertising.co.uk* for more information). The key point in successfully implementing this strategy is using peripheral elements in order to increase advertising attractiveness. It is not important whether the elements are related to the advertising message or not! However, it is important that the advertising design must be unique. If marketers are able to design an extraordinary advertisement, it is possible that their advertisement is capable of increasing customer brand awareness; for example,

Timesonline.com has introduced the 10 top viral advertisements (see *business.timesonline.com*).

ADS AS A COMMODITY STRATEGY

There are some companies in which the marketers introduce advertising as a commodity. For example, *mypoints.com* and *clickrewards.com* are two remarkable companies that utilized this strategy successfully. In displaying advertising as a commodity, the publishers gather relevant interests on their websites and ask users to register their priorities. Then they publish an announcement to identify appropriate marketer that can meet the customers' registered wants. The publishers send the marketers products in the form of advertising to customers' emails and persuade them to react. The advertising involves various kinds of information like a product's price, size, color, and delivery time. Publishers earn a fee if the advertisement persuades customers to visit the marketers' websites.

ASSOCIATED ADVERTISING DISPLAY

Associated ad display exclusively belongs to the Internet medium. In this strategy, users' interests are traced through their keywords inserted into search boxes when they are surfing from one website to another. As they search, they receive a parallel banner advertisement on their requested web page. The alignment between an associated ad and desired content is called associated advertising display. Due to its relationship with a customer's current motive and that it presents the results that the customer is looking, associated ad display is one of the best strategies for Internet marketing because it motivates the customer to click on associated advertisements.

Figure 8. A sample of an online catalogue

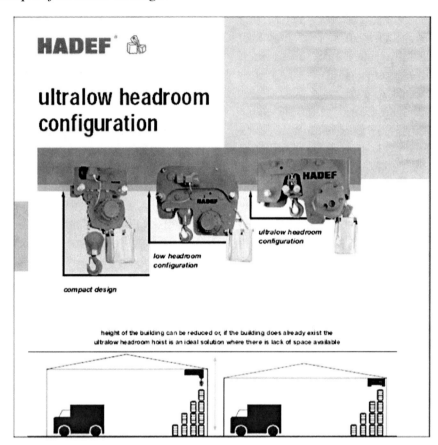

FORCED ADVERTISING STRATEGY

One of the most irritating online strategies is the advertising strategy. The phrase is derived from the situation in which advertisements enter customers' e-mailboxes or servers without permission and publish their message. Whereas, some scholars believe that this is an irritating method with negative effects (Edwards, Li, &Lee, 2002), others think it can be a good method for increasing customer awareness of new brands. Using the pop-up format of online advertising is an appropriate way to implement this strategy, especially when entering new markets (see Chapter 4). Since pop-ups are developed using rich media technology and advertisers can use animation and video within them, even if the advertisement is closed immediately by the customer, due to its appeal, the customer

will keep it in mind. The forced advertising strategy is the best choice for those services that are unfamiliar to customers and for users who have no awareness of product features. In such cases, the advertisers intrude their advertisements into the users' privacy in order to increase customer information about new products.

CONCLUSION

Advertising strategies are promotional practices that are designed to promote business dissemination actions and campaigns whereby a corporation can achieve its goals and grow faster than its competitors. The advertising strategy or the publicizing solution is defined usually on the basis of an organization's limited resources and environment analysis to achieve a predicted organizational goal. There are some differences in disseminating advertising in traditional offline and modern online media. Forming a new role for consumers in disseminating information is known as interactivity and results in creating new strategies for the online environment. A number of questions have emerged in marketers' minds. For example, what is the right online advertising strategy? What is the best practice for developing web-based advertising? How are marketers able to start up an innovative advertising strategy in an organizational framework?

Marketers must determine their goals for advertisement publishing. To determine appropriate and timely goals, marketer must recognize the needs which lead to broadcasting to a targeted audience. To determine the main criteria in advertising orientation, business owners must discover why and how to respond to the needs for which they are advertising. There are three major objectives for any advertising campaign: informative objectives, protective objectives or comparative objectives, and influencing objectives. Being aligned with the company's market position is the core orientation in setting advertising objectives. If the firm is a leader, challengers or followers must be taken into account when developing its proportionate objectives.

In online media, there are new strategies like the push-interactive-pull model, the SEA strategy, the informative strategy, image-making strategies, the online direct selling strategy, the viral advertising strategy, the advertising as a commodity strategy, the associated advertising display strategy, and the forced strategy. Marketers must develop the right online advertising on the basis of their exclusive requirements. There are different methods for employing these strategies; for example, developing a combination strategy that stems from an informative strategy, image-making strategies and an online direct selling strategy is effective for high involvement products.

REFERENCES

Abhishek, V. (2007). *Key words generation for search engine advertising using semantic similarity between terms*. India: Fair Isaac Company.

Berger, P. D., Lee, J., & Weinberg, B. D. (2006). Optimal cooperative advertising integration strategy for organizations adding a direct online channel. *The Journal of the Operational Research Society, 57*, 920–927. doi:10.1057/palgrave.jors.2602069

Besla.org. (2010). *Advertising and the convergence TV, film and technology on the internet*. Retrieved from http://www.besla.org.

Briggs, R., & Hollis, N. (1997). Advertising on the web: Is there response before click-through. *Journal of Advertising Research, 37*(2), 33–45.

Cheung, R. C. T. (2006). Case study of successful internet advertising strategy in Hong Kong: A portal for teenagers. *Marketing Intelligence & Planning, 24*(4), 393–405. doi:10.1108/02634500610672125

Cleary, J. M. (1999). P & G's consumer centric approach to the web. *Direct Marketing, 62*(5), 47–50.

Cornin, M. J. (1996). *Global advantage on the internet*. New York, NY: Van Nostrand.

Edwards, S. M., Li, H., & Lee, J. H. (2002). Forced exposure and psychological reactance: Antecedents and consequences of the perceived intrusiveness of pop-up ads. *Journal of Advertising, 31*(3), 83–96.

Emarketer.com. (2005). *SEMPO*. Retrieved from http://www.emarketer.com.

Fastoso, F. (2007). International advertising strategy: The standardization question in manager studies. *International Marketing Review, 24*(5), 591–606. doi:10.1108/02651330710828004

Godin, S. (1999). *Permission marketing*. New York, NY: Simon & Schuster.

Gretzel, U., Yuan, Y., & Fesenmaier, D. R. (2000). Preparing for the new economy: Advertising strategies and change in destination marketing. *Journal of Travel Research, 39*, 146–156. doi:10.1177/004728750003900204

Hagel, J. (1999). Net gain: Expanding markets through virtual communities. *Journal of Interactive Marketing, 13*(1), 55–65. doi:10.1002/(SICI)1520-6653(199924)13:1<55::AID-DIR5>3.0.CO;2-C

Hoffman, D. L., & Novak, T. P. (1995). *Marketing in hypermedia computer-mediated environments: Conceptual foundations*. Working Paper. Nashville, TN: Vanderbilt University.

Hultman, K. (1998). *Making change irresistible: Overcoming resistance to change in your organization*. Palo Alto, CA: Davies-Black.

Kaplan, R. S., & Norton, D. P. (2001). *Strategy-focused organization: How balanced scorecard companies thrive in the new business environment*. Boston, MA: Harvard Business School Publishing Corporation.

King, L. T. Y. (2002). Internet advertising and selling strategies. *Malaysian Journal of Technology, 36*(D), 71-82.

Korgaonkar, P. K., & Wolin, D. L. (2001). Web usage, advertising, and shopping: Relationship patterns. *Internet Research: Electronic Networking Applications and Policy, 12*(2), 191–204.

Kotler, P. (2001). *Marketing management* (10th ed.). Upper Saddle River, NJ: Prentice-Hall, Inc.

Levinson, J. C., & Rubin, C. (1995). *Guerilla marketing online*. New York, NY: Houghton Mifflin.

Limaconsulting.com. (2007). *The 9 essentials to effective online marketing best practice guide*. Retrieved from http://www.LimaConsulting.com.

Management-report.com. (2007). *Search engine advertising is essential for modern marketing*. Retrieved May 2007, from http://www.Management-reports.com.

Margrethe, D. T. (1996). *Advertising on the internet*. Masters Dissertation. Westminster, UK: University of Westminster.

Okazaki, S., & Rivas, A. J. (2002). A content analysis of multinationals' web communication strategies, cross-cultural research framework and pretesting. *Internet Research: Electronic Networking Applications and policy, 12*(5), 380-390.

Perry, M. (2002). Fortune 500 manufacturer web sites: Innovative marketing strategies or cyber brochures. *Industrial Marketing Strategies, 31*, 133–144. doi:10.1016/S0019-8501(01)00187-0

Porter, E. M. (2001, March). Strategy and the internet. *Harvard Business Review*.

Sands, M. (2003). Integrating the web and e-mail into a push-pull strategy. *Qualitative Market Research: An International Journal, 6*(1), 27–37. doi:10.1108/13522750310457357

Schlosser, A. E., Shavitt, S., & Kanfer, A. (1999). Survey of internet users' attitudes toward internet advertising. *Journal of Interactive Marketing, 13*(3), 34–71. doi:10.1002/(SICI)1520-6653(199922)13:3<34::AID-DIR3>3.0.CO;2-R

Schwartz, E. I. (1998). *Webonomics: Nine essential principles for growing your business on the world wide web*. New York, NY: Broadway.

Sterne, J. (1997). *What makes people click: Advertising on the web*. Indianapolis, IN: Que Corporation.

Timesonline. (2010). *The top ten viral ad campaigns*. Retrieved January 15, 2010, from http://www.Business.timesonline.uk.

Zeff, R., & Aronson, B. (1999). *Advertising on the internet* (2nd ed.). New York, NY: John Wiley.

Chapter 9
Advertising and E–Business

ABSTRACT

How do websites earn revenue? Many websites enter this field with a so-called "bright perspective," then end up adding their name to the dotcom failure statistics.

In today's online marketing arena, there are remarkable concepts which are rarely available for public study and consideration. For instance, the e-business models are considered trendy by many Internet specialists who do not consider superior operational efficiency as a critical factor for success in companies such as Cisco, EBay, Dell, and Amazon. However, they believe that the business model or method adopted in modern technology is the basis for their success. With the implicit awareness of success in these kinds of companies, few of them have explicit insight regarding this success; therefore, they cannot distinguish the different kinds of businesses and business models utilized by giant merchants. Thus, this chapter introduces e-business and draws a line between e-business and e-commerce. Also, different kinds of e-business models are examined because an advertiser should know the business models of the websites which may be publishing his advertising. Above all, at the end of this chapter, the reader will be able to distinguish between the businesses and business models of commercial and non-commercial websites and understand their earning methods.

E-BUSINESS AND E-COMMERCE

While many people consider e-business and e-commerce to be the same, these concepts are different in many respects. E-business includes e-commerce and a variety of other applicable programs; many applications and advantages are derived from e-business. E-commerce focuses solely on the customers of an organization, finding new channels and resources for the organization and maximizing profit through modern media. On the other hand, e-business develops the communication of the organization between suppliers, staff and partners. Mass communication is a prominent strategy of e-business. Therefore, e-business is considered the second wave in the Internet revolution (Bigg, 2001). E-commerce includes such

DOI: 10.4018/978-1-4666-0885-6.ch009

transactions as ordering, payment and delivering the orders to the customers. In e-commerce, the users do not have access to electronic data for products and services via the Internet, Intranet and Extranet, so e-commerce transactions require human interaction. E-commerce transactions are considered to be contract-driven processes, for customers' demands are met through updating or contracting directly with the company. When comparing e-commerce with e-business, it can be concluded that e-commerce is slower than e-business as e-commerce adds to the information available to the user to improve the company's marketing capacity. Besides, the focus on e-commerce is on one side of the company, i.e. the customers, and there is no close relationship with staff and suppliers. That is why e-commerce is limited to customer-serving software and is not supported by organizational servers. In addition, the e-business infrastructure is much more complicated than that of e-commerce. E-business usually deals with utilizing the Internet and its relevant technologies to develop the organization and provides the facilities for sharing the information in different places online. Finally, it can be claimed that e-commerce attempts to establish a relationship between customers and the organization, while e-business is a set of infrastructures and methods which speed up the information exchange of the organization with the outside world where he customer plays a crucial role.

The greatest dream of successful organizations is to have the same success in online world as in the real world. In other words, they want to change their traditional business to e-business. To achieve these goals, they must understand e-business and its models. According to the Health Industrials Today Institute, e-business includes utilizing electronic data standards with automatic computerized technology for integrated information, and integrating internal and external data systems and business processes among business partners. The most important function of e-business is connecting and interacting with a network. One of the consequences of an online business is the removal of some of the human roles like data reprocessing. Therefore, thanks to the online environment and the computerized system, efficiency is increased and the possibility of errors is decreased. E-business enables the service providers to interact with suppliers and consumers (Follit, 2000) which results in customer loyalty and, in the long run, increases a company's profitability and competitive advantage.

E-Business Components

E-business creates affiliations between customers, suppliers, employees, and business partners via the Internet, Intranet, and Extranet. Web-based systems manage customers' transactions and allow them to utilize e-commerce. The most important factor in e-business is the Internet which is constantly used in interactional and transactional processes and in data-sharing. In addition, the information that flows from and to business partners is facilitated by developing Extranets which provide companies with strategies and advantages of e-business. They also allow suppliers to have an integrated relationship with customers.

E-Business Model

The term e-business came into vogue when the number of PCs used by businesses and customers rapidly increased and access to the global network became easier. The term was first coined by Dan Bricklin and then adopted by MIT University. E-business is one of those concepts which is not clearly understood by users, and for this reason, there are many definitions for it. The definitions are not derived from an integrated approach consisting of four basic elements including product innovation, infrastructure management, customer relationship and financial aspects. The researchers' definitions of an e-business model are gained from an elementary and/or strategic point of view (Osterowalder & Pigneur, 2002) so a comprehensive category of an e-business model cannot be provided (Lambert, 2003).

Business models have been defined in many ways. Business models are scenarios or real stories which describe how a business institution will operate going forward (Magretla, 2002). Peter Drucker, the most renowned author in management, believes that a model is a method which determines who the customers are and what the values are for them. He also believes that all managers should decide how they can earn income from this business. What is the basic rationale which can create value for the customer and minimize expenses? Two other definitions of business models include: a business model consists of the structure of the flow of information, service and products, and a description of the administrator's interests and income resources (Timmer, 1998); and a business model is the procedure of doing business in a way that the organization can earn revenue (Turban, 2006).

Although many studies have been done on turning real-world business models into e-business models, still there exists no clear reason to do that (Drew, 2003). Some researchers believe that there is no difference between e-business models and business models (Porter, 2001). Others believe that because of the changing environment, there are some differences between e-business and business models (Canzer, 2003). One model on this issue of using the Internet in business was proposed by Adam in 2002. This model analyzes the extent of use of the Internet in different businesses and categorizes them into four classes.

On one side are pure dotcom businesses whose models are entirely electronic. On the other side are pure brick-and-mortar businesses which are unfamiliar with the Internet and its relevant businesses. There is a case to be made for each group.

Different Kinds of Business Models

There are many e-businesses on the World Wide Web, which depend on websites to manage their income methods. Advertising is one of the most important factors in a majority of these models. According to the method of revenue earning or the business model, most financial institutions are in one way or another dependent on advertising. From an unprofessional point of view, discussing e-business and its related models may not be important; however, understanding the process of designing a website, employing experts, providing the infrastructures and adopting an appropriate business aimed at forming a good advertisement may reveal a new outlook. In fact, by choosing the right e-business model, an organization adopts an appropriate way of advertising so that profitability increases. In addition, as discussed in Chapter 8, one of the forms of advertising is the website itself.

Merchandizing and earning income through the Internet has resulted in the creation of so many business models (Rappa, 2005). Interaction and transaction with merchants emphasizes the importance of recognizing the various models used on these websites. Different categorizations have been made by online business researchers, three of are introduced here:

Rayport and Jaworski (2004) categorized e-business models as follows: 1) *Freshest Information, Highest Quality, Widest Assortment, Lowest Prices,* and *Most Personalized* (Rayport & Jaworski, 2004, p. 132); 2) Laudon and Traver (2007) introduced e-business models including *Advertising, Subscription, Transaction Fee, Sales,* and *Affiliate* (Laudon & Traver, 2007, p. 62); and 3) Rappa (2005) categorized e-business models into *Brokerage, Advertising, Infomediary, Merchant, Manufacturer, Affiliate, Community, Subscription,* and *Utility.*

Upon investigation, we see that some companies are classified into different categories (*see their references at the end of this chapter).* As mentioned before, lack of a clear definition of any particular business model and lack of standards and features for classifying these models are the basis for these differences. However, there are other kinds of e-business models which are defined and patterned by today's outstanding companies in order to be pioneers in the e-marketplace. What is observable much more than any other factor is the innovation and creativity of these advertisers. Owners of these businesses introduce new concepts to the World Wide Web via new and intelligent innovations. Below, some of these models are introduced and discussed, and e-business models, their revenue sources, and some examples of each are introduced in Table 1.

PORTAL MODELS

Portals provide the opportunity to find everything that users may need. These websites provide information on professional domains like *Medicine* or *Law*. For instance, *Webmd.com* provides a selection of medical documents and other medically related information. It also helps users find their favorite physicians or specialists who are members of this site. Membership to this website lets users update their information by way of medical announcements, read the newest scientific magazines, and be able to connect with other members. *Mdscape.com* and *Drkoop.com* are other portals that deliver medical information.

Table 1. Different kinds of e-business models

Business Model	Source of Revenue	Examples
Advertising	• An advertising model has content of the highest quality to gain a competitive advantage. Cost of space and sources of revenue in such sites is valuable.	• Yahoo.com • Aol.com • Msn.com • Lycos.com
Membership Fee	• In a membership fee model, visitors pay a fee to receive things like information and software.	• Listen.com • Netflix.com • WSJ.com
Customizing	• In a customizing model, a website take leads from Lead Generation companies to deliver the right product and service to the consumer.	• Sevencycles.com • EDiets.com
Web Analyzers	• A web analyzer site delivers a kind of software, statistics and solutions to merchants to optimize their business.	• Clicktraks.com • Coremetrics.com • Omniture.com
Broadest or Widest Array	• A broadest array sells products to customers. This type of business model may have the lowest price or the highest quality.	• Amazon.com • Allbooksforless.com • Ashford.com
Affiliation	• An affiliation model redirects customers to an advertiser website. For this purpose, the website pulls traffic through gifts, prizes, andcontests. Other affiliation models focus on agencies' technical talent and attempt to deliver an appropriate plan for affiliation marketing	• Affiliatefuel.com • Affiliatefuture.com • Darkblue.com • Incentaclick.com • Linkshare.com • Mypoints.com
Ad server	• An ad server model offers a comprehensive approach for ad publishing. This type of e-business model attempts continually increases its sub-websites or integrated websites. One of the success features in this model is the number of integrated websites. Advertising by this model is published on its own sub-websites or integrated websites.	• Epilot.com • Gorillanation.com • Drivepm.com • Doubleclick.com • Eyeblaster.com • Valueclick.com • Aquantive.com

Advertising Insight 1: Yahoo! Shopping

Yahoo is a *horizontal website*, linked to a countless number of other websites and online catalogs. This portal provides the customer with unlimited capacity for shopping. Customers can link to online stores and buy their favorite items via Yahoo. When they are finished with shopping and are ready to pay, they can simply pay for all their purchases through Yahoo. To limit the number of invoices from different online retailers, shopping-cart technology is utilized to substantially decrease e-shopping time. The customer clicks on *Yahoo Shopping* on the upper part of the Yahoo homepage. Searching a product or product keyword, the customer can visit *Featured Stores*. From among other important icons, gift Registration, Hot Products, What is Selling Now and Yahoo Prizes can also be accessed. To use the shopping cart technology, the customer must register in Yahoo selecting a user name and password. After registering, the user can continue searching for products and can click on the "add to the cart" icon for any product. Yahoo shopping is only one example of services provided by this portal. There are other kinds of horizontal portals on the net including *Aks.com*, *Ask jeeves*, *Av.com*, or *AltaVista*. *Ask jeeves* is a portal designed to answer users' questions. *Alta-Vista* links users to all domains on the Internet and provides free service. *Metacrawler.com* and *Gomez.com* are other horizontal portals.

Other vertical portals are known as *Legal Portals*. Services available on these portals are partly free and partly related to licenses for legal companies. *Lexis.com* and its partner, *Nexis.com,* are two examples. *Lexis.com* makes information and case studies on legal issues and news articles available on the Internet. However, there are other types of community portals which work in domains like age or target groups. *Bolt.com* is a portal containing subjects for teens and young adults; it provides online chats, message boards, surveys and shopping. The website promotes ongoing and repeat visits by means of accessing desired information and interaction with peers.

Advertising Insight 2: American Online (AOL.com)

Joining Time Warner Entertainment CO. was the AOL starting point. Twenty years ago, AOL was created by Steve Case in his bedroom; it now is one of the biggest Internet portals and one of the most profitable e-business models. Networks and companies working under AOL control include: CompuServe, Netscape, Digital City, ICQ, and AOL Movie Phone. Thanks to a presently powerful and user-friendly community, users of AOL can connect and interact with everyone everywhere. Via AOL, nearly 25 million users are able to search, download, and chat online as well as e-mail.

Ivillag.com is a portal which is designed for women where news and information on women's health is available for free and includes a message board for questions. A similar portal designed for 15-to-20-year-old women is *Iemaily.com*. *Opinions.com* is a portal which allows users to convey information like interests, strategies and favorite media. Users pay a specified amount for each message. *Opinions.com* is one of the largest websites where users find information on products and services. The last kind of vertical portals discussed here is *Internet.com*. The contents of this website are concentrated on the Internet and electronic business, and information on this site is free.

DYNAMIC PRICING MODELS

The Internet has revolutionized business practices. In a real-world transaction, the vendor sets a price and, if the customer agrees, there will be an exchange. In the cyber world, the mechanism is rather different. Companies like *priceline. com* and *Imandi.com* enable users to set a price for services like hotels and travel. In the past, customers had to visit many wholesale and retail centers to bargain for and finally purchase their desired goods and services. Today, they can get all they need at home and at the lowest price by a few simple clicks. Mass shopping will always result in discounts and lower prices.

Advertising Insight 3: Priceline.com

Using a Name-Your-Price Model has brought priceline.com world fame. At this site, customers can bid (suggested price) for plane tickets, hotel reservations and car rentals. This model has been registered by priceline.com as a patent and is called a demand-collecting system. In this system, a shopping bot gathers all bids and delivers them to priceline.com to be analyzed. Some businesses use an intelligent agent to promote their website's level of service; these agents are usually used to search for data saved in a database to answer special inquiries.

The shopping process on priceline.com is quick and easy. For example, when a customer wants a ticket for a flight, the start date, destination, suggested price, and number of tickets needed are input. Then the flight number, airport, and destination are selected. This system has a great deal of flexibility, but even more important, the customer can buy the ticket at the desired price.

Priceline.com delivers the price suggested by the customer to the airlines. Then the website negotiates to reach an agreement under the customer's bid. If the company agrees, priceline.com keeps the margin between the agreed price and the customer's price. The whole process takes less than an hour. In the airline industry, thousands of vacant seats are available daily; priceline.com helps the airlines to sell these vacancies. Since the flights do not depend on the fullness or emptiness of the seats, *Priceline* convinces the companies to accept the customer's price and fly with fewer vacant seats.

Name-Your-Pricing Model

The Name-Your-Pricing business model lets the customers set the price for products and services (see *priceline.com* insight). Some businesses that provide this service have formed relationships with the managers of hotels, financial institutions and retailers. The managers receive the price desired by the customers and then decide whether or not to sell the service or product. If the customer's price is not accepted, a new bid is proposed by the customer.

Comparative Pricing Model

The comparative Pricing model lets customers compare many prices and purchase the product or service at the lowest price (advertising insight 4). These companies usually earn their income through interaction with traders, so customers should be careful when working with them, because the best price may not be revealed to them, and instead they may end up buying the item at a price suggested by the traders who are related to the website.

Advertising Insight 4: BottomDollar.com

BottomDollar.com uses intelligent agent technology to search sites for the best possible price for customers. Intelligent agents are programs that search, classify, and report a large body of data. Using *BottomDollar.com*, customers can search and analyze product catalogs in different groups. *BottomDollar.com* scrutinizes thousands of retailers in seconds in search of the best price. To understand the volume of the operation, imagine searching one thousand online stores one by one to find the best price.

Intelligent agents are changing the shopping habits of customers. Instead of going personally to the stores, customers can use these services and sites, which give them the best price in the shortest time possible. The pressure of these modern technologies on retailers forces them to keep their prices in a competitive position.

There are other websites like *dealertime.com*, *Deja.com*, and *mysiman.com* which use the comparative pricing business model. Unlike other sites using this model, *Deja.com* chooses the trade on the basis of income, reputation and last records of a customer's shopping. *Deja.com* is a multipurpose website, which manages chatting groups, customer classification and comparative selling. Customers can also search the prices of the most famous retailers after seeing the search results.

Demand-Sensitive Pricing Model

The Internet enables customers to meet their demands for faster and cheaper service. One factor that facilitates decreasing the prices is group shopping. The demand-sensitive pricing Model means that when a lot of customers intend to buy a product, the individual cost decreases. Individual shopping could be expensive for one customer; vendors must price their products so that they can cover their selling costs. When customers shop in large volumes, these prices are prorated, and the gross earnings increase. *Mercata.com* utilizes this method in selling products like electronics and computers. Thanks to this model, customers show greater loyalty to a company for the company helps them to save more. *Mobshop.com* is another website which uses this model. There is of course, a difference, because *Mobshop.com* presents a comparative service so customers can visit other websites before making a buying decision.

Bartering Model

Another well-known method in e-business is the cambium or Bartering Model. *Ubarter.com* is a website which allows customers and companies to suggest their list of products. In this method, the vendors provide a preliminary draft of products to gain customer agreement to bartering goods.

There is a wide range of products for barter on this site. Another site which is using the bartering model is *Isolve.com*, which helps businesses that want to get rid of products stored and unsold for a long time. At *Isolve.com* products can be bartered or exchanged directly. Prospects send their suggested prices to the website, and the administrators analyze their prices. The transaction is often made via an exchange rather than cash.

Rebates Model

Rebates Models help websites to find more customers. Some companies use an everyday-low-price method to encourage users to visit the website again. *Ebates.com* is an electronic store which refunds a part of their customers' money after each shopping experience. This website interacts with other online wholesalers and retailers which offer rebates. The above-mentioned companies consider these discounts for customers' next payments and discharge their accounts. This kind of rebating encourages customers to view their previous discount as a positive reason to revisit the site for shopping. Similarly, the website tries to use the added value of repeat visits to satisfy the users and make them more loyal.

Offering Free Product and Service

Many employers adopt the Advertising-driven Revenue Stream Model. Radio and TV networks use advertisements to gain more revenue. In cyberspace, there are websites which offer free products in order to entice more advertisements. Some of these methods have been developed through interaction with other websites. That is to say, some websites let other websites sell their products for free and thus introduce the website to the customer.

Freemerchant.com utilizes this model. This website offers all the requirements of an e-business for free, including shopping cards, traffic log and auction facilities. Strategic partners of the site supply these costs and in return, they use the spaces on new websites to introduce their products and services. Some of these sites include *Iwon.com, startsampling.com, Free-program.com, Free-staff center.com* and *Emazing.com.*

Advertising Insight 5: ETrade.com

One of the leading companies in online business is E*Trade. E*Trade was established in 1982 in order to price the stocks of America's holding companies. To develop an Internet and WWW presence, *e.Trade.com* was created. With the establishment of the website, investors could manage their own investments, eliminating the need for consultants. E.*trade.com* users can exchange stocks, or search bonds and mortgage loans. If the user does not have enough knowledge of online business and stock marketing, *e-trade.com* offers a game where users can gain experience in online business. The program aims at educating and creating proficiency in potential investors. There is also news about the stock market, stock ups and downs, analytical information and statistics of the experts, and changes in stocks over the past five years.

B2B SERVICE PROVIDER

B_2B e-business includes operations like shopping, selling, exchanges, partnerships and trade between two or more e-businesses. B_2B e-business revenue reached 1.5 thousand billion dollars at the end of 2004. B_2B has been one of the fastest-growing businesses in the e-commerce field. Some of these models have been created which earn their revenue by meeting the requirements of e-businesses and also improving procedures and customer services. For example, *Aviba.com* is a B_2B service provider whose strategies and solutions include supply chain management, procurement and logistics and customer service. *Freemarkers.com* is a marketplace which develops a relationship between buyer and vendor. Companies which have a large amount of inventory can use this website to sell their overstocked or unsold products. *Freemarkers.com* has the specific ability to sell any equipment, raw materials and stock which has low customer demand. Delivering customer satisfaction is crucial, especially in today's competitive online market. Since the number of websites offering the same services are many, delivering an exclusive service to customers and using troubleshooting tools on a website will play a key role. *Liveperson.com* has developed a new method for improving customer service; it offers a product which links customers to a product service center or a text chat. The customer can communicate and negotiate with the staff or product provider with a simple click. Other websites which provide B_2B services are *ceverything.com* and *Magnifi.com.*

ONLINE LENDING MODELS

One of the other fast-growing issues in e-commerce is E-stock trading. Stock trading in the past was only facilitated through dealers and their commissions, but with the emergence of e-business, dealers established sites which let investors manage their stock transactions. These kinds of businesses usually are cheaper than buying and selling stock through brokerage businesses. *Schwap.com* is one of these websites which operate online trading and lending. Others include *Dljdirect.com, Fidelity. com, businessweek.com,* and *Thestandard.com* which are respected resources in this field.

ONLINE LENDERS

Via an online lending model, An Internet user can find loans with a smaller interest rate on the Web than rates in the real world. *Eloan.com* provides services like credit cards, loans and equipment necessary for decision-making and awareness in lending. The most well-known websites in the field of online lending are *Gomez.com* and *Mortgage. com*. *Mortgage.com* lets its users find a bank near their business which is likely to offer a lower interest rate. *Ecredit.com* is another leading website in this field, allowing users to search for e-loans. This company also interacts with well-known financial institutions which offer large loans and utilizes this advantage to meet its users' needs quickly. When businesses are successful in making a loan, *e-credit.com* helps them to spend the assets in a proper way. *Ecredit.com* has giant customers like Intel and Hewlett-Packard; this reputation is key in attracting new customers. Other companies are also active in the field of e-lending but may have different services. For instance, *loansdirect. com* represents a comparative service on its site, allowing customers to search and choose the best option for their loan.

RECRUITMENT ON THE WEB

The Internet is also useful for employee recruitment and job finding (see insight 6: *Monster.com*). Job seekers can learn how to write a resume, and then through online searches, find the most appropriate job compatible with their abilities. Employers can also advertise jobs on the Internet to attract job seekers. There are many companies which execute online recruitment, such as *Dice. com*. *Dice.com* is largely related to computer science. Revenue is gained on the basis of a fee paid by each user for introducing their resume to different companies. Free search of job and recruitment is among this site's services.

Guru.com is another website which introduces contractual jobs. Independent contractors, consultants and private tutors can refer to this site to find short- and long-term jobs. There are many articles on this website offering users information about their favorite industry and how to negotiate a contractor manage a business. Users can also learn how to supply requirements and how

to deal with legal issues. In addition, *Guru.com* has an online store where customers can find the products needed for their business, and companies can create a profile for themselves to register their inquiries if they need a contractor. *Sixfigurjobs. com* is a recruitment website designed for senior managers. Executive senior positions often require a great experience; therefore, finding an appropriate person may take more time. This website is created for vacancies in management positions, and sending documents is free. The other company which is active on the Web is *Refer.com*. This site awards a prize to its users for introducing available jobs on the website. The revenue for the website is considerable, because for favored jobs, thousands of dollars for both the owners and users of the website may be obtained. For introducing a friend or a family member to the site and for sending their resume to companies, users receive awards and a fee. These websites were just a few examples that work on recruitment. Some of them are specialists targeted toward a limited group, while others offer services to any user.

Advertising Insight 6: Monster.com

Comparative advertising and an efficient job-finding system has made *monster.com* a famous online brand. *Monster.com* allows jobseekers to send resumes, search job lists, and view announcements and information about the process of finding a job and developing a career. Access to the Internet is easy for jobseekers and employers as well who can send their job lists to *monster.com*, and study the database of resumes.

Employers from around the world send their information to this website. *Monster.com* also has a resume-making system which helps users create their resume in only 30 minutes. Some companies also send their application forms directly to the website, and users are allowed to delete or change their information.

ONLINE NEWS SERVICE

As we move into the information age, we fill the gap even more between Internet industries and the real world and its relevant industries. Giant news agencies like *Newsweek* and *The Wall Street Journal* use the Web as a dynamic news outlet. In fact, *wsj.com* is one of the best-selling e-newspapers around the world and updates its content every 24 hours. Unregistered users only have access to a limited amount of information, but after a simple registration, they can also enjoy the comments of *Barrons.com* (a database containing papers and comments by expert investment analyzers).

Espn.com presents the most recent sports news. This website provides the opportunity to search and read detailed information about favorite teams, players, and coaches. The website also displays sports events through live video, voice and text for its viewers. The quality of newspaper publication has changed as publication and distribution does not matter anymore. because publishers can convey their ideas easily through creditable online sources.

Segmentation and message broadcasting on the basis of different market segments is a core approach in advertising context. Introducing different kinds of websites along with diverse business models shows that different e-business models have different requirements and users, and consequently need different online advertising methods to succeed. For example, the same advertisements (especially the same format with the same cue) will not be successful in both sports and general newspapers.

INTERNET TRAVEL SERVICE

Users can manage all their requirements for a vacation or business trip via the Internet and save money. Formerly, customers had to visit a travel agency to effect their travel plans, but today this has been replaced by the Internet, and users can have access to relevant information through websites (Advertising Insight 7: Travelocity.com). Websites suggest the best time and opportunity that fits with the customer's desired time. For example, *Microsoft* offers travel services via their *Expedia.com* website, which enables users to reserve all their travel requirements such as hotels and transportation. Membership is free, and all information is available for all users. Another website which provides users with discounts on hotels, flights, resorts and car rentals is *Cheaptickets.com*. Its users have access to the website's database and can view and select flights based on schedules.

Some travel websites focus on business trips. *Biztravel.com* is a website with truly unique services. If a customer faces the problem of a cancelled flight, lost luggage or poor service, the website refunds all the costs. The other website adopting business travelers for its business model is *Getthere.com*. To drop the costs and offer more convenience, the website lets customers negotiate on airline, hotel and car rental costs directly through the website.

ONLINE ENTERTAINMENT

The Web is formed by the communication of high-quality information and high-quality multimedia which lets users transfer pictures, text, voice and videos. Manufacturers in the entertainment industry recognized this and began using the Web sell movie tickets, albums and other materials. There are, of course, some controversies over this kind of business, including unauthorized application or copyrights that affect the business model of those websites.

Icast.com is a multimedia entertainment website where downloading of music and movies is free for visitors. Any article is accompanied by a supporting multimedia file. For example, news about actors may be matched with a review of their last movie. There is also a free version of iCast Media Player for users to use to watch and listen to their favorite movies and music. The slow connection speed is one of the limits of this business model.

The Internet movie Database, *IMDB.com*, has combined the greatest movie databases and has become the biggest website within this business model. The website employs an exceptional design. Applicable menu lists and desirable content has attracted a lot of users. *IMDB.com* gives new information about actors to the users and helps them find the websites which contain the most information about their favorite actors. *IMBD. com* is one of the most successful companies under Amazon's control.

ONLINE AUTOMOTIVE

Many companies let users search their websites for cars to buy. This business model allows users to be involved in the car-manufacturing process, and in this way, car-makers can ensure users' satisfaction. Through these websites, users can interact during the preliminary processes and negotiate the prices and materials of different automobiles.

One of the most powerful automotive websites is *Autobytel.com* for both selling and buying cars. Users can view advertisements about the newest cars and search the best prices from wholesalers and retailers. Those who seek to repair their cars can easily communicate with insurance companies, and this website offers insurance services to users as well. *Autoparts.com* is an online auction for trading spare auto parts. When users register, the website searches the database to find their desired spare parts with information like desired model and production date,. *Aut.com* is another website with a combined business model. The website belongs to the *Detroit Free Press* and is the best source for the most recent news and information on the automotive industry.

Advertising Insight 7: Travelocity.com

The travel industry has been extremely successful on the Web in recent years. Customers reserve their travel much cheaper and easier than having a physical presence at travel agencies. *Travelocity.com* offers services to its users which let them manage all issues of their trip in one simple online visit. The website takes advantage of a shopping bot. The user enters the time and flight code for each trip and waits to receive the information. At the same time, the shopping bot reviews the airlines' databases and introduces the best option together with a ticket-buying icon.

ENERGY ONLINE

Some companies have made buying and selling energy available on the Internet. These companies sell electricity and crude oil, and their distribution systems and equipment on the Internet. *Huston-street.com* is an e-marketplace for businesses and merchants who are searching for equipment and raw materials. They can buy and sell crude oil, infiltration equipment and electricity easily on this site. *AltraNet.com* is also an online store where users and involved companies can purchase natural gas, electricity and oil. *AltraNet.com* and its sub-companies have substantially increased the speed of buying and delivering energy and its distribution systems. *RetailEnergy.com* is a comprehensive index for energy industries. This site was created by the Power Marketing Association and contains an integrated list of energy providers as well as information on changes in the price of natural gas and electricity.

SELLING BRAINPOWER

Some companies buy people's brainpower and register it as their own patent. Since investing in research and development is not possible for small businesses, one of the compensation strategies is to buy others' brainpower.

Companies who need help with complicated projects can find their favorite specialists on *HelloBrain.com*. When the business owner reports unfinished projects, the website searches through contractors and companies, and provides a list of these to the above-mentioned businesses.

Questionexchange.com is a website which lets users troubleshoot programming and customer service. Companies must register and pay a membership fee to have access to a database of 10,000 questions, answers and strategies. *Yet2. com* is designed to help organizations by selling brainpower by the patent and trademark method. The website is supported by giant industrial companies which are willing to trade for brainpower.

ONLINE ART DEALERS

The Internet is a new market for showing or selling popular art materials. Users can buy or sell their artistic items for the best price. Shopping carts and similar other technologies allow sellers to deliver customer products in a short time after ordering.

Art.com authorizes its users to select their favorite items among artworks like pictures, posters and animation. Users can search for artists, media, decorations, and artistic and literary styles in the website's database. There is also a list of popular artists separately displayed on this website. *Guild. com* is among those websites which offer art and literary pieces in massive volume to users; most of these more than 7,000 items are in the form of documents, and their prices are estimated from hundreds to thousands of dollars. Other websites in this field include *Autonet.com* and *Atomfilm.com*.

E-LEARNING

Since more and more people have access to a computer, e-learning and teaching has grown at a fast rate. Universities and institutions offer virtual learning on the Internet. Some institutions have been created to provide online services and products for publishers and take a membership fee from them. There are also improvements in the quality of education because of technological developments and the compatibility of more programs like voice, film, and video conferencing.

One of the leading websites active in e-learning is *clic2learn.com*. This website has a perfect database for equipment and services in e-learning which helps students and schools. The website also has a measuring system which meets each user's educational needs. In addition, institutions that want to develop their educational systems can accomplish this through the tool book of the website. They can also sell their educational courses via the Web. Whenever a user shows his willingness to participate, the course is ready to begin. *Saba. com* is another website which provides e-learning courses. Institutions can enroll and create an online store for their e-learning products. Customers can use *Saba.com* as a portal for searching for educational items. Other websites active in the field are *Deitel.com*, *Blackboard.com* and *Webct.com*.

CONCLUSION

This chapter recognized new channels of Internet advertisement and online marketing, and introduced different kinds of e-business models. At first sight, introducing e-business models in a book which is developed with the purpose of broadcasting online advertising seems out of sync, but from a marketing point of view, recognizing the different channels is the main ingredient in developing successful advertising. As different broadcasting channels meet different customers' needs, they use a variety of publishing strategies for attracting and serving their customers. In this regard, aligning with publishing strategies is the key to success in the advertising process.

It is obvious that message disseminating and delivering require a customer's attention. As mentioned in Chapter 1 and will be mentioned in Chapter 11, different publishers broadcast their content toward different target markets because customers enter into the Web with various motivations; in addition, different advertising formats are targeted to different customers. Therefore, online marketers must utilize diverse appeals and cues to push and pull consumers toward their websites. However, due to the lack of appropriate knowledge among advertisers, the same advertising, with the same cues, appeals and formats, is applied in all the websites which are responsible for broadcasting. That is hardly in conflict with the core advertising practice that says that advertising must be published in the right format, in the right media, for the right customer, at the right time. In sum, introducing more than 20 new e-business models in this chapter can be an appropriate pattern for pioneers of e-business.

In this chapter, we first explained the differences between e-business and e-commerce. Then we mentioned e-business components and defined e-business models. Next, we explored the different kinds of e-business models. Some of the e-business models discussed include: portal models (vertical portal, horizontal portal), dynamic pricing models, B_2B service provider models, online lending models, recruitment online models, online news service models, online travel service models, online entertainment models, online automotive models, energy online models, selling brainpower models, online art dealers models and e-learning models. Also in this chapter, we presented a new category of different kinds of e-business models which, in comparison with former ones, is applicable with today's online technologies.

REFERENCES

Adam, S. (2002). A model of web use in direct and online marketing strategy. *EM Electronic Markets: International Journal of Electronic Markets*. Retrieved from http://www.electronicmarkets.org / modules/pub/view.php/ electronicmarkets-418.

Canzer, B. (2003). *E-business strategic thinking and practice*. Boston, MA: Houghton Mifflin Company.

Dragan, R. (1998). Microsoft site service 3 commerce edition. *PC Magazine*. Retrieved from http://www.zdnet.com /filters/printerfriendly/ 0,6061,374713-3,00.html.

Drew, S. (2002). E-business research practice: Towards an agenda. *Electronic Journal of Business Research Methods*. Retrieved from http:// www.ejbrm.com /,Accessed1.

Fletcher, J. (2000, June 12). The great e-mortgage bake-off. *The Wall Street Journal*.

Laudon, K. C., & Traver, C. G. (2007). *E-commerce: Business, technology, society*. Upper Saddle River, NJ: Prentice Hall.

Magretta, J. (2002). Why business models matter. *Harvard Business Review*, *80*(5), 86–92.

Methvin, D. W. (1999, August). How to succeed in e-business. *Windows Magazine*, 98-108.

Osterwalder, A., & Pigneur, Y. (2002). *An e-business model ontology for modeling e-business*. Paper presented at Ecole des HEC. Bled, Slovenia.

Porter, M.E. (2001). Strategy and the internet. *Harvard Business Review*, *79*(3), 62–78.

Ranjay, G., & Garino, J. (2000, June). Bricks to clicks. *Silicon India*, 75-78.

Rappa, M. (2005). *Managing the digital enterprise*. Retrieved from http://digitalenterprise.org /index.html.

Timmers, P. (1998). Business models for e-commerce. *Electronic Markets, 8*(2), 3–7. doi:10.1080/10196789800000016

Timmers, P. (1999). *Electronic commerce: Strategies and models for business to business trading.* New York, NY: John Wiley and Sons Ltd.

Turban, E. (2006). *Electronic commerce: A managerial perspective.* Upper Saddle River, NJ: Prentice Hall.

Chapter 10
Effectiveness Solutions in Online Advertising

ABSTRACT

As one of the core concepts in advertising campaigns, effectiveness is realized more in Internet advertising. Basically, the Internet has the potential to convey marketers' advertisements in a buying position. For example, when an advertisement can captivate customers' interests, they are able to click instantly and be in a situation where essential requirements about the product are ready for them to view. They also can negotiate with advertisers or give a personalized order. On the contrary, when they observe an advertisement in traditional media, they must find other channels to contact the advertiser. The broad function of Internet advertising is caused by horizontal integration in the three marketing channels of communication, transaction, and distribution. It is also a result of the vertical integration of marketing communication (Li, 1999). As discussed in the first and second chapters, marketing communication includes advertising, public relations, sales promotion, personal selling, and direct marketing.

To understand Internet advertising effectiveness, special features of advertising formats should be assessed. In this regard, marketers must develop new criteria for measuring online advertising effectiveness. First, the effectiveness criteria should be totally revised, and a set of new features must be defined so that marketers can utilize the new criteria for online advertising measurement. Then, advertisers must develop a typology of different online advertising formats and scrutinize scholars' research in an online context. In this chapter, Internet advertising is discussed from two points of view: first, from a general viewpoint (effectiveness in advertising as whole), and then from each format's viewpoint.

OBJECTIVES AND EFFECTIVENESS

Any discussion of advertising effectiveness requires that marketers incorporate organizational goals into advertising management. Goals act as a criterion to direct the managers' decisions to predetermined orientations. For example, when advertisers choose an appropriate media for broadcasting, their selection undoubtedly is relevant to the advertising objectives. Goal-setting and using related promotional tools must be determined along with one orientation. Goals are also useful in assessing results as they are indicative of what a

DOI: 10.4018/978-1-4666-0885-6.ch010

business wants to achieve. Questions that must be answered include: Are the advertising campaigns doing well? Are they able to create a profit for the company? Are they designed in a way that can increase the number of customers in the target market who know the brand? Predetermined goals and criteria allow marketers to investigate their achievements and also recognize the best direction for their advertising efforts.

Finally, the most important issue is that goals direct the advertising campaigns toward a deeper understanding of basic processes and special problems. For instance, a rational advertising goal cannot be determined without awareness of how advertising functionscrowdfunding Thus, there are two main separate issues in the management of advertising campaigns: first is setting the goals, and second is measuring the results. These two issues have the same by means of use and function of effectiveness criteria (Li & Leckenby, 2004).

EFFECTIVENESS CRITERIA

Thanks to its central role in setting goals and measuring results, effectiveness criteria have a long record with the promotion mix in general and advertising in particular. In 1898, Luis, the first writer of advertising, developed the famous four-term method: attention, interest, desire and action. After that, criteria became a basic issue in advertising. First, Lavidge and Steiner (1961) introduced the hierarchy of effects or CAB (Cognitive, Affection, and Behavior). In this hierarchy, which was based on the stepladder method, attention resulted in interest, interest resulted in ideas, ideas resulted in desire and finally desire resulted in action. These factors were then classified into the three larger classes of cognition, affection and attempt, which later turned into behavior. Cognition is related to the information-processing abilities of individuals, including perception, learning, remembering, judging and problem-solving, and it refers to the forming and abstraction of knowl-

edge in the mind. Affection deals with emotional and attitudinal aspects of meaning like love and hate, and behavior is related to the visible actions of people.

Researchers believed that setting goals and measuring advertisement effectiveness should be done with all three criteria of CAB rather than using one or two of them because customers have complete emotional responses to promotional efforts based on a combination of cognitive, affective and psychological responses (Kershel, 1984). Therefore, it is expected that advertising goals management and the results of effectiveness criteria can be performed in the same framework.

Criteria and Control Ownership

The completing variable in CAB hierarchy is interaction, which was a minor consideration in previous studies because there were no interactive tools for communicating between advertisers and customers like there are today. One of the critical subjects in interaction and effectiveness criteria is control ownership. Control ownership implies how much of the communication surroundings on the Internet are under the control of the user and how much are under the control of the advertiser. To describe and distinguish the control between user and advertiser, Pavlou and Stewart (2000) conducted a study introduced two distinctive aspects of control: process control and result control. Process control is a part of the communication process which is strictly controlled by the user, and results control is related to outcomes which emerge from the customer's perception of an advertisement. Process control measures the first motivations for using online media: information seeking, attention and information processing. These scales are mostly dependent upon the behavior in which the user has formed a relationship with the message and attempts to control it. Results control measures the outcome and message efficacy after the user viewed the online advertisement. Efficacy of advertising involves any desired changes (brand awareness, creating a positive attitude, or buying intention) in a company's target publics which are created by broadcast, promotion, advertising, publishing, publicizing or narrowcasting the messages.

Advertising is an independent variable while standard scales of CAB like attention, attitude and intention are dependent variables. Process control, of course, is partly under the control of the advertiser who designs and posts the message online, and partly controlled by the customer who receives and absorbs the message.

Regardless of the amount of control on both sides, it is necessary to measure control ownership to create a framework of Internet advertising effectiveness. Either aspect of control ownership can be considered under the three criteria of effectiveness: cognition, affection and behavior. Li and Leckenby (2004) showed a classified measuring model of CAB and control ownership aspects. Their model states that users with low efficiency in searching are less interactive; this is a cognitive function. Customizing factors are most likely to result in emotional responses and interaction on the user's side during message processing. Involvement and participation in a message as a behavioral response is dependent upon the user's tendency and the attractive formats of the advertisement designed to appeal to the user.

MANAGING ADVERTISING CAMPAIGNS

To optimize Internet advertising, some measures should be taken into account. These include considering a general recognition framework and performance of the campaigns which can be accomplished through special procedures. Successful advertisers use a regular procedure, are loyal to assignments, know what are their responsibility is in any situation, and are continuously trying to improve that procedure. Marketers should first set t advertising objectives and then, based on those goals, determine the measuring scales and improve the operations within the structure of a predesigned framework. Finally, advertisers must assess the results carefully to recognize the practices which optimize their future activities. DoubleClick (2006) has an appropriate fourth step procedure by which marketers can improve their advertising campaigns. That framework includes:

- **Setting explicit goals**: Determining the business goals so that advertising campaigns are designed based on those goals, and more precisely, defining scales whereby marketers are able to evaluate the goals.
- **Segmenting the users**: Recognizing those users who are most likely to respond to advertising messages or click on them actively.
- **Optimizing the media**: Improving the advertising programs with regard to more harmony within the target market, and improving the landing page aligned with message content and advertisement placement on the Web.
- **Revising, evaluating and improving**: Conducting a comprehensive investigation at the end of a campaign to find out what factors were efficient and helped to reach the advertising goals. After that, the scales should be scrutinized to see whether they can evaluate the goals or whether the determined goals were real ones. The results of these investigations are useful experience for future campaigns (Double Click, 2006).

MANAGING REACH AND FREQUENCY

Advertising activities display the brand and get a direct response from users. In all advertising activities, the ideal situation is maximization of users who see the advertisement (reach). Advertising reach is the penetration degree of an online advertisement among target audiences' desired websites so that the ad can create at least one change in the users' behavior regarding brand awareness, positive attitude or buying intention. In addition, advertisement broadcasting is ideal when an optimal number of advertisements is published for each user (advertising frequency). However, in most cases, advertisers cannot control their campaigns, and consequently, they publish more advertisements for fewer visits. That means a lot of published advertisements are wasted.

Reach and frequency are proportionally related in that publishing an online advertisement for users who have not seen it is developing and expanding the advertising reach. Publishing for target audiences who have seen the advertisement before increases advertising frequency. It seems that the right frequency (the ideal times that consumers must be exposed to one advertisement) is not clear as few studies have been conducted in this area, and their results differ by product type, advertising objectives and other factors. The conventional way which is considered an appropriate frequency among advertisers and advertising agencies is publishing four to seven advertisements per user (Double Click, 2006).

One of the challenges in managing reach and frequency is that all users do not visit the same pages. In 2004, *Double Click* and *Com Score Networks* conducted a study of 1.5 million visitors of Com Score Networks where monthly visits were classified into three categories. Users with 19 visits were considered as heavy, 11 to 19 as medium, and 10 or less considered as light users. According to this classification, it was discovered that 36% of the users were light, 25% were medium and 39% were heavy users of this website. The point was that heavy users had visited 73% of the pages of the website, while the light ones had just visited 6% of them. Hence, the challenge for advertisers is to reach the third group that visits only 6% of the website. At the same time, they must prevent publishing the advertisements for the 73% group

too frequently, because overexposure of an advertisement creates a negative attitude toward the advertisement and its brand.

Strategic Website and Its Role

How can we control frequency to get the maximum reach? The first method is to position a frequency primer in a publisher's or advertiser's server so that cookies (the data sent by the server to the browser to recognize the user and its reach) prevent the over-displaying of the advertising to previous users. However, due to technical problems, installing such a primer of frequency in a server is difficult.

The second method is the most efficient way to control frequency. In this method, the advertisement is positioned in a strategic website. In 2002, Jupiter Media Metrix conducted a study which showed that publishing four million advertisements can reach one third of users as long as they were published by three giant websites rather than one giant website or many small ones. The basic principle in this strategy is using the wide range and number of sub-pages of giant websites to increase the number of users and achieve high reach with just a few frequencies.

Temporary Targeting

The timing of advertisement broadcasting based on a part of the day in TV and radio is common. The times when TV and radio have the most audience are the most expensive for advertising broadcasting. However, on the Internet, this method is not effective except in some industries like hot-food companies which publish their advertisements around noon.

Temporary targeting or targeting by time or part of a day or a day of the week (such as weekends) can be a successful strategy for managing advertising reach and frequency. For example, as the Double Click (2006) study shows, the number of users who watch the video part of Yahoo.com are amazingly more on the weekend in comparison with other days of week (Double Click, 2006). The advertisers believe that more leisure time on the weekend is the reason for this outstanding increase in visits to entertainment websites. Thus, the publisher's server should be designed to display the advertisement on special days of the week. Also, if the advertisement is going to be published every day of the week, the advertisement publishing timing should be programmed in a way that it will be displayed mornings and evenings, because, unlike TV which has one prime time, the Internet has two prime times. According to tracing and tracking, which have been conducted about customer Internet usage times, morning and the first hours of the night are times when the Internet is most used (Korgaonkar & Wolin, 2002). Marketers and advertisers will have the most distribution by focusing on these times. Temporary targeting in this segment of the market is one of the strategies to reach more users with less frequency.

MANAGING GEO-TARGETING

Geo-targeting is a highly applicable method for market targeting and online advertising. Organizations which operate locally, and whose products or services are available in regional or domestic markets, use geo-targeting. These advertisers should also pay attention to their non-targeted markets as their non-targeted advertisements may be seen by international users. American servers traces shows that most websites are viewed by 25 percent international visitors (Double Click, 2006).

For most of the service providers and Internet advertisers, geo-targeting may not be important, but for websites that have challenges of global delivery, advertising operations should continue regardless of time and place. Multinational companies have subsidiaries around the world which are obliged to obey appropriate geo-targeting

aligned with local requirements. To this end, company branches in host countries publish their promotional messages through local websites which are most aligned with their organizational framework. Another operational method used by many websites for targeting involves zip codes. This method is frequently used in Asian countries by completing initial information forms (the information is processed online and when confirmed, the user is allowed to pass) and tracing IP connections.

TRACING VEIW THROUGH EFFECT

The click-through rate is a new advertising paradigm in which a company's potential and active users are able to respond directly to online advertising and obtain immediate information. This scale has become more popular and has turned into a criterion of effectiveness measuring as it forces the advertiser to incorporate navigators and incentives in the advertisements in order to encourage the users to click on them.

However, the main objective of advertising campaigns is NOT to increase the click-through rate! This type of advertising is developed in order to influence the target market's attitude toward the brand and to create a buying intention. When the advertising objective is to attract and push the user to the website, clicking is secondary; the users who are exposed to the advertisement and do not click on it may visit the website later to satisfy their needs. This is called the view-through effect. The view-through effect is when advertising redirects customers to behave according to the marketer's promotional actions and follow the advertisement's lead. To help with this, marketers can use cookies and tags (in the programming language of HTML any commands that insert < >)on the website in order to measure the view-through effects on users. In user tracing, when a user is on a website, the tags recognize the observable cookie files, and the server can determine whether the user is directly in (has actually clicked on the advertisement) or indirectly (for example, through search engines or where a browser entered the website ID). Studies show that half of customer visits from marketers' websites are affected by advertising view-through effects rather than direct clicks or click-through rates (DoubleClick, 2006).

Some marketers trace the effects of their advertisements; however, since advertising also takes place via standard channels like TV, radio and newspapers, they still wonder how many of the website visits are affected by seeing an advertisement on the Web and how many are accidentalcrowdfunding For example, the customer may see the brand on TV and have some questions about the advertisement in his mind. He then visits the website to find answers. The customer may also be loyal to the organization, and advertisement influence is not the reason for his presence on the advertiser's website. In this regard, the advertiser can use a control group. In 2004, a case study on airlines was conducted by Double Clickcrowdfunding In this study, all campaigns and applications were studied for a full month, and then new advertisements were published. These advertisements were Red Cross service advertisements that marketers developed in order to identify a control group. During this time, all campaigns were under scrutiny to make sure that the control group did not see the experimental advertisement. At the end of the month, the users of the website were analyzed to find out how many of them in each group, without clicking on the advertisement first, visited the website and made a purchase. Users affected by the advertisement after three exposures were more likely to buy the advertised item than those who entered the website via the Red Cross advertisement. The result was that 2/3 of users were affected by environmental factors. Hidden visits or affected by advertisement exposure, forms an investigating behavior in users to find the website. Thus in future weeks, products or services which are publicized will sell more.

CREATING CURIOSITY

Psychologists have studied curiosity and its role in human behavior regarding childhood, nurturing, scientific discoveries and behavioral disorders (Loewenstein, 1994). Creating curiosity is a key element in leading users to follow an advertisement. An advertising strategy which generates curiosity increases interest more than a strategy which merely lists information about the product.

Different methods and procedures have been proposed by scholars to provoke a sense of curiosity in customers. One theoretical plan for creating curiosity is redirecting customers toward a knowledge gap feeling. A knowledge gap is defined as the difference between two quantities: the information someone knows, and the information someone would like to know. Curiosity flourishes when people are aware of the knowledge gap in special fields or are faced with inconsistent, unclear and incompatible stimuli or that which reverses their expectations. These situations magnify their knowledge deficiency (Menon & Soman, 2001). The knowledge gap creates an annoying feeling of deprivation or unhappiness which is only soothed by acquiring the needed information to bridge this gap. As a result, there will be considerable willingness in customers to enhance their information structure (Berlyne, 1960). The initial challenge in advertisement effectiveness is to make sure that the advertising not only draws the attention of target customers, but also creates a sense of interest in the advantages of the products (Aker, Batra, & Myers, 1992). The challenge of creating interest is mostly related to Internet advertising, because, unlike TV and print media advertisements, Internet advertisements are presented in one format and must attract users' attention to motivate them to interact with the message in order to get the necessary information. Studies show that creating curiosity is a much more successful strategy than a passive message (Ries & Ries, 2000). That is why the proficient publishers of advertisements are likely to have a role in designing the advertisement content and nurturing customers as they try to increase the sense of curiosity in users (Maddox, 2001).

To increase advertisement effectiveness, Menon and Somen (2001) conducted a study in which advertising strategies based on curiosity were introduced in four elements:

- Creating curiosity by making a gap in current knowledge.
- Creating a clue to redirect the existing involvement toward clarifying the curiosity.
- Enough time to overcome the curiosity and build confidence that there are solutions for puzzling out the curiosity.
- Evaluating customer involvement and learning in order to measure advertisement effectiveness.

MOTIVATING AND PREPARING THE CONSUMER

Internet advertising is published in different formats, and each one has different features. In interacting with online advertising, users must do something to be exposed to and communicate with them (as an example, clicking and then searching). However, Internet advertising is successful only if the customer has enough motivation to click. Thus, to motivate the customer to interact with the medium and get precise information, and to make the Internet advertisements (especially banner ads) more successful, some mechanisms must integrate. In addition, the advertiser should actively teach and train customers about target products, shopping patterns and inquiries for catalogs. Encouraging users to search for information to facilitate learning is one of the basic requirements of successful online advertising strategies (Manon & Soman, 2001).

USING LARGE FORMATS

When advertising is aimed at getting a direct response from customers and also is focused on brand awareness, larger formats are preferred. As an example, Double Click made a study of 136 online publishers in which a direct relationship was confirmed between the size of a banner ad and a strong click rate. In this study of approximately 20 million publications (banners and bottoms), 14 standard click rates were compared. The study found that the more the banner size increased, the more the click percentage went up.

EFFECTIVENESS OF DIFFERENT FORMATS

According to IAB (2007), percentages of revenue for each eight methods of online advertisement formats are as follows:

- Banners 21%
- Searches 42%
- Lead Generation 7%
- Classified Ads 14%
- Sponsorships 3%
- Digital Videos 2%
- E-mails 2%, and
- Rich Media or Animated Advertisements 9%.

In comparing these statistics with former parts, it is clear that substantial changes have occurred. For example banner share was 56% in 1998, a significant decrease in comparison to 2007. The other formats also show the same trend, as sponsorship advertisement went from 33% in 1998 to just 3% in 2007. On the other side, rich media moved from 2% in 2000 to 9% in 2007. However, the greatest change is in searches, which had only 1% in 2000, and moved to more than 42% in 2007, experiencing the greatest change.

Banner Effectiveness

As mentioned in Chapter 4, banners, or display advertisements, often contain text, pictures, images and animation. IAB (1996) determined eight standard sizes for banners and increased these to 14 standard sizes in 2001. In improving the effectiveness of this kind of format, the main focus was on direct response or the click-through rate. However, in the mid 1990s (when the click-through rate was 3%), a big change took place in the banner click-through rate, and it reached an unheard rate of 28%. This suggested that the banner format was not effective anymore and could not be considered as a successful online advertising format.

Recognizing the reduction in the banner click-through rate, researchers looked for new ways to both increase the click-rate and make it more effective. After that, the attitudes toward advertisement effectiveness changed, and clicking on a banner did not indicate online advertising effectiveness. It was proven that a banner can increase brand awareness and cognition perception because when users are online, and especially when surfing at the website, they are exposed to the brand's advertising which causes a change in the user's attitude toward the brand (Briggs & Hollis, 1997). Thus, two factors in advertising seem crucial in order for marketers to reach the above-mentioned outcomes:

- **Physical features**: Size, animation, stimuli and incentives of banners cause more effectiveness in both the click-through rate and informative aspects (Li & Bukovac, 1999). Incentives designed in banners increase the click-through rate by creating positive emotions in the user. On the other hand, if animation is incorporated into the banner, users will become more fascinated

will want to click on the advertisement (Xie, et al., 2004).
- **Right placement in website**: Where is the focal attention of customers when they first enter a website? To answer that question, scholars have developed some linear and nonlinear models (Chuang & Chong, 2004). The right placement on a website must be taken into consideration before publishing an online advertisement. It is not a matter of how much more they should pay; it is a matter of whether their banner is exposed to their targeted audience or not. The right placement has an exclusive definition for each advertising campaign. It depends on attributes like whether the advertisement is trying to promote an emotional-based product or a rational-based one. If the advertisement consists of an emotional-based product, the marketer must target and buy the upside of the host website as the targeted public for this kind of advertising is more likely to be Internet surfers who are willing to investigate fascinating items which usually appear first on websites. However, if marketers are trying to broadcast a rational-based advertisement, that target audience is more likely to be logical and wanting to seek the website for specific objectives. In this situation, it is enough to redirect them to information storage via the banner.

Sponsorship Effectiveness

Sponsorship advertisements put the advertiser's logo or brand on a host website. In improving sponsorship effectiveness, marketers must first recognize or develop the brand's effective features. One feature which plays an important role is the degree of alignment between the brand and the host website's content. The extent to which the advertisers' brands are published on websites that have similar content or the same business model is an indicator of how successful they will be. For example, travel agencies should advertise on transportation organizations' websites.

Using Rich Media

Advertising by Rich Media, in comparison with GIF formats and JPG formats (picture formats), are more applicable for appealing to the user's attention. Rich Media usually has an advanced flash format which has the possibility of zooming beyond standard size and attaching to all web pages. They also may have or be attached by video clips. The large, image-based Rich Media also usually have a higher click-through rate than standard image-based advertisements. As examples, interstitials,, a kind of Rich Media, have 10 clicks per hour and pop-ups have 50 clicks per hourcrowdfunding Rich Media results in a 50 percent increase in buying intention in comparison with the GIF and JPG formats of advertisements (Double Click, 2006).

Digital Video Effectiveness

Due to the rapid growth of the Internet and increase in bandwidth, watching video advertisements has become a common event in cyberspace. Digital video methods have been transferred from TV to the Internet with one big difference: the span of control has been divided between customer and advertiser (Dynamic Logic, 2007). Along with developing digital video advertisements, marketers must consider what attributes can make these kinds of advertisements more effective; they know that a key factor in improving digital video advertisements is innovation. Such advertisements will capture users' interest so that pressing the replay button will be the first reaction after watching the advertisement. Secondly, the advertisement must be created in a way that can form a positive attitude in the user's mind. In other words, the

brand message should be prevalent in the user's mind so that it can be memorized easily. To make sure that the brand has found a place in the user's mind, the advertisement should have a link to the advertiser's website. The link must be developed with the purpose of persuading the customer to want to obtain more information and to eventually buy from the advertiser's website.

The next issue in video format effectiveness is display duration. The extent to which a digital video advertisement is designed in a shorter time is in direct relation to how much the video advertisement will be watched. Longer advertisements may make users frustrated and may force them to close the video. Sometimes the user may close the window of an advertisement in as few as 15 seconds. Therefore, the critical issue in developing a digital video format is displaying an advertisement effectively in seven or eight seconds. How can marketers display a brand's story in that short time?

With short display duration, scene-making and attracting attention toward the brand are the most crucial factors, because the story must end in 8 seconds and there is no time for prefacing. Online short-time advertisements must also focus on one key message during the display time (Dynamic Logic, 2007). Regardless of the lack of time, when marketers try to convey more than one promotional message in one online digital video, it is possible that customers cannot absorb different messages and the promotion is faced with failure.

There are two ways for conveying a brand scenario in a video advertisement. First concerns the display sequence of an advertisement, and the second is exaggerating in advertising. In the display sequence of an advertisement, the advertisers will show advertisements in the frame of the main scenario step by step, developing a parallel character aligned with their brands so that the message stays alive for a long time in the user's mind. A parallel character for advertising is something like the victor who never fails in scenario courses. On the other hand, customers are expected to want to watch or hear him again, so sequences of the digital video will follow, and marketers will be able to complete their promotional messages in several video advertisements.

The second technique is exaggerating in advertising where marketers must develop an exciting and controversial advertisement in order to captivate users and push them to watch the rest of the advertisement on the advertiser's website (Dynamic Logic, 2007). Creating controversies and conflicts is an outstanding method, because it involves the user's mind directly with the brand video, and motivates the user to mentally review it again. The satisfaction and excitement ensures that the user will never forget the advertisement. Advertisers should create an exciting role for a brand or key message when designing advertisements so that the user can constantly review the information and does not forget the brand in the short run. On this basis, the advertisement forms a mental readiness in the user's mind so that with only a tiny hint of the brand, (for example, talking about the group of services to which that brand belongs) the excitement is rekindled. According to studies, video advertisements are the most applicable formats for encouraging users to become interested in and purchase a brand (Double Click, 2006).

CONCLUSION

Any discussion on advertising effectiveness requires that marketers involve organizational goals in advertising management. The goals indicate what a business wants to achieve and direct the advertising campaigns to consider a deeper understanding of basic processes and uncommon problems. Basically, in measuring advertising prosperity, marketers should develop some criteria that enables them to orient the whole campaign in one direction. Criteria like attention, interest, desire and action or cognition, affection

and behavior help marketers measure advertising results easier. In effectiveness criteria developed for new media, marketers must consider some complementary issues like interaction and control ownership. Control ownership indicates how much of the communication surroundings on the Internet are under the control of the user and how much is under the control of the advertiser. Control ownership is comprised of two separate aspects: process control, which is a part of the communication process strictly controlled by the user, and result control, which is related to outcomes that emerge from the customer's perception of the advertisement. Process control measures the first motivation of using the media: information seeking, attention and information processing. Results control attempts to find the efficacy of advertising, involving any desired changes in a company's target public which are created by broadcast, promotions, advertisements, publishing, publicizing, or narrowcasting the promotional messages.

Marketers must aware that in optimizing Internet advertising, some measures should be taken into account, including considering a general recognition framework and performance of the campaigns which can be done through special procedures. In improving their advertising campaigns, marketers must consider a four-step procedure which involves: setting explicit goals, segmenting the users, optimizing the media, and revising, evaluating and improving the campaign. In all advertising activities, the ideal situation is maximization of the users who see the advertisement, called advertising reach. Also, advertisement broadcasting is ideal when an optimized number of advertisements are published for each user, termed advertising frequency. In managing reach and frequency, it is necessary that two issues be considered by marketers: a strategic website and its role, and temporary targeting. Also, marketers should handle their targeting and geo-targeting in order to keep both local and international customers satisfied.

Nowadays, the click-through rate is not the only way to measure online advertising effectiveness; there are other scales like the view-through effect, creating curiosity in customers and their desire to follow. The view-through effect is the advertising affect on customers that redirects them to behave aligned with the marketer's promotional actions. Creating curiosity is a key element in getting a user to follow an advertisement. One of the theoretical plans for creating curiosity is redirecting customers toward a situation in which they feel a knowledge gap. Acknowledge gap is defined as the difference between two quantities: the information someone knows, and that which someone would like to know. In this regard, advertisers must prepare consumers with enough motivation to follow the advertisement, perhaps with the use of large formats.

The advertising effectiveness which is examined in this chapter also scrutinizes the effectiveness of each online advertising format. For banners, it is necessary that two features be viewed carefully by marketers: physical features and the right placement on a website. In sponsorship, if advertisers' brands are published on websites that have similar content or the same business model, they will be successful. In the Rich Media case, the large image-based format of Rich Media usually has a higher click-through rate than standard image-based advertisements. In digital video, advertisements must be able to capture the user's interest in order that pressing replay button will be the first reaction after watching the advertisement. The next issue in video format effectiveness is display duration. The digital video advertisements that are designed to display a shorter time will be watched by more users. Marketers must also be aware of about issues like display sequence of advertisement, exaggerating in advertising and developing a parallel character for advertising.

REFERENCES

Aker, D., Rajeev, B., & Myers, J. G. (1999). *Advertising management*. London, UK: Prentice-Hall International.

Briggs, R., & Hollis, N. (1997). Advertising on the web: Is there response before click through? *Journal of Advertising Research, 37*(2), 33–45.

Chuang, T. T., & Chong, P. P. (2004). Searching advertising placement in cyberspace. *Industrial Management & Data Systems, 104*(2), 144–148. doi:10.1108/02635570410522116

Double Click. (2002). *Internet audience dynamics: How can you effectively use online as a reach medium?* Retrieved from http://www.Doubleclick.Net.

Double Click. (2003). *Rich media: What? Where? Why: A Double Click white paper*. Retrieved June from http://www.Doubleclick.Net.

Hanson, W. (2000). *Principles of internet marketing*. Cincinnati, OH: South-Western College Publishing.

IAB. (2007). *Internet advertising revenue report: 2007 full-year, May*. Retrieved from http://www.Iab.Net.

Korgaonkar, P. K., & Wolin, D. L. (2002). Web usage, advertising, and shopping: Relationship patterns. *Internet Research: Electronic Networking Applications and Policy, 12*(2), 191–204. doi:10.1108/10662240210422549

Lavidge, R., & Steiner, G. (1961, October). A model for predictive measurements of advertising effectiveness. *Journal of Marketing*, 59–62. doi:10.2307/1248516

Li, H. (1999). *Conceptualization of internet advertising: Practical and theoretical issues*. Working Paper. East Lansing, MI: Michigan State University.

Li, H., & Bukovac, J. L. (1999). Cognitive impact of banner ad characteristics: An experimental study. *Journalism & Mass Communication Quarterly*, *76*(2), 341–353. doi:10.1177/107769909907600211

Li, H., & Leckenby, D. J. (2004). *Internet advertising formats and effectiveness*. Retrieved from http://www.Ciadvertising.Org /Studies/Reports/ Measurement/ Ad_Format_Print.Pdf.

Loewenstein, G. (1994). The psychology of curiosity: A review and reinterpretation. *Psychological Bulletin*, *116*(1), 75–98. doi:10.1037/0033-2909.116.1.75

Maddox, K. (2001). Outlook brightens for web advertising. *B to B, 86*(15), 10.

Menon, S., & Soman, D. (2001). Managing the power of curiosity for effectiveness web advertising strategies. *Journal of Interactive Marketing*, *31*(3), 1–14.

Moorey-Denham, S., & Green, A. (2007). *The effectiveness of online video advertising*. Retrieved from http://www.Dynamiclogic.Com.

Pavlou, P. A., & Stewart, W. D. (2000). Measuring the effects and effectiveness of interactive advertising: A research agenda. *Journal of Interactive Advertising, 11*. Retrieved from http://Jiad.Org/Vol1/No1/Pavlou.

Ries, A., & Ries, L. (2000). *The 11 immutable lows of internet branding*. New York, NY: Harper Business.

Rodgers, S. (2003). The effects of sponsor relevance on consumer reactions to internet sponsorships. *Journal of Advertising*, *32*(4), 68–76.

Sundar, S. S., & Kalyanaraman, S. (2004). Arousal, memory, and impression-formation effects of animation speed in web advertising. *Journal of Advertising*, *33*(1), 7–17.

Xie, F. T., Naveen, D., Ritu, L., & Osmonbekov, T. (2004). Emotional appeal and incentive offering in banner advertisements. *Journal Of Interactive Advertising*, *4*(2). Retrieved from http://Jiad.Org/Vol4/No2/Xie

Chapter 11
The Right Internet Advertising Format (RIAF)

ABSTRACT

This chapter will reveal the appropriate answers to the following questions: (1) What advertising format should be developed by advertisers for different goods and services? (2) Which ad formats meet the needs of marketers and advertisers of a product or service? (3) What criteria and features should be considered for advertising a certain product or service? And (4) How can we define the right Internet advertising format for a certain good or service?

This chapter will develop a general framework to illustrate the factors, criteria, and features that are involved in determining the proper format of Internet advertising, and then compare these criteria with alternative advertising formats to provide the appropriate Internet advertising format. In sum, the present chapter classifies various possible scenarios and selects the most appropriate Internet advertisement format from each group.

INTRODUCTION

Increased access to the Internet has turned it into a dynamic and user-friendly medium for advertising. As a method of marketing through communication, advertising has essentially two primary components: marketing, whose target is communicating value to the customer (Darroch, et al., 2004), and communication, which encompasses creating a united idea between a sender and a receiver (Schramm, 1955; Dibb & Simkin, 1991). According to Sepstrup (1991), the ideal advertisement is the one with the highest possibility of access to a wide range of well-defined audiences (selectivity) that provides good feedback at a low cost. However, mass communication often forces advertisers to accept a wide range of ill-defined audiences that do not provide proper feedback in order to achieve a reasonable cost-effectiveness (Thomsen, 1996). This definition raises a question in advertisers' minds: which medium has the potential to provide the ideal type of advertisement?

DOI: 10.4018/978-1-4666-0885-6.ch011

According to IAB, the share of the four major types of Internet advertising studied in this research from the total incomes was 34 percent at the end of 2008. The four major Internet advertising types are: 1) Display Ads (21%) including Banners, Hypertexts, and Skyscrapers; 2) Rich Media (7%) including Pop-Ups and Pop-Unders and Interstitials; 3) Sent Emails (2%); and 4) Digital Video (3%).

Although large investments are made on Internet advertising, the advertisers and marketers are not yet aware of the effectiveness of the various forms of Internet advertisements or the appropriate audience of each. The great variety of Internet advertising formats and insufficient knowledge of advertisers have added to the complexity of online advertising activities. It is useless to recommend that an advertiser use the right format (Heinz, 2004) when the advertiser does not understand what that is (Burns & Lutz, 2006).

BACKGROUND

Advertising Models

As discussed in Chapters 3 and 7, few conceptual and qualitative Internet advertising models have been proposed, such as the Interactive Advertising Model (IAM) (Rogers & Thorson, 2000) and the structural equation model (Ko, et al., 2005). The IAM introduces the motivations and initial reasons for entering into the Internet within the framework of users and advertisers, and then examines the factors that are influential on processing the information by the users and the output resulting from that processing.

Based on previous studies on the uses and gratifications theory and Internet interaction, the structure equation model (Ko, et al., 2005) demonstrates the relationships among motivation for using the Internet, duration of time at a website, interactivity, attitudes and purchase intention of online customers in a structural framework.

Whereas in the IAM, the general assumptions are based on the merit of information processing in an interactive environment and are related to functional structure. This model classifies the different types of online advertising and recognizes their features. It also attempts to find the effective factors which shape and influence the user's attention, memory and attitude.

The distinction between the study conducted by Rogers and Thorson and the present study is that while Rogers and Thorson investigated information processing from a customer's viewpoint, this chapter investigates the issue from an advertiser's viewpoint in an attempt to provide the right model for Internet advertising. The other model (Ko, et al., 2005) examined the interactivity construct in terms of its antecedent and consequences and illustrated the interaction between the user and the advertisement.

Previous investigations mostly reflected the general attitude toward Internet ads (Ducoffe, 1996; Previte, 1998; Scholsser, et al., 1999) and toward different types of Internet advertising (Burns & Lutz, 2006). Li and Leckenby (2004) introduced the relationship between the content of a website and Internet advertising, while Sundar and Kalyanaraman (2004) investigated the effects of animated banner speed and found fast animations to be more attractive. According to these two studies, fast animations can elicit greater psychological arousal compared to slow animations.

Most of the research conducted on the effectiveness of Internet advertising is concerned with the steps taken after selecting an Internet advertising format. In other words, the assumption is that users are already exposed to an advertisement. In that case, how should the impact of advertising be enhanced to yield a higher click-through rate (Sundar & Sriram, 2004; Burns & Lutz, 2006)? The present study takes some neglected aspects of Internet advertising into account. The specifications of a given product or service must be considered a priority when deciding on a proper advertising format, and the next step is the study of ad impact and it effectiveness in increasing the click rates by identifying the main actors in the context of advertising development.

Product Involvement

Product involvement means "how the product fits into a person's life" (Cushing & Douglas-Tate, 1985, p. 243). From an information-processing perspective, involvement is related to the accuracy of elaboration and the amount of attention dedicated to advertising messages (Gardner, et al., 1985). Involvement is also influential on processing, keeping and retrieving information (Salmon, 1986).

Involvement, particularly product involvement, has been proven to be a major determinant of a consumer's behavior and response to a certain ad (Laurent & Kapferer, 1985; Celsi & Olson, 1988; Zaichkowsky, 1985). When product involvement and complexity are high, consumers process advertisements more actively (Krugman, 1965; Warrington & Shim, 2000), devote more time and cognitive effort to the advertisements (Celsi & Olson, 1988) and focus more on the product-related information of the ads (Petty, et al., 1983; Celsi & Olson, 1988). This was also verified by (Petty, et al., 1983; Petty & Cacioppo, 1984).

When product involvement is low, consumers are less likely to process written brand message claims (Chattopadhyay, 1998) because those claims require more cognitive effort to be processed compared to advertisement execution elements (Chattopadhyay & Nedungadi, 1992; Chattopadhyay, 1998), and consumers are not motivated to devote much cognitive effort to low-involvement products (Warrington & Shim, 2000). Consumers are more willing to devote their cognitive effort to high-involvement products and are then more likely to process the brand message claims of advertisements (Dahlén, et al., 2004).

Moreover, product involvement affects the design of the advertising messages. Advertise-

ments of low- or high-involvement products differ in advertising appeals. Research findings support the idea that rational advertising appeals can help market high-involvement products, whereas emotional appeal has been proven to be good for low-involvement products (Crocker, et al., 1983; Holmes & Crocker, 1987; Wills, et al., 1991).

In his study, Vaughn (1986) takes four types of involvement into account and believes them to be the determining features of a given product or service to be considered when selecting the right Internet advertising format. Our first hypothesis is based on this viewpoint.

H1: Type of product or service involvement has a positive impact on determining the right Internet advertising format.

Audiences

The way the Internet is used has a considerable effect on the users' interest and willingness to follow online ads and purchase goods and services. Furthermore, the type of responses users provide to an advertisement is, to a large extent, based on their beliefs and attitudes toward the Internet (Bruner & Kumear, 2000).

The time users spend on the Internet is a determining factor in forming such beliefs and perceptions. In this respect, Internet users are divided into three groups: heavy users, medium users and light users (Korgaonkar & Wolin, 2002). Heavy users include PC owners using the Internet at their homes or offices, as well as well-educated people using the Internet at universities (Anderson & Bickson, 1995), men (Sheehan, 1999) who earn a higher income, (Katz & Aspden, 1997) and people who use the Internet excessively for their occupational purposes (Korgaonkar & Wolin, 2002).

A heavy user spends up to five hours per day on the Web and usually visits three websites an hour. Heavy users believe Web advertising to be amusing, enjoyable, informative, trustworthy and helpful. They also feel that Internet advertising decreases expenses, and they have a positive attitude toward Internet advertisements.

The medium users are among the most educated and the highest income earners of Internet users. Compared to heavy users, they believe that Internet advertising is boring. Medium users spend up to three hours per day on the Web, mostly visiting websites of their own interest, and they visit two or three websites an hour (Korgaonkar & Wolin, 2002).

The time spent by light users on the Web is about an hour, and no clear-cut usage pattern exists for this group in terms of the time they spend each day on the Web. Light users are second only to medium users in terms of income and education (Korgaonkar & Wolin, 2002).

Classifying users into three groups has been confirmed by other studies, too. For example, Double Click (2004) conducted a study in which users were divided into heavy, medium and light according to the number of times they used the Internet monthly. Heavy users were those who used the Internet 19 times, those using the Internet 11 to 19 times were the medium users, and those using the Internet less than 11 times were classified as light users.

When publishing an online advertisement, the advertiser should be mindful of the users' motivation for going online, because users have distinctive motivations for surfing a given website. In fact, people use the Internet not only to retrieve information, but also to entertain themselves (Korgaonkar & Wolin, 2002; Ko, et al., 2005). The marketers' task is to identify the right audience, because each audience has a unique behavioral reaction to the Internet (Cho & Roberts, 2005). Regarding the distinctive perceptual backgrounds of Internet users and audiences, one Internet advertising format is likely to have a different impact on each group. A hypothesis has been developed on this basis:

H2: The type of audience has a positive impact on determining the right Internet advertising format.

Advertising Type

According to Thorson (1996), all advertisements can be classified into one of five basic categories: product/service, Public Service Announcement (PSA), issue, corporate, and political. Each of these ad types represents the general structure in which an ad is seen; that is, the ad type itself provides an indicator of the types of possible consumer responses.

Ad type often will determine the types and the extent of the cognitive tools (outlined earlier) that audiences will use. For example, attention may be heightened by ads that promote a political candidate who is strongly favored by the consumer. Additionally, memory for an issue ad may be poor in instances where the ad promotes a health or public message that is irrelevant to the user.

It is known from traditional advertising research that PSAs (Public Service Announcements) outperform other types of ads in terms of credibility and perceptions of social responsibility (Haley & Wilkinson, 1994). The general ad type will predict whether and how much cognitive effort is devoted to the task of processing online ads. Ad type will also interact with the user's motives to influence outcomes or consumer responses. Based on this point, a third hypothesis is suggested as follows:

H3: The type of advertising has a positive impact on determining the Internet advertising format.

Pull or Push Strategy

A pull strategy involves advertising promotion as a means of persuading consumers to order the product. This is especially appropriate when there is a high brand loyalty and high involvement in the category; people understand brand differences and usually choose before they go to the store (Kotler, 2001, p. 279). When users have a high level of loyalty, they tend to look for the corporate brand. Therefore, the only thing a manufacturer needs in these cases is to design a website and wait for its users to visit (Turban, et al., 2006, pp. 172-173). Depending on their attitude toward the products and services, customers search the Internet to find relevant information (Turban, et al., 2006, p. 171). However, when companies provide products or services that are unfamiliar to the customers, or when customers are not motivated enough to follow the ads, a push strategy is used. In a push strategy, the company's sales force and trade promotions induce intermediaries to carry, promote and sell the product to end users. In this situation, various tools are applied to push the users toward a company's website. On this basis, another hypothesis is formed:

H4: The type of strategy plays an important role in the selection of the right Internet advertising format.

The Status of an Audience's ICT Condition

In some developing countries, the level of user access to the Internet is not the same as in Western countries. According to an Iranian Ministry of Telecommunication and Information Technology (ICT.com, 2007) report, a low-rate connection with a transfer rate of 56 kbps is mostly suitable for home connections, and a high-rate connection with a transfer rate of 128 kbps is mostly used by organizations and institutions. Since copper wires are used for the connections in Iran, a faster rate of data transfer is not achievable. The fifth hypothesis mentioned below is based on the fact that different types of advertisements require different bandwidths:

H5: The status of ICT or the audience is a determinant in the selection of the right Internet advertising format.

In this study, data transfer at the rate of 128 kbps is referred to as "high-speed Internet" which is shown by "H," while data transfer at the rate of 56 kbps is referred to as "low-speed Internet" illustrated by "L." However, recently higher rates of data transfer have been achieved in these countries as a result of using fiber-optic cables, and sometimes data can be transferred at the rate of several megabytes per second. They were not included in this study for two reasons: first, it is not cost-effective to develop and expand fiber-optic networks for home users; and second, in the universities and organizations using fiber-optic networks, the high number of users reduces the rate to less than 100 kbps.

Advertising Features

So far, the external features' effects on Internet advertising formats have been discussed; however, the advertisement itself has some features that seem to affect the selection of the right Internet advertising format (Holbrook & Lehmann, 1980). These features or specifications are divided into two categories: subjective features and objective ones. Subjective features include typeface, appeal type, number of sentences, movement and Interactivity, sound level, sound clarity, telepresence, realism, and number of choices. Objective Features, on the other hand, include excitement, flow, current information, attitude toward ad and friendly navigation (Thorson & Leavitt, 1986). On this basis, the following hypotheses are formed:

H6: Subjective features of advertising are a determinant in the selection of the right Internet advertising format.
H7: Objective features of advertising are a determinant in the selection of the right Internet advertising format.

In this chapter, objective features such as typeface, appeal type, movement and interactivity, as well as subjective features such as attitude toward ads are considered. Although Thorson and Leavitt (1986) included more features under both subjective and objective categories (reviewed by

Rodgers & Thorson, 2002), those features are not covered in this study as they are stylistic and subject to variation based on either the advertising company or the advertiser's ideas.

CONCEPTUAL MODEL

Right Internet Advertising Format (RIAF)

Based on a review of the literature leading to the development of the seven mentioned hypotheses, a conceptual model was designed for the selection of the right Internet advertising format (Figure 1). The model is a scoring process, initiated by the product or service intended to be advertised. The next steps are determination of the type of product/ service to be advertised, the pertinent audience, the most effective advertising strategy, the ICT status and finding out the audience's Internet connection speed. After calculating the scores allocated to the external variables, the process focuses on two internal advertising variables. This chapter deals with the type of online ad suitable for a given product/service.

RESEARCH METHODOLOGY

In order to identify the right Internet advertising format, this study provides a general framework as a scientific method. First, the selection criteria were identified from international studies and classified into seven groups which were then confirmed by the experts. A questionnaire within the framework of the website *IARFM.com* was designed and distributed to the experts via email.

Sample and Data Collection

The required data was collected between February 2009 and June.2009. Considerable effort was made to find the e-mail IDs for marketing, DBA, MBA, IS, and E-commerce experts. Most of the experts selected were either jury members of various journals or faculty members of universities. Ultimately, more than 1500 IDs belonging to international experts and 200 IDs belonging to Iranian experts were identified (which itself was deemed a valuable asset for future studies). A questionnaire was designed in the form of a website (*IARFM.com*), and e-mail invitations including a hypertext were sent to the above-mentioned experts to motivate them to participate

Figure 1. Right internet advertising format (RIAF)

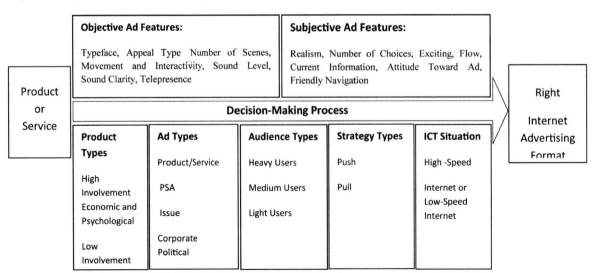

in the survey. From 1700 experts receiving the invitations, 370 replied by completing the questionnaires, indicating a response rate of 0.217. The questionnaire included seven hypotheses based on a five-point Likert-type scale (Newman, Stem, & Sprott, 2004). Since six out of the seven hypotheses in this article are based on international studies performed in other domains, and the study was performed in Iran at that time, the opinions of the Iranian experts were regarded as weightier. As to the third hypothesis referring to the users' type, since the classification presented was specifically in line with American society, a parallel survey was developed to study and classify Iranian users. Encompassing all conditions, the Korgaonkar and Wolin (2002) survey inquired as to the number of weekly visits paid to the Web. The study revealed the same results as those of Korgaonkar and Wolin's (2002) study. Based on these results, Iranian users, like users in other parts of the world, are divided into three groups: heavy users, medium users and light users. The finding was included in the questionnaire so the experts could assess it as true or false. All pertinent documentation is accessible for future researchers. After collecting the questionnaires, (illustrated in Tables 1 and 2 via a strict assessment ($\mu \geq 4$)), all experts confirmed the research. Consequently, a core ideal framework was designed based on TOPSIS to compare the alternatives intended to be used as a tool for the selection of the right Internet advertising format. The TOPSIS method is a multi-criteria decision-making approach based on distance from and closeness to the ideal. It ranks the solutions by defining the main and subsidiary ideals. According to the TOPSIS philosophy, a solution is considered proper if it is closest to the main ideal solution and furthest from the subsidiary solution. The authenticity of these findings has been verified in previous studies (Hanafizadeh, Moosakhani, & Bakhshi, 2009).

Selecting a Process for the Right Internet Advertising Format

In order to select the right Internet advertising format, first the advertising core ideal framework should be designed according to the confirmed features, i.e. the features of the product or service, and the features of the advertisement itself. This framework serves as a criterion to evaluate the features of the scenario and possible advertising alternatives. It is noteworthy that the term "scenario" here refers to a product/service about which the advertiser tends to send information to his potential customers (i.e. to advertise). To advertise a scenario, it must first be located within this framework to identify its ideals. In addition, this framework serves as a criterion to show the ideal scenario of any given advertising alternative (Table 3). In fact, it identifies the appropriate type of advertising for a given scenario (product or service). Later, this scenario is compared to the ideals of the main advertising alternative, and

Table 1. Product/service student's T test statistical computing

Statistics	$f(x-)^2$	$(x-)^2$	fx	f	x	Product / Service Types
= 4.35	78.557	11.2225	7	7	1	
Sx= 0.85	22.09	5.5225	8	4	2	
Critical value = -1.65	67.432	1.8225	111	37	3	
T= 7.92	15.19	0.1225	496	124	4	
	83.655	0.4225	990	198	5	
	266.925		1612	370		

Table 2. Hypothesis, validity, and reliability

| Results | Examination Statistics: t _student_ | | | | | μ ≥ 4 |
	Examination Statistics	Critical Value	Sx	M.	N.	Hypothesis
Accept	7.92	-1.65	0.85	4.35	370	Product/Service Types
Accept	3.574	-1.65	0.89	4.165	370	Advertising Types
Accept	7.08	-1.65	0.815	4.3	370	Audience Types
Accept	0.53	-1.65	1.08	4.03	370	Strategy Types
Accept	-0.68	-1.65	1.125	3.96	370	Situation ICT
Accept	-1.113	-1.65	1.19	3.93	370	Ad Subjective Features
Accept	2.24	-1.65	0.945	4.11	370	Ad Objective Features

the closest advertising type is selected as the right Internet advertising format.

Elements of the Main Ideal Framework

The details of the five features (involvement, audience, ad type, strategy, and ICT status) are located in the "Hypotheses" section. There are five advertising features, four of which (appeal, interaction, movement and size) are categorized under objective features, while "attitude toward ads" belongs to the subjective category. These features are the base for making a distinction among various types of Internet advertising. Therefore, each has been elaborated in detail under different Internet advertising types. This chapter solely deals with the appeal type, because it is directly related to the customers' type of involvement with the product or service. Appeal is divided into two groups: emotional factors, represented here by "E," and rational factors, represented by

"R." As mentioned earlier, product and service advertisements to low-involvement customers can be effective by applying emotional factors, while those to high-involvement customers may influence their audience by applying rational appeals.

INTERNET ADVERTISING FORMATS

As mentioned earlier, the four types of Internet advertising formats discussed here are Display Ads (including banners, skyscrapers, and hypertexts), Rich Media (including pop-ups and interstitials), Sent E-mails, and Digital Video. This section discusses each type, explaining the distinctive features of each. Furthermore, each advertising type is evaluated based on the advertising criteria of Appeal Type, Movement and Interactivity, Typeface, Attitude Toward Ad, Strategy, Audience, Involvement, ICT Status, and the Type of Advertisement, which have already been mentioned under "Main Framework Elements."

Table 3. Core ideal framework

| Other Features | | | | | Ad Features | | | | | Product or Service |
ICT	Strategy	Ad Type	Audience	Involvement	Attitude	Size	Interactive	Animation	Appeal Type	
										Ideal

Banners

A banner typically appears as rectangular-shaped box located at the top, on either side or at the foot of the webpage (Faber, et al., 2004). It enables consumers to connect to an advertiser's website by clicking on it (Briones, 1999). At present, two major banner formats exist: static and rich media (IAB, 2000). Static banners are interactive but stationary, and generally appear in the size of 2.5cm × 12.5cm or smaller. Rich media banners, on the other hand, are more interactive (Briones, 1999). Banner advertisements are effective in motivating evoke click-throughs for high-involvement users (Dahlén, et al., 2000; Dahlén & Bergendahl, 2001; Dahlén, 2002). A banner is the smallest Internet advertising format (usually 468 × 60 pixels). Efforts made to tempt people to click on such ads through misleading messages have fostered a sense of dislike in the consumers as to this format. Although the information included in a banner is usually limited to the brand name and a brief slogan, it can serve as a means to improve brand awareness (Faber, et al., 2004; Briggs & Hollis, 1997). However, audiences cannot interact with it and, hence, a banner is neutral from this point of view.

Banners seem to be effective for those products whose owners apply a pull strategy and try to enhance customer awareness (Dahlén, 2004; Double Click, 2006). Due to their low file size, banners do not require a high bandwidth; the available bandwidth of 56 kbps seems adequate to display and view these ads (Table 3).

Pop-Ups

Pop-ups usually appear in a separate window at the top of the webpage. The pop-up window does not disappear until the user closes it voluntarily. A recent study reveals that pop-up ads are irritating and annoying to users (Edwards, et al., 2002; Faber, et al., 2004) and seem to be due to the disruption that such ads cause for the users when they are engaged in a specific activity on the Web (see Table 4).

Since pop-ups have a high rate of movement, they are categorized under large Internet advertising types because the smallest pop-up is 250 × 250 pixels, while the largest one may be 550 × 480 pixels (IAB, 2007). Pop-up size and movement are important because a bigger size and higher rate of movement result in a higher number of clicks. From an interactive point of view, a pop-up is designed to lead the audience to a certain website, without providing an explanation about the target product /service. In fact, pop-ups provide their audiences with no interactive information.

Pop-ups appeal mostly to light users, first because such users have little information about advertising types, and second because these users get online basically for entertainment. Such audiences do not have any particular query (Bruner & Kumar, 2000), thus they react to appealing objects and are more influenced by emotional appeals rather than rational ones (Korgaonkar & Wolin, 2002).

Table 4. Banners and pop-ups core ideal framework

Other Features					Ad Features					Features Alternatives
ICT	Strategy	Ad Type	Audience	Involvement	Attitude	Size	Interactive	Animation	Appeal Type	
L	Pull	ALL	H, M, L	H_1, H_2	-				R	Banners
H	Push	ALL	L	L_1, L_2	-	+		+	E	Pop-ups

Interstitials

Interstitials are considered annoying by users (Cho, 2000) as they cover the whole page (Ragers & Thorson, 2000), and users have little control over them because unlike pop-ups, there is no "exit" option to stop or delete an interstitial. However, customers show somewhat of a more positive attitude toward such ads because they are bigger than pop-ups, provide customers with more information and thus are easier to interact with.

Just like pop-ups, interstitials can effectively advertise products and services which are unfmailiar to users, where a push strategy is applied to provide the required information. Interstitials, just like pop-ups, have a lot of movement due to employing rich media technology along with applying numerous appealing and emotional factors to influence users. As mentioned above, audiences of an interstitial are primarily light users because this group is more susceptible to emotional appeals. Moreover, this type of advertising suits those users who have access to a connection speed of 100 kbps.

Skyscrapers

Skyscrapers are the most popular Internet advertising format (IAB, 2007) and are considered to be large Internet advertisements (600 × 120 pixels). Skyscrapers are especially effective for advertising products and services of high customer involvement. Since they are positioned on the right side of the webpage, the information they provide mostly includes companies' brands and logos. Because these customers look for products and services with high involvement, they comfortably interact with skyscrapers. A skyscraper contains a lot of GIF files and animation, and its background color constantly changes to attract users' attention. Skyscrapers are more appealing to heavy and medium users who use the Internet for highly rational and emotional motives. These people surf the Internet to find their targets. Skyscrapers are effective for

advertising familiar brands, and advertisers with such products should use a pull strategy in their advertisements. An Internet connectivity rate of 56 kbps seems to be enough for users exposed to skyscrapers.

Hypertexts

Hypertexts come under the oldest and cheapest category of Internet advertising. They appear within the content of webpages in the form of highlighted text. Hypertexts are interactively neutral, because most of the time they include only one or two words, or a relatively short phrase. Since the only things that users see are a number of words possibly related to a search option, a hypertext is not interactive (Hanafizadeh & Behboudi, 2008, p. 92).

Hypertexts are neutral from the typeface and movement points of view, as they are offered in the form of text and might be ignored by some users. The required speed is a mere 56 kbps. Heavy users and high-involvement products are potentially the best targets (Salmon, 1986; Hanafizadeh & Behboudi, 2008, p. 93) of hypertexts. Through employing an inexpensive pull strategy, and locating the hypertexts in frequently visited websites, the product owner may facilitate users' access to the website. Since hypertexts play an important role in decreasing advertising expenses and do not appear to be disruptive, users have a positive attitude toward them (Hanafizadeh & Behboudi, 2008, p. 93).

E-Mail Advertising

Advertising through e-mail is one of the major instruments of a push strategy. The targets of this method are mainly middle and heavy users, because light users rarely tend to check their mailboxes (Hanafizadeh & Behboudi, 2008, p. 81). The lowest connectivity speed, 56 kbps, seems to be adequate for this method. Movement and size have nothing to do with emails because they are specifically for those ads which occupy space on the Web. Used as a push strategy, follow up e-mails trigger a user's emotional, not rational, involvement, first due to the large number of spam and lack of trust in e-mails, and second because of the effectiveness of appeal factors. In e-mail advertising, emotional motives play a determining role persuading users to follow up on the e-mails; otherwise, they will be easily ignored by the users. This method provides a low level of rational interaction. The attitude toward e-mails is positive, and e-mails are popular with users (IDC, 2001). Moreover, studies reveal that Internet users are keen on receiving e-mails to stay informed (Intermarketgroup.com, 2002) and hence, tend to fill out application forms on the Web quite often.

Digital Video

This method has successfully shifted from TV to the Internet; however, both advertisers and consumers contribute to controlling it (Dynamic Logic, 2007). Digital video has a high interaction rate as it can be recalled and analyzed as long as the logo of the advertising company is displayed. Customers have a positive attitude toward this method due to its dynamism and appealing images. According to a study carried out by the Jupiter Institute (2005), compared with text-type advertising, video advertising has a deeper effect on customers' attitudes. Video advertising is more influential on light and medium users than heavy users due to the emotional appeal. High-speed Internet connections are required for this type of advertising, and it is appropriate for unfamiliar or new products and services. Video advertising is used both for pull and push strategies.

The Variables of the Model

The model includes two groups of features presented in Table 5:

- The "R" represents "rational appeal" and is related to those products with which the customer has a high rate of mental involvement and gathers a lot of information in order to buy them.
- The "E" represents "emotional appeal" and is related to those products with which the customer has a low rate of rational involvement and purchases due to emotional motives.
- The "□" stands for those features that do not apply to the option or have a zero value.
- The "-" sign stands for features of negative value.
- The "+" sign stands for features of positive value.
- H_1 and H_2 stand for high customer-product involvement. H1 stands for those rational-based purchases (like furniture), while H2 represents emotional-based purchases (like jewelry or cosmetics).
- $L_{1 \& } L_2$ stand for low customer-product involvement, both from a logical and an emotional point of view.
- H, M, and L stand for "Heavy" user, "Middle" user and "Light" user, respectively.
- In the ICT section, L represents "low connection speed," and H represents "high speed."

When the ideal framework for each advertising alternative is defined (Table 3), a comparison is made between the scenario and each individual alternative to choose the most appropriate framework for the product.

Case Study

Here "Job search" was the study case. Job search ads are categorized under "issue ads" (Devlin, 1995).

Table 5. Core ideal framework based on 10 features and 7 alternatives

Features Alternatives	Ad Features					Other Features				
	Appeal Type	Animation	Interactive	Size	Attitude	Involvement	Audience	Ad Type	Strategy	ICT
Banner	R	□	□	□	-	H_1, H_2	H, M, L	ALL	Pull	L
Pop-up	E	+	□	+	-	L_1, L_2	L	ALL	Push	H
Interstitial	E	+	+	+	-	L_1, L_2	L	ALL	Push	H
Skyscraper	R	+	+	+	+	H_1, H_2	H	ALL	Pull	L
Hypertext	R	□	□	□	+	H_1, H_2	H	ALL	Pull	L
E-mail Ad	E	□	□	□	+	L_1, L_2	H, M	ALL	Push	L
Digital Video	E	+	+	+	+	L_1, L_2	H, M	ALL	Push, Pull	H

- Involvement: high
- Appeals: rational and logical
- Audience type: all users
- Ad type: issue
- Strategy: pull
- ICT: lowest connection
- Attitude: negative
- Interactivity: positive and high
- Size and animation: neutral

The scenario presented in Table 6 is considered as the core ideal framework for Job Search based on 10 variables. This ideal framework is compared to the individual ideals of all advertising items (Table 5), and the alternative, having the most corresponding ideals with the scenario ideal, will be selected as the right Internet advertising format for Job Search.

As illustrated in Table 7, banner advertisements are closest to the Job Search scenario with only one difference. According to this model, banners proved to be the most effective type of Internet advertising method for Job Searches. To evaluate and assess the accuracy of the model, a content analysis was performed on Persian weblogs and websites to observe and record Job Search ads. Eventually, the proposed model was strongly confirmed because the majority of Job Search ads were in the form of banners.

Considering the fact that banners may be the most common format of Internet advertising and since relying merely on one advertising format may not be reliable enough to prove it to be efficient, another case study was developed. Just as with the banner scenarios, an assumption emerged. According to this assumption, skyscrapers were assumed to be the best solution for advertising a film due to customers' high emotional involvement. The proper strategy to be used is a pull strategy because users look for this type of product. In this case, customer-product interaction is high, because users scrutinize the ad looking for the names of the actors and the director. They may even refer to the website to seek additional infor-

Table 6. Core ideal framework for job search

Other Features					Ad Features					Job Search
ICT	Strategy	Ad Type	Audience	Involvement	Attitude	Size	Interactive	Animation	Appeal Type	
L	Pull	Issue	H, M, L	H_1, H_2	-	□	+	□	R	Ideal

mation. As to the ICT status, minimum speed can satisfy this demand. To apply the model, an approach was defined. First, a visit was paid to *Webgozar.com*, an Iranian source of statistics providing monthly reports introducing websites most-visited by users within the previous month. It also provides a list of most-visited websites by users within a year and a list of the 150 most-visited websites within the previous year. Next, entering into each URL, pertinent data was collected (as stated in Appendix 1). The website was checked to confirm whether it accepts the ad or not, and then the type of product to be advertised and the advertising format were checked. The findings revealed that from 150 websites, there were 111 accepted ads. 65 had already accepted film advertising, 45 of which accepted ads in the skyscraper format, 20 in the banner format, and the remaining were as follows: 1) filtered and damaged ones = 14, 2) Skyscrapers= 6; Banners = 21; and Bottoms = 5 which displayed ads of some other products. According to the content analysis, the skyscraper is the most frequently used format (the right format) for film advertising, and thus it can be concluded that the model is functionally efficient.

DISCUSSION

Categorization of Likely Scenarios

Finding a potential framework that helps classify the possible scenarios is considered as the most significant achievement of this study. Based on the main ideal framework, decisions can be made

as to what advertising format suits which scenario best. An advertisement likelihood scenario is the closest thing to reality. For instance, in the aforementioned case study, banners proved to be the best advertising method once the ideal framework was defined. On this basis, one classification may be as follows:

Scenarios that are closest to the following features are categorized in the "banner" group:

- High mental involvement and data processing complexity
- Pull strategy
- Type of advertisement (product/service, issue, public service announcement, corporate and political)
- Heavy, medium and light users
- Negative attitude toward the product or service
- Neutral interaction, size and movement
- Rational appeal type

A banner is the appropriate advertising alternative for those scenarios identified with these features. Actually, this classification can be equally applied to six other types of Internet advertising formats. Each Internet advertising method has specific characteristics that make it the best advertising alternative for the scenarios categorized in this group.

CONCLUSION

To identify the right Internet advertising format, this chapter proposed a general framework using

Table 7. Core ideal framework for banner

Other Features					Ad Features					Banner
ICT	Strategy	Ad Type	Audience	Involvement	Attitude	Size	Interactive	Animation	Appeal Type	
L	Pull	ALL	H, M, L	H_1, H_2	-	□	□	□	R	Ideal

the TOPSIS approach. Applying the proposed model, the likelihood of an ideal group of advertising formats for different types of products/services was defined. The hypotheses were evaluated by international and Iranian experts. In order to complete and extend this research, further research can be performed on the ad types and the way they contribute to choosing the right Internet advertising format. Therefore, more comprehensive studies seem to be required to assess the effect of advertising methods on the selection of the right Internet advertising format.

This chapter discovered a general theoretical framework for defining the course of action required to study Internet advertising. The chapter consolidated the findings of previous studies and introduced the main pillars for making decisions about the selection of the right Internet advertising format. This text opens a window for researchers through which they may observe the various branches of a subjective features model (ICT situation, strategy type, audience type, ad type, product type, and subjective and objective features) which is effective for making decisions as to Internet advertising, and develop the required delves. It is noteworthy that the main criteria included in this text was extracted from 50 sources. Business firms tend to use the Internet as an advertising medium, and may use this model to select an advertising format that suits their product/service best. They may also develop their advertising activities based on the defined criteria to improve the efficiency of their ads.

REFERENCES

Anderson, R., & Bickson, T. (1995). *Universal access to email: Feasibility And societal implications*. Santa Monica, CA: Rand Corporation.

Briggs, R., & Hollis, N. (1997). Advertising on the web: Is there response before click-through. *Journal of Advertising Research, 37*(2), 33–45.

Broines, M. (1999). Rich media may be too rich for your blood. *Marketing News, 33*(7), 4–5.

Bruner, R. E. (2006). *Best practices for optimizing web advertising effectiveness*. Retrieved from Www.Doubleclick.Com /Insight/Pdfs/ Dc_Bpwp_0605.Pdf.

Burns, K. S., & Lutos, J. R. (2006). The function of format. *Journal of Advertising, 35*(1), 53–63. doi:10.2753/JOA0091-3367350104

Cacioppo, J. T., & Petty, R. E. (1984). The elaboration likelihood model of persuasion. *Advances in Consumer Research. Association for Consumer Research (U. S.), 11*(1), 668–672.

Celsi, R. L., & Olson, J. C. (1988). The role of involvement in attention and comprehension processes. *The Journal of Consumer Research, 15*, 210–224. doi:10.1086/209158

Chattopadhyay, A. (1998). When does comparative advertising influence brand attitude? The role of delay & market position. *Psychology and Marketing, 15*(5), 461–475. doi:10.1002/ (SICI)1520-6793(199808)15:5<461::AID-MAR4>3.0.CO;2-5

Chung-Chuan, Y. (1997). An exploratory study of the effectiveness of interactive advertisements on the internet. *Journal of Marketing Communications, 3*, 85–91.

Cushing, P., & Douglas-Tate, M. (1985). The effect of people product relationships on advertising processing. In Alwitt, L. F., & Mitchell, A. A. (Eds.), *Psychological Processes And Advertising Effects: Theory, Research, and Applications* (pp. 241–259). Hillsdale, NJ: Lawrence Erlbaum Associates.

Dahlén, M. (2002). Thinking & feeling on the world wide web: The impact of product type and time on world wide web advertising effectiveness. *Journal of Marketing Communications, 8*, 115–125. doi:10.1080/13527260210142347

Dahlén, M., & Bergendahl, J. (2001). Informing & transforming on the web: An empirical study of response to banner ads for functional & expressive products. *International Journal of Advertising, 20*(2), 189–205.

Dahlén, M., Ekborn, Y., & Mörner, N. (2000). To click or not to click: An empirical study of response to banner ads for high & low involvement products. *Consumption. Markets and Culture, 4*(1), 57–76. doi:10.1080/10253866.2000.9670349

Dahlén, M., Malcolm, M., & Nordenstam, S. (2004). An empirical study of perceptions of implicit meanings in world wide web advertisements versus print advertisements. *Journal of Marketing Communications, 10*, 35–47. doi:10.1080/1352726042000177391

Darroch, J., Miles, M. P., Jardine, A., & Cooke, F. E. (2004). The 2004 AMA definition of marketing & its relationship to a market orientation: An extension of Cooke, Rayburn & Abercrombie. *Journal of Marketing Theory & Practice, 12*(4), 29–38.

Devlin, P. L. (1995). Political commercials in American presidential elections. In Kaid, L. L., & Holz-Bacha, C. (Eds.), *Political Advertising in Western Democracies: Parties & Candidates on Television* (pp. 186–205). Thousand Oaks, CA: Sage Publications, Inc.

Dibb, S., & Simkin, L. (1991). Targeting, segments & positioning. *International Journal of Retail & Distribution Management, 19*(3), 4–10. doi:10.1108/09590559110143800

Ducoffe, R. H. (1996). How value & advertising on the web. *Journal of Advertising Research, 36*(5), 21–35.

Edwards, S. M., Li, H., & Lee, J. H. (2002). Forced exposure & psychological reactance: Antecedents & consequences of the perceived intrusiveness of pop-up ads. *Journal of Advertising, 31*(3), 83–96.

Gardner, M. P., Mitchell, A. A., & Russo, J. E. (1985). Low involvement strategies for processing advertisements. *Journal of Advertising, 14*(2), 4–12.

Hairong, L., & Leckenby, J. D. (2004). *Internet advertising formats & effectiveness.* Retrieved from http://Www.Ciadvertising.Org /Studies/ Reports/Measurement/ Ad_Format_Print.Pdf.

Haley, E., & Wilkinson, J. (1994). And now a word from our sponsor: An exploratory concept test of PSAs vs. advocacy ads. In *Proceedings of the 1994 Conference of the American Academy of Advertising*, (pp. 79-87). American Academy of Advertising.

Hanafizadeh, P., & Behboudi, M. (2008). *Internet advertising: New opportunity for promotion.* Tehran, Iran: Termeh Publication.

Hanafizadeh, P., Moosakhani, M., & Bakhshi, J. (2009). Selecting the best strategic practices for business process redesign. *Business Process Management Journal, 15*(4), 609–627. doi:10.1108/14637150910975561

Heinz, M. (2004). It's the message, stupid. *Imedia Connection.* Retrieved from http://Www.Imedia-connection.Com /Content/3084.Asp.

Holbrook, M. B., & Lehmann, D. R. (1980). Form versus content in predicting starch scores. *Journal of Advertising Research, 20*, 53–62.

IAB.com. (2000). *Internet ad revenue report.* Retrieved April 23, 2001 from http://Www.Iab. Net /News/Pr_2001_04_23.Asp.

IAB.com. (2007). *Pop up guidelines & table.* Retrieved September 16, 2007 from http://www. Iab.Net.

IAB.com. (2008). *Internet advertising revenue report, 2007 full-year, May.* Retrieved from http:// www.Iad.Net.

IAB.com. (2009). *Internet advertising revenue report, 2008 full-year results, March 2009.* Retrieved from http://www.Iad.Net.

ICT.com. (2007). *Communication ministry online report on internet bandwidth.* Retrieved from http://Www.ICT.Com.

Intermarket Group L. P. (2004). *The internet commerce briefing, online advertising & digital marketing report.* Retrieved from http://Www.Intermarketgroup.Com.

International Data Corp. (2002). *Email marketing.* Retrieved from http://www.Idcresearch.Com.

Jupiter Institute. (2005). *Digital video report.* Retrieved from http://www.Jupiter.Com.

Katz, J., & Aspden, P. (1997). Motivations & barriers to internet usage: Results of a national public opinion survey. *Internet Research: Electronic Networking Applications & Policy, 7*(3), 170–188. doi:10.1108/10662249710171814

Ko, H., Chang, H. C., & Roberts, M. S. (2005). Internet uses & gratifications structural equation model of interactive advertising. *Journal of Advertising, 34*(2), 57–70.

Korgaonkar, P. K., & Wolin, L. D. (2002). Web usage, advertising, & shopping: Relationship patterns. *Internet Research: Electronic Networking Applications & Policy, 12*(2), 191–204. doi:10.1108/10662240210422549

Laurent, G., & Kapferer, J. (1985). Measuring consumer involvement profiles. *JMR, Journal of Marketing Research, 22*(1), 41–53. doi:10.2307/3151549

Mehta, A., & Sivadas, E. (1995). Direct marketing on the internet: An empirical assessment of consumer attitudes. *Journal of Direct Marketing, 9*(3), 21–32. doi:10.1002/dir.4000090305

Mills, P. K., & Margulies, N. (1980). Toward a core typology of service organizations. *Academy of Management Review, 5*(2), 255–265.

Morris, J. D., & Woo, C. M. (2003). Internet measures of advertising effects: A global issue. *Journal of Current Issues & Research in Advertising, 25*(1), 25–43.

Newman, J. E., Donald, E., & David, S. E. (2004). Banner advertisement & website congruity effects. *Industrial Management & Data Systems, 104*(3), 273–281. doi:10.1108/02635570410525816

Petty, R. E., Cacioppo, J. T., & Schumann, D. (1983). Central & peripheral routes to advertising effectiveness: The moderating of involvement. *The Journal of Consumer Research, 10*(2), 135–146. doi:10.1086/208954

Previte, J. (1998). *Internet advertising: An assessment of consumer attitudes to advertising on the internet.* Paper Presented at the 1998 Communication Research Forum. Canberra, Australia.

Rodgers, S., & Thorson, E. (2000). The interactive advertising model: How users perceive & process online ads. *Journal of Interactive Advertising, 1*(1), 26–50.

Salmon, C. (1986). Perspectives on involvement in consumer & communication research. In Dervin, B., & Voigt, M. (Eds.), *Progress in Communication Sciences* (pp. 243–268). Norwood, NJ: Ablex.

Scholsser, A. E., Shovitt, S., & Kanfer, A. (1999). Survey of internet user's attitudes toward internet advertising. *Journal of Interactive Marketing, 13*(3), 37–46.

Schramm, W. (1955). How communication works. In Schramm, W. (Ed.), *The Process & Effects of Mass Communications* (pp. 3–26). Urbana, IL: University of Illinois Press.

Sheehan, K. B. (1999). An investigation of gender differences in online privacy concerns & results behaviors. *Journal of Interactive Marketing, 13*(4), 24–38. doi:10.1002/(SICI)1520-6653(199923)13:4<24::AID-DIR3>3.0.CO;2-O

Sundar, S. S., & Kalyanaraman, S. (2004). Arousal, memory, & impression-formation effects of animation speed in web advertising. *Journal of Advertising, 33*(1), 7–17.

Thomsen, M. D. (1996). *Advertising on the internet.* Masters Dissertation. Wesminster, UK: The University Of Westminster.

Thorson, E. (1996). Advertising. In Salwen, M. B., & Stacks, D. W. (Eds.), *An Integrated Approach to Communication Theory T Research* (pp. 211–230). New York, NY: Taylor & Francis.

Thorson, E., & Leavitt, C. (1986). *Probabilistic functionalism & the search for taxonomy of commercials.* Unpublished Paper.

Turban, E., King, D., Viehland, D., & Lee, J. K. (2006). *Electronic commerce: A managerial perspective.* Upper Saddle River, NJ: Prentice Hall.

Vaughn, R. (1986). How advertising works: A planning model. *Journal of Advertising Research, 26*(1), 57–66.

Warrington, P., & Shim, S. (2000). An empirical investigation of the relationship between product involvement & brand commitment. *Journal of Psychology & Marketing, 17*(9), 761–782. doi:10.1002/1520-6793(200009)17:9<761::AID-MAR2>3.0.CO;2-9

Wills, J., Samli, A. C., & Jacobs, L. (1991). Developing global products & marketing strategies: A construct & a research agenda. *Journal of the Academy of Marketing Science, 19*(1), 1–10. doi:10.1007/BF02723418

Zaichkowsky, J. L. (1985). Measuring the involvement construct. *The Journal of Consumer Research, 12*(3), 341–352. doi:10.1086/208520

Zenithoptimedia.Com. (2009). *Advertising expenditure press release.* Retrieved April 14, 2009, from http://www.Zenithoptimedia.Com.

Chapter 12
Lead Generation and Behavioral Marketing

ABSTRACT

According to an IAB (2009) report, the total revenue of lead generation as one of the main elements of Internet advertising at the end of 2008 was more than seven percent of the total 23,448 million dollars in the US. How lead generation companies achieve this amount of income and how they help the marketing and advertisement process are the subjects of this chapter. Being virtual and tracing virtual behavior are new issues in the area of user behavior. Being virtual has many advantages for advertisers and marketers; perhaps the greatest is the possibility of observing the real behavior of the customer. Marketing research shows that in offline atmospheres, customers do not often behave as they think or say, and in fact behave differently when confronted with environmental variables. However, cyber space and developed technologies have denied these variables to online users so that it is no longer possible for them to show different behaviors. In this regard, lead generation companies have achieved a defined pattern of wants, interests, and needs motives for persuading customers by tracing and recording behavior (customer clicks) over a long period.

The importance of introducing lead generation is that it is the most basic activity before publishing an advertisement or conducting any other strategic activity on the Internet. Advertisements formed by a true understanding of the target customers, their wants, motives, and the main reasons for purchasing are more efficient and effective. Thus, marketers always try to adapt their solution based on the sensitive needs and wants of their audience. These efforts of marketers on the one hand, and emergence of new technologies in interactive media on the other, have led to the creation of a new concept of lead generation in marketing and online advertising with the responsibility of collecting information, trends, and surfing methods of various customers. This chapter focuses on lead generation as a new responsibility of interactive agencies and its role in B2B and B2C. Also, the way of launching a successful lead generation strategy will be reviewed, and new concepts such as behavioral targeting and behavioral marketing will be mentioned. Meanwhile, by studying forums and online communities, the chapter will show how focus groups based on traditional marketing research are being replaced by free online focus groups. The main emphasis of this chapter is the application of new technologies for making Internet advertising more effective.

DOI: 10.4018/978-1-4666-0885-6.ch012

WHAT IS LEAD GENERATION?

In today's digital world, through the emergence of concepts such as RSS, Social Bookmarking, Social News, Social Recommendation Engines, Photo Sharing Sites, Social Search Engines, Video Sharing Sites, Social Networks, Widgets, and Wikis, marketers are able to address their customers with a rather complete background (see Figure 1). When a user registers at a publisher's website, this information results in lead generation offers being provided by the advertisers. During registration, the user might record interests, fill in several forms or provide Personally Identifiable Information (PII). The user may also allow the sharing of PII with the advertiser or third parties. In general, publishers provide the advertisers with two kinds of online lead generation forms: (1) simple offers in which the user might sign up to receive the current offers without entering extra information; (2) custom offers in which the user is required to enter extra information in order to receive offers (IAB, 2008). Information entered in registration forms includes first name, last name and email address. Additional contact information such as physical address and phone number, or demographic information such as household income and other pertinent information for the offer, such as average monthly mortgage payment, may also be collected.

Lead generation is a winning approach for both buyers and sellers; buyers can get information from several companies, and sellers have the opportunity to fit their goods and services with the people who want them. The lead generation approach is becoming more and more popular due to the following reasons: Pricing on the basis of the primary leads provided by the customer.

- Focusing on the products which are more compatible with customer preferences.
- Selecting the target market according to the regions in which the company does business.
- Controlling the number of leads the organization receives in each period, helping with budgeting.

Figure 1. Social media and its new technologies

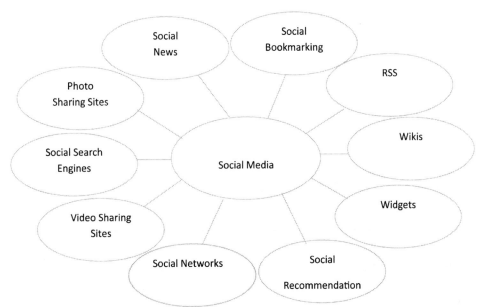

- Optimizing advertisements. Considering the expenses of weak advertising activities such as direct posts, yellow pages and flyers, expenses will be reduced and advertising efficiency will be increased. Advertisement efficiency involves issues like accuracy, ease and measurability. By examining the expenses for buying the leads versus the number of customers added, marketers will easily be able to evaluate their ads' efficiency.

We define lead generation as follows:

Lead generation is the process of online data gathering with the purpose of creating and promoting customers' personalized profiles whereby companies are able to create and deliver customized product and services to those customers.

DIFFERENT KINDS OF LEAD GENERATION

Lead generation involves two main operational areas: B2B lead generation and B2C lead generation. B2C is more related to that group of Internet sales areas which are in direct contact with the end-users and must continuously identify customers' IPs in order to create profiles. In contrast, lead generation in the B2B area relates to businesses which are in contact with their agencies rather than the users of the products.

B2B Lead Generation

B2B electronic business is experiencing accelerating growth and is predicted to own a major share of the e-business market. According to International Data Corporation (IDC) (2004), the volume of B2B exchanges has risen to 2.4 trillion. B2B refers to transactions between businesses conducted electronically over the Internet, extranets, intranets or private networks (Mahadevan, 2003; Haig, 2003). Nowadays, 85 percent of electronic exchanges

are conducted in the B2B area (Cunningham, 2001). In addition, the creation of 5th generation organizations in B2B (Gartner Inc, 2004) has made this market completely distinctive and has caused organizations using full technology-driven methods to outsmart their rivals. One of the main issues in applying new technologies in B2B is the issue of advertisements and the new technologies.

As the name implies, the aim of advertising in the B2B arena must be inclined toward governmental organizations, semi-governmental businesses, and private economic agencies, customers who buy to process not to consume, and customers who use the purchased products or services for the production of other products or services to sell to their end-users. According to eMarketer.com (2003), industries like electronics and computers, transportation and warehousing, petro-chemistry, automobiles, paper goods, food stuffs and agriculture have pioneered the B2B electronic business. Purchasing patterns in this segment of the market are governmental ones, thus the advertising targeting and appeal differs greatly from that of the consumer market. Due to a high volume of purchasing, this segment of the market pays more attention to the offers that meet their demands and requirements. Companies acting in the B2B area are usually inquiry-based, and these inquiry-based buying. Companies usually buy through an online ordering method whereby they collect the inquiries of various providers and negotiate with them before finalizing the purchase.

Offering an appropriate inquiry as a promotional tool encourages the customer to choose a desired company from among the inquiries offered by all competitors. Since, in this segment of the market, it is the customer who requires information, advertising and promotion are already one step further along in the process. Unlike in the consumer market, B2B marketers do not need to use motivational strategies to persuade customers to click on their advertisements. Instead, the key objectives of advertising in this market segment is designing and developing the right content for the inquiry. The right content includes the customers' needs and wants, which are revealed on the basis of probing and tracing previous orders, problems and purchases.

Marketers must be aware of the real needs of the customers in order to design good content for the inquiry. "Real needs" are not the wants which the customer has recorded in his order; rather, the aim is to identify the customer's real problems. In a B2B market, the issue of problem-solving is more important than need-satisfying. For example, the Kayson Company has offered a request to the Hadef Company to buy a number of cranes. Kayson's request includes specifications for a number of cranes with certain lifting capacity and in a certain price range. But what is the real problem of the Kayson Company as an oil supplier? Finding the answer to this question will definitely guide the Hadef Company in preparing and developing the right content for the inquiry. The advertising department must collect leads relevant to this company in order to find the answer to this question. For, today, with high accessibility to secondary data, the same inquiry cannot be offered to all customers. Marketers can utilize two methods for collecting leads in a B2B market:

- **Creating a marketing network and integrating databases:** This is the most important activity that marketers must do for the prosperity of their companies. Having a strong network of high-quality providers presents an ideal opportunity for on-time delivery. By creating and developing a marketing network and integrating databases, marketers become aware of the previous activities of these companies and can better provide their customers with inquiries. The network enables marketers to be informed of the capabilities of each provider so they can choose the most appropriate case. By creating an appropriate section on the home page of their website,

marketers can invite new members to their marketing network. Sharing databases enables companies to collect specific leads by tracing customers throughout the network.

- **Buying leads:** Marketers must trace the previous behavior and orders of their customers in order to offer the right content for the inquiry. Previous buying behaviors as well as accepted inquiries can show marketers the appropriate direction for developing the right inquiry content.

As *Marketwisesolution.com* (2010) reports, every business needs sales to survive; therefore, every business needs a sales pipeline containing a steady flow of qualified prospects to whom it can sell products and services. B2B lead generation is the process that consistently keeps qualified prospects steadily flowing through the sales pipeline. B2B lead generation is the heart and soul of business-to-business sales. Organizations cannot survive without actively seeking new customers unless they are a monopoly (*Marketwisesolution. com*, 2010).

B2C Lead Generation

The issue of lead generation and collecting data relevant to customers' wants in the area of B2C is somewhat different from those of the B2B area. In B2C, businesses continuously face needs, wants, and demands which are first, very limited, i.e. their buying volume is small and light; and second, lacking clear understanding of the IP owners who are offering or requesting service. Although it seems that segmentation is easier on the Web, which provides the validity of users' IP addresses, that premise does not always hold true, because it is possible that at different times, different people use one IP for different purposes. Therefore, the general assumption of following and recording the behavior of one IP cannot be accepted as a basic trend of the wants of a user. Rather, this trend must be realized by filtering and examining tools, and the identity of the online user must be verified.

According to Professor Kotler, "If you really find an unmet need and do a good job of providing a solution, you don't have to do much selling." The main orientation in B2C markets is identifying and satisfying the customer's unmet needs. Unmet needs form the main motives of a potential customer for following promotional hints, clues, cues, decoys and messages. What is relatively important in businesses which are directly in contact with end-users is understanding this main unmet need. This means understanding that the previous values offered to the customer were not able to meet this intensified need, so the user is still searching the market for those solutions.

At each visit, customers have a specific unmet need, so it is natural for them not to show a predefined behavior on various visits. Marketers should pay special attention to this issue. What would be the perception of the customer who enters the Web with a specific need who faces the same offer as viewed on a previous visit? Thus, the first activity of the marketers in the B2C area is identifying the probable needs of customers their motives for surfing the Web. Then, a value-delivering career for the customers 'expected service must be formulated on the basis of their primary motive. We define the value-delivering career for a customer's expected service as follows:

All marketer's actions and answers to customer wants during a visit which are designed for the purpose of meeting customers' unmet needs.

As mentioned earlier, marketers must simultaneously do two activities to achieve the goal of meeting customer needs. First, they must identify the primary motive for a user's entrance into the site, and then they must develop a value-delivering career for the customer's expected service. In this regard, Ko *et al* (2005) showed that the primary motives for the user to enter a website are summarized in four main categories: social interaction, convenience, information and entertainment. According to the findings of this study, it is enough for the marketers to use the four standard forms developed on the basis of the requirements of each motive instead of one standard form. Marketers must create four segments by defining and developing the range of each of these four segments. Therefore, the main task of marketers in the first stage is using lead generation to identify and categorize customers into one of the four segments. Then, they must move on to the next stage and develop the expected values of each segment by offering distinctive services for each.

To gather correct and useful data, the website must develop dynamic registration forms instead of static ones. Reading the data transferred into the database of the website by tracing, the registration forms must identify the users and recognize the groups to which they belong. Then, it must provide offers relevant to that segment with the help of leads recorded by the users. This strategy is a segmentation strategy on the basis of standardization. In other words, instead of offering the same service to every individual present on the Web, customers are first categorized, and then service is provided to the correct target audience group.

LEAD GENERATION IMPLEMENTATION STRATEGIES

Lead generation plays an important part in each strategy implemented by organizations for developing their business. The degree of importance of lead generation is evident when marketers notice that customers collect their information on goods and services from the Internet. Changing the Internet into a central point of users' searches emphasizes that business owners must develop a comprehensive lead generation strategy on their websites to obtain the needs and wants of their customers in the online environment. Developing a lead generation strategy involves methods by which a company can maximize online requests, effectively turning visitors into prospects.

Understanding organization prospects is vitally important as this helps the company determine the range of business operations and specify target markets. Organizations that consider prospects will be able to exactly identify those prospects' information and physical needs, and focus on meeting them. This is also true in relation to online communications. In order to make a good relationship as the center point of the advertisement, organizations must be well aware of the features of their target markets. This requires a data collection process called lead generation. There is a set of tools and methods for launching and administering a comprehensive lead generation strategy which are addressed in this section.

Online Feedback

Before anything else, an organization must know what it really offers to public. Are its offers really responsive to the needs and wants of the target public? In order to obtain true answers, owners of electronic businesses must conduct activities that enable them to hear the voices of their customers. Among these activities is motivating their customers to express their opinions by offering incentives. Online feedback is the first lead each organization looks for in its lead generation process for these reasons:

- First, it specifies what the customers are really looking for. In other words, it identifies which products customers are buying.
- Second, it specifies the main competitive advantage of the company or the reason the customers buy from the company.

To put it simply, it shows what solutions the company's offers provide customers which are not seen among the offers and solutions of competitors. In order to obtain this important information, a set of strategies must be employed. One useful strategy is polling and arranging an appropriate place for it on the website. Marketers are faced with challenges for polling, including devising a polling mechanism. Polling can be developed and conducted in a way that users can see important features confirmed by others after announcing the results, or polling can show new users the importance assigned to each feature by previous users.

Depending on the product or service to be advertised, each of these approaches can be efficient and useful in their own way. However, the method suggested here is to follow a binary purpose; in this way, organizations can use polling as an effective advertisement. For this purpose, it is sufficient to ask the users to take part in the poll and not to show the amount of votes received for each feature in the polling chart. This is because the voters' opinions, consciously or subconsciously, will be influenced by the numbers in the chart, and this will threaten the validity of the poll. However, if polling is conducted in a way that the visitor is not aware of the previous votes, not only is the validity of the poll preserved, but also it can be used as an influential Internet advertisement methods as the poll indicates the competitive advantage of the company in relation to its competitors. Also, it shows the reason for the customer's visit to the website and any purchases. The objective for using polling must be changed from a tool for lead generation to a tool for publishing information. Features identified by present users as a competitive advantage must be introduced to new users so that they have a reason for their purchase. This also causes the present voting customers to get after-sale support and protects them from the uncertainties they may feel when facing competitive brands by emphasizing the positive reasons for their purchase. Therefore, leads obtained from customers can align and optimize both the interests of the organization and those of the customers. Using this method results in achieving several goals from one path -- the process called cost energy by the management scientists (Kaplan &Norton, 2001, pp. 25-30).

In general, in the world of electronic business, there are two classification of websites, each of which has special importance for marketers. The first category, top-tier websites, includes websites which are considered as the primary portals of most Internet users. Due to excessive usage, these websites are visited once during almost every Internet session. Google, Yahoo, AOL and MSN are examples of this category. The second group, known as second-tiers, consists of the websites which have attracted a rather homogenous group of users with the same interests. Blogs, social networks, entertainment sites and niche content are among the websites belonging to this group. Users' tendency to use and accept second-tier websites has had considerable growth in recent years. However, despite this trend of users to accept second-tiers, the revenues of Internet advertisements are still earned through the CPM method. Earning income in second-tiers is difficult because this kind of website lacks the technical capability for targeting an audience and does not have enough users to attract direct advertisements. In this respect, new business technologies and models are growing in line with promoting targeting in second-tier websites. The aim of employing these business models is to create a considerable value for Internet advertisers. As we will discuss in this chapter, technologies such as behavioral targeting and lead generation are among the models which attract target users so that the owners of these websites can benefit from the profits of publishing an advertisement to an appropriate target public.

All content websites want to be able to directly negotiate with the advertisers to publish their advertisements; however, this requires having high traffic, professional content, a high rank among similar websites and an attractive market for the advertisers. Direct advertisement of a brand is appropriate for top-tier websites like AOL, Yahoo, and MSN, where a CPM equals $50 for each visit. However, a large number of users spend a lot of time at second-tier websites (user-generated sites, social networks, niche content, blogs and convenience sites which have neither a large audience nor content which is in line with the products of

advertisers). According to Kinzelberg and Wienbar (2008), there are more than 70 million blogs having over 1.5 million daily posts. At present, MySpace, Facebook, and YouTube comprise 16% of all the time spent online. Also, children's online gaming websites like *Pogo*, *Runescape,* and *Neopets*, were among the 25 first websites of 2007. Without the ability to directly attract advertisers, most of these second-tier websites rely on Google Adsense or join vertical advertising networks whose result is CPMs less than $1-2$.

ONLINE COMMUNITY AND LEAD GENERATION

Sellers spend a lot of time on focus groups whereas virtual communities of users are focus groups, which are available 24/7 and provide the organization with countless learning opportunities. Community websites attract users with membership opportunities on the website, online chats with friends and the availability of exceptional information.

Undoubtedly, the most important goal of social media is lead generation. Especially in today's economic climate, getting in touch with potential clients is the lifeblood of any company (*Socialmediab2b.com*, 2010). But how can companies leverage social media to get more leads without blatantly revealing users' referrals?

Free offers given to users in return for their registration must be sufficiently attractive because filling in the registration forms requires strong motivation. Thus, the important issue in designing a lead generation structure is creating strong motivation in the users to follow the proposed offer so that the website and lead generation companies can collect the leads. For this purpose, marketers can secretly become members of online communities that are in line with their products and services and be in close contact with potential customers. A presence in online communities and building relationships with other users enables marketers to identify customers' real needs and wants. Then marketers can place the goods or services that meet those needs into the website and put the direct link of the website into the community. In this way, marketers are able to create necessary motivation for filling in the registration forms.

More importantly, unlike other traditional media, Location Based Advertising (LBA) is not only used principally for advertising, but also doubles as a means of researching consumers. "Consumers are constantly providing information on their behavior through mobile Internet activity" (Ferris, 2007, p. 33). With a location-based service, surveys can take place in the real world, in real time, rather than in halls, focus group facilities or on a PC. Mobile surveys can be integrated with a marketing campaign, and the results of customer satisfaction research can be used to guide the next campaign. For example, a restaurant that is experiencing increased competition in its area is able to use the specific database—a collection of small mobile surveys of those customers that had used coupons from the LBA in the geographic area—to determine dining preferences, times and occasions. Marketers can also use customers' past consumption patterns to forecast future patterns and send special dining offers, such as Mother's Day specials and Thai food fare deals, to the target population at the right place and right time, in order to build interest, response and interaction with the restaurant.

FORM DEVELOPMENT

Have you thought about your web forms? How much information are you asking for before you have earned your customers' trust?

Marketers must know when they are dealing with a high involvement sale as most people do not visit a website for buying; they come to a website for information. Also, potential customers are often hesitant about giving up too much information on registration forms before marketers have earned their trust.

Behavioral Targeting

Behavioral targeting, as a necessary element of advertisement, has grown on Facebook. The nature of this website involves sending and receiving valuable information on age, lifestyle, gender, interests, and personal information—information that is recorded on the registration forms. The reason is that there is a halo effect on these kinds of websites which has been able to overcome distrust and avoidance to offering personal information and interests. Behavioral targeting uses this unique opportunity to collect and aggregate Internet usage methods and deliver more purposeful advertisements. Hence, in this method, advertising is based more on user interests than on site content. Many companies have emerged that provide customer following and tracing services to marketers to predict future customer behavior (for more information, see *Tacoda* BT in platform-a.com).

BT and Lead Generation

BT is an appropriate lead generation strategy. One of the problems marketers face is getting the right information on the lead form. Behavioral targeting enables lead generation to retarget because there are many users who initially show interest in the website but then give up after a short time.

What motivates users to click and what discourages them from following is the question that can be answered by lead generation. The first thing to be specified is what percentage of the users present on the host website gave behavioral responses to the solutions offered by the website or advertiser, and developed the motivation necessary for its following. If the percentage of individuals who gave a positive behavioral response to the solution is high, it can be concluded that the stimulant used in the offer to attract the user fits with the stimulants entered by the user into the web. What happens when this motivation wanes? Lead generation companies must know that users mostly visit these websites with the initial motivation of leisure and entertainment (Ko, et al., 2005), and in fact are surfers. That is, as stated in Chapter 7, they are sensitive to environmental variables and thus have a higher conversion rate. Presence in a new environment makes them notice the features of a new webpage, and if they see a new strong stimulant, they will be attracted by it, thereby avoiding continuing filling out the registration forms (because they usually open several webpages and visit several screen servers at the same time). Timely identification of these changes in users' trends results in offering new solutions with new motives to return the users to their main path, i.e. completing the lead form.

Along the same line, a study by Ansari and Mela (2003) discussed e-mail customization based on Click-Stream Information (CSI) that the user leaves behind when, for instance, using a firm's webpage. Response rates could be increased by more than 60 percent by customizing e-mail using this information.

Behavioral Marketing

Behavioral marketing was created with the emergence of the Internet and the unique technologies of this medium in the business environment. The aim of developing behavioral targeting is to enable marketers to build stronger and better relationships with commercial and interactional capacities in online media.

Marketing myopia is different from individuals' shortsightedness and marketing. In the new marketing world, the purpose is to empower customers while satisfying them. Marketing is a tool in the users' community for organizing them by creating appropriate methods and empowering them for a better life experience. Production creates value, but consumption creates motivation for value-making. Thus, marketing is the facilitator of the value-making process, not the provider of the end products which are at one end of the producer value chain and at another end of the consumer value chain. The meaning of a value-making process facilitator is different from that of a sales facilitator. From the new viewpoint, the consumer is an implicit designer of the product whose implicit design changes into a clear one though marketing research. Consumers are not pure users of the produced value; rather, they are member of the consumption society that help producers to invest in value-maker ideas.

Easy access to information of different goods and provisions of various products results in a lack of commitment to a product. In this situation, the consumer is no longer motivated to buy, but buys for solving a problem. In such a circumstance, consumption is a tool for self-presenting, and people consume to seem more presentable and credible in social environments. Thus, marketers must be aware of the new motives of consumers and send the right promotional messages. The hyper-competitive climate dominating the market prevents the consumer from having loyalty to a brand. The messages sent by competitors developed on the basis of new technologies make customers believe that competitors' products are more compatible with their wants. Therefore, they change from loyal consumers to selective ones. Formation of selectivity in consumers, particularly in relation to Internet-based products, requires producers to create a new structure in their organizations, so the consumption chain undergoes a basic change.

ONLINE CONSUMPTION CHAIN AND LEAD GENERATION ROLE

As Figure 2 shows, with the emergence of lead generation, the consumption chain changes from a one-way chain to a two-way chain. First, producers display new offers via advertising messages. Customers, after viewing the advertisements and obtaining primary information about the goods or advantages, start searching. At this time, advertisers watch for keywords entered by the consumers, and if there is a relationship between the keywords and the advertisements displayed, they send an email to the consumers containing complementary information. This is also done if tracing shows that the audience has not seen the advertisement but a search indicates that their wants are compatible with the advertised goods. It is important to emphasize this process because searching and giving positive response to emails are among the methods which help advertisers determine if their advertisement has been able to create a follow-up motive in the users.

In addition, by way of other promotional tools, a company tries to directs consumer attention to itself. All these actions and reactions formulated by marketing (as a facilitator in the consumption chain) between producers and consumers are recorded by lead generation companies cooperating with producers. Marketers reexamine and analyze these records, and produce a customized offer in accordance with the implicit wants identified from consumer behavior. Afterwards, obtaining information related to a user's click-stream on other websites, they publish a personalized advertisement for the target user which is developed specifically on the basis of the appeals and cues motivating the consumer. In this situation, when an advertisement is completely personalized, the consumer is predicted to show a differentiated reaction and follow the advertisement with a stronger motive. If the producer wishes to survive in the online consumption chain, he must change from a traditional producer to an agile one and become a producer who has high flexibility in response to environmental changes and diverse consumer wants. Besides, marketing plays a role more important than that of a facilitator. In this respect, marketing, instead of creating and managing demand, provides a customized demand

Figure 2. Online consumption chain and lead generation role

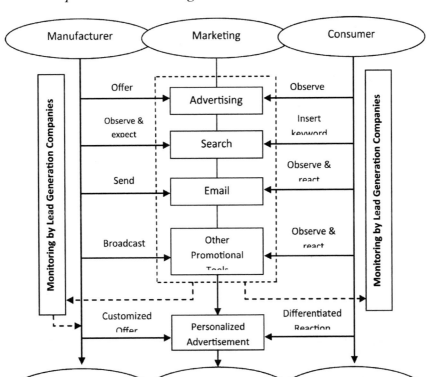

which leads to the creation of a new concept in marketing referred to as personalized supply. Behavioral marketing, using tracing and targeting technologies of lead generation companies, changes a customer uncommitted to a brand and living in multiplicity of various goods to a loyal one. However, consumers in the online consumption chain change from unaware consumers who have little information about new goods and services, and who take months for them to find new products. Online consumers are transactional consumers who unintentionally switch from one brand to another due to being continuously in contact with advertisements and strategic messages.

In general, there are two kinds of tracing for recording the leads of potential customers: direct tracing and indirect tracing. Direct tracing involves activities related to collecting leads from customers that are accomplished through their clicks and keywords used. In this kind of tracing, a website attempts to motivate its target customers to insert information by entering ports or boxes on the homepage or most-visited pages. Of course, as mentioned before, in order to encourage users to enter information, a website includes a set of offers to be provided to the user as soon as he fills in the information. Providing offers is a comprehensive unwritten law to ensure the motivation of customers to volunteer information.

Indirect tracing is intangible tracing of the user on the advertising website or other websites visited by target users. Direct and indirect tracing must be conducted simultaneously so that marketers can verify the information entered by the users through indirect tracing and measure the sustainability of the wants and present needs of users at the same time. Indirect tracing enables marketers to know if their target users search other websites to find similar products or services to meet their needs or to determine if their response to advertisements is more a transactional reaction to environmental attractiveness.

Avery Company is a good example in this regard. Avery.com has been successfully able to employ lead generation companies, using direct and indirect methods, to trace its customers.

In terms of direct tracing, by positioning an appropriate place on its website, Avery has provided its users the opportunity to record their wants on the website and to receive a customized service. After entering the information, the website sends a welcome message in order to ensure that the user is a high-involvement user. Then, creating a profile for each customer, to the website sends promotional messages to the users based on their profile facts. With the help of lead generation companies like Omniture.com, Avery indirectly traces its users and their reactions. In this way, Avery.com knows whether its offers were in line with the wants of its customers and whether its answers were able to meet the expectations of its customers.

We know from Williams and Mullin's (2008) study that "The offer is the supplier's answer to the customers' needs meeting the customers' expectation" (p. 26). The main purpose of all marketers is achieving customer welfare in line with societal welfare; using the least amount of resources possible, i.e. short-term welfare, with the lowest amount of damage to the surrounding environment, and creating necessary infrastructures for good competition until the long-term welfare of customers is achieved. To understand good competition, it is necessary to look into the area of competition and its definition. There are two kinds of competitors from this point of view. According to the first definition, competition is a match between the companies offering the same goods or services and the target market. Thus, they continually try to persuade customers to select their products or services.

In the second definition, competition is an effort made by a company to hear the voice of the customer ahead of similar companies and provide solutions based on customers' present needs and wants. According to the second definition, competition does not mean more sales; rather, it means better value-giving. Hence, the first attempt made by companies is defined as bad competition because at this level of competition, consumers are not a priority, and competitors try more to get sell their products and goods rather than providing customers with more welfare. Whereas, the second definition, good competition, which is the main purpose of authoring this book and particularly this chapter, involves the application of new technologies such as lead generation for hearing the voices of customers and offering high-quality products on the basis of customer's wants and needs.

CONCLUSION

The emergence of new technologies in interactive media has resulted in a new concept called lead generation in online marketing and advertising whose task is the collection of the information, trends and surfing methods of customers. Lead generation is a win-win approach both for sellers and purchasers, because purchasers are able to request information from several companies offering their desired products and services. On the other hand, sellers have the opportunity to fit their products and services with those who have permitted them to do so. Lead generation has two main operational areas: B2B lead generation and B2C lead generation. Lead generation in B2C is more related to that group of Internet sales areas which are in direct contact with the end-users, and must continuously identify customers' IPs and create profiles. In contrast, lead generation in the B2B area relates to businesses which are in contact with their agencies rather than the users of the products.

Companies acting in the B2B area are usually inquiry-based, and their buying method is called inquiry-based buying. In this method, companies try to select the right inquiry by collecting the inquiries of various providers and negotiating with them to finalize the purchase. Advertisers must be aware of the real needs of the customer in order to design a good content for the inquiry. Real needs are not the wants which the customer has recorded in his order; rather, the marketer must identifying the real problems. In a B2B market, problem-solving is the important issue, not need-satisfying. Marketers can use two methods, namely, buying lead and creating a marketing network for integrating databases.

The issue of lead generation and collecting data relevant to customers' wants in the area of B2C is somewhat different than those of the B2B area. In B2C, businesses continuously face customer needs, wants and demands which are limited, i.e. their buying volume is small and case-oriented, and also there is no clear understanding of the IP owners' offering or requested service. Although it seems that segmentation is easier on the Web with providing the validity of users' IP addresses, that does not always hold true, because it is possible that at different times, different people use one IP for different purposes. Therefore, the general assumption of following and recording the behavior of one IP cannot be accepted as offering a basic trend of the wants of a user. Rather, this trend must be realized by filtering and examining to verify the reality of the online user.

In this chapter, discussions other than those mentioned above, such as strategy administration, online community, and lead generation, were addressed. Also, behavioral targeting as a necessary component of advertising was addressed, as well as which factors encourage customers to click and which discourage them. At the end, the distinctive service provision model was presented which involves the supply and demand process of an advertisement fitting with customer wants. In this model, it was stated how lead generations can aid customer welfare.

REFERENCES

Ansari, A., & Mela, C. F. (2003). E-customization. *JMR, Journal of Marketing Research, 40*(2), 131–145. doi:10.1509/jmkr.40.2.131.19224

Cunningham, M. J. (2000). *B2B: How to build a profitable e-commerce strategy.* Cambridge, MA: Peruses Book Group.

Emarketer.com. (2003). *Has B2B e-commerce stagnated?* Retrieved April 2003 from http://www.Emarketer.Com.

Ferris, M. (2007). Insight on mobile advertising, promotion, and research. *Journal of Advertising Research.* Retrieved from http://www.docstoc.com/docs/31089160/Insights-on-Mobile-Advertising-Promotion-and-Research.

Gartner Inc. (2004). *Gartner G2 key business issues study: Web casting.* Retrieved from http://www.gartner.com.

Haig, M. (2003). *The B2B e-commerce handbook.* London, UK: Kogan Page Ltd.

IAB. (2008). *Online lead generation: B2C and B2B best practices for U.S.-based advertisers and publishers.* Retrieved from http://www.Iab.net / Lead_Generation.

IAB. (2009). *Internet advertising revenue report, 2008 full-year results, March 2009.* Retrieved from http://www.Iab.Net.

IDC. (2004). *Worldwide dynamic pricing B2B ecommerce sales volume 2003-2008 forecast.* Retrieved March 2005 from http://www.Idc.Com/Getdoc.Jsp?Containerid=30892.

Kaplan, R. S., & Norton, D. P. (2001). *Strategy-focused organization: How balanced scorecard companies thrive in the new business environment.* Boston, MA: Harvard Business School Publishing Corporation.

Ko, H., Cho, C. H., & Roberts, M. S. (2005). Internet uses and gratifications structural equation model of interactive advertising. *Journal of Advertising, 34*(2), 57–70.

Mahadevan, B. (2003). Making sense of the emerging market structure in B2B e-commerce. *California Management Review.* Retrieved from http://www.iimb.ernet.in/~mahadev/cmrb2b.pdf.

Marketwisesolution.com. (2010). *B2B lead generation.* Retrieved February 8 from http://www.Marketwisesolutions.Com /B2b-Lead-Generation.Htm.

Socialmediab2b.com. (2010). *Increase B2B lead generation using social media.* Retrieved February 13 from http://Socialmediab2b.Com /2009/07/B2b-Lead-Generation-Social-Media/.

Wienbr, S., & Kinzelberg, C. (2008). New targeting technology strategy for internet advertising boom. *Thomson Venture Capital Journal.* Retrieved from http://www.Scalevp.Com /Downloads/News/Vcj_Scalevp.Pdf.

Compilation of References

Abhishek, V. (2007). *Key words generation for search engine advertising using semantic similarity between terms*. India: Fair Isaac Company.

Adage.com. (2006). *Top 20 search engine marketing and optimization companies*. Retrieved from http://www.twistimage.com/.../advertising-age-gives-you-the-search-marketing-fact-pack-2006/.

Adage.com. (2006). *Top 50 interactive agencies, agencies report 2006*. Retrieved from http://www.adage.com/datacenter/article?article_id=108866.

Adam, S. (2002). A model of web use in direct and online marketing strategy. *EM Electronic Markets: International Journal of Electronic Markets*. Retrieved from http://www.electronicmarkets.org /modules/pub/view.php/electronicmarkets-418.

Advertising.com. (2007). *Banner audio/video guidelines*. Retrieved from http://www.platform-a.com/search/node/video%20advertising.

Age, A. (2007). *How to make effective online video ads*. Retrieved from http://www.adage.com.

Aggarwal, G., & Hartline, J. D. (2005). Knapsack auctions. In *Proceedings of the First Workshop on Sponsored Search Auctions*. ACM Press.

Aguirre, M. S. (2001). Family, economics and the information society - How are they affecting each other? *International Journal of Social Economics, 28*(3), 225–247. doi:10.1108/03068290110357645

Akamine. (2009). *Generalized second-price auctions (GSP)*. Retrieved September 18, 2009, from http://expertvoices.nsdl.org/cornell-info204/2009/02/25/generalized-second-price-auctions-gsp/.

Aker, D., Rajeev, B., & Myers, J. G. (1999). *Advertising management*. London, UK: Prentice-Hall International.

Alvin, J. S. (2001). The emerging position of the internet as an advertising medium. In *Netnomics* (pp. 129–148). Dordrecht, The Netherlands: Kluwer Academic Publishers.

Alwitt, L. F., & Prabhaker, R. P. (1992). Functional and belief dimensions attitudes to television. *Journal of Advertising Research, 32*(5), 30–42.

American Marketing Association. (2006). *Marketing terms dictionary*. Retrieved from http://www.marketingpower.com /index.

Amiri, A., & Menon, S. (2003). Efficient scheduling of internet banner advertisements. *ACM Transactions on Internet Technology, 3*(4), 334–346. doi:10.1145/945846.945848

Anderson, R. E., & Srinivasan, S. S. (2003). E-satisfaction and e-loyalty: A contingency framework. *Psychology and Marketing, 20*, 123–138. doi:10.1002/mar.10063

Anderson, R., & Bickson, T. (1995). *Universal access to email: Feasibility And societal implications*. Santa Monica, CA: Rand Corporation.

Andrade, E. B., Kaltcheva, V., & Weitz, B. (2002). Self-disclosure on the web: The impact of privacy policy, reward, and company reputation. *Advances in Consumer Research. Association for Consumer Research (U. S.), 29*, 350–353.

Ansari, A., & Mela, C. F. (2003). E-customization. *JMR, Journal of Marketing Research, 40*(2), 131–145. doi:10.1509/jmkr.40.2.131.19224

Asdemir, K. (2006). Bidding patterns in search engine auctions. In *Proceedings of the Second Workshop on Sponsored Search Auctions*. ACM Press.

Association of Advertising Agencies of America. (2011). *Website*. Retrieved from http://www.aaaa.com.

Atlassolutions.com. (2006). *Atlas ad serving platform*. Retrieved from http://www.atlassolutions.com / news_20061101.aspx.

Auction Papers. (2011). *Website*. Retrieved from http:// www.cramton.umd.edu /auction-papers.htm.

Bakos, Y. (1998). The merging role of electronic marketplace on the internet. *Communications of the ACM, 41*(8). Retrieved from http://portal.acm.org /ft_gateway.cfm?id =280330&type=pdf&CFID=18384839&CFTOKEN=72 033081doi:10.1145/280324.280330

Balachander, S., & Kannan, K. (2006). *Pricing of advertisements on the internet*. Purdue CIBER Working Papers. Retrieved from http://docs.lib.purdue.edu /ciberwp/47/.

Barker & Gronne. (1996). *Advertising on the world wide web*. Thesis. Copenhagen, Denmark: Copenhagen Business School.

Barnes, S. J., & Scornavacca, E. (2004). Mobile marketing: The role of permission and acceptance. *International Journal of Mobile Communications, 2*(2), 128–139. doi:10.1504/IJMC.2004.004663

Barnes, S. J., & Vidgen, R. T. (2003). Measuring web site quality improvements: A case study of the forum on strategic management knowledge exchange. *Industrial Management & Data Systems, 103*(5), 297–309. doi:10.1108/02635570310477352

Belk, R. W. (1975). Situational variables and consumer behavior. *The Journal of Consumer Research, 2*, 157–160. doi:10.1086/208627

Bennett, D. P. (1995). *Dictionary of marketing terms* (2nd ed.). Chicago, IL: American Marketing Association.

Bergen, M., Dutta, S., & Walker, O. C. (1992). Agency relationships in marketing: A review of the implications and applications of agency and related theories. *Journal of Marketing, 56*(3), 1–24. doi:10.2307/1252293

Berger, P. D., Lee, J., & Weinberg, B. D. (2006). Optimal cooperative advertising integration strategy for organizations adding a direct online channel. *The Journal of the Operational Research Society, 57*, 920–927. doi:10.1057/ palgrave.jors.2602069

Berkowitz, D. (2004). *Responsys responds to email challenges*. Retrieved April 9, 2011, from http://www. emarketer.com.

Berthon, P., Leyland, F. P., & Watson, R. T. (1996). The world wide web as an advertising medium: Toward an understanding of conversion efficiency. *Journal of Advertising Research, 36*(1), 43–54.

Besla.org. (2010). *Advertising and the convergence TV, film and technology on the internet*. Retrieved from http:// www.besla.org.

Bettman, J. R., Johnson, E. J., & Payne, J. W. (1991). Consumer decision making . In Robertson, T. S., & Kassarjian, H. H. (Eds.), *Handbook of Consumer Behavior* (pp. 50–84). Englewood Cliffs, NJ: Prentice Hall.

Bettman, J. R., & Kakkar, P. (1977). Effects of information presentation format on consumer information acquisition strategies. *The Journal of Consumer Research, 3*(4), 233–240. doi:10.1086/208672

Bilchev, G., & Marston, D. (2003). Personalized advertising, exploiting the distributed user profile. *BT Technology Journal, 21*(1), 84–90. doi:10.1023/A:1022460428681

Blumler, J. G. (1979). The role of theory in uses and gratification studies. *Communication Research, 6*(1), 9–36. doi:10.1177/009365027900600102

Briggs, R., & Hollis, N. (1997). Advertising on the web: Is there response before click through? *Journal of Advertising Research, 37*(2), 33–45.

Broines, M. (1999). Rich media may be too rich for your blood. *Marketing News, 33*(7), 4–5.

Brooks, N. (2004). *The atlas rank report, part 2: How search engine rank impacts conversion. Technical Report*. New York, NY: Atlas Institute.

Brown, S. P., & Stayman, D. M. (1992). Antecedents and consequences of attitude toward the ad: A meta-analysis. *The Journal of Consumer Research, 19*(1), 34–51. doi:10.1086/209284

Bruner, E. R. (2006). *Best practices for optimizing web advertising effectiveness*. Retrieved from http://www.doubleclick.com.

Bruner, G. C. II, & Kumar, A. (2000). Web commercials and advertising hierarchy-of-effects. *Journal of Advertising Research, 40*(1/2), 35–42.

Bucy, E. P., Lang, A., Potter, R. F., & Grabe, M. E. (1998). *Structural features of cyberspace: A content analysis of the world wide web*. Paper presented at the 1998 Conference of the Association for Education in Journalism and Mass Communication, Theory and Methodology Division. Baltimore, MD.

Burns, K. S., & Lutos, J. R. (2006). The function of format. *Journal of Advertising, 35*(1), 53–63. doi:10.2753/JOA0091-3367350104

Cacioppo, J. T., & Petty, R, E., Feinstein, J., & Jarvis, W. B. G. (1996). Individual differences in cognitive motivation: The life and times of people varying in need for cognition. *Psychological Bulletin, 119*, 197–253. doi:10.1037/0033-2909.119.2.197

Cacioppo, J. T., & Petty, R. E. (1984). The elaboration likelihood model of persuasion. *Advances in Consumer Research. Association for Consumer Research (U. S.), 11*(1), 668–672.

Cagley, J. W. (1986). A comparison of advertising agency factors: Advertiser and agency perceptions. *Journal of Advertising Research, 26*(3), 39–44.

Canzer, B. (2003). *E-business strategic thinking and practice*. Boston, MA: Houghton Mifflin Company.

Celsi, R. L., & Olson, J. C. (1988). The role of involvement in attention and comprehension processes. *The Journal of Consumer Research, 15*, 210–224. doi:10.1086/209158

Chattopadhyay, A. (1998). When does comparative advertising influence brand attitude? The role of delay & market position. *Psychology and Marketing, 15*(5), 461–475. doi:10.1002/(SICI)1520-6793(199808)15:5<461::AID-MAR4>3.0.CO;2-5

Chellappa, R. K. (2001). *Consumers' trust in electronic commerce transactions: The role of perceived privacy and perceived security*. Retrieved from http://asura.usc.edu /~ram/rcf-papers/sec-priv.pdf.

Chen, J., & Ringel, M. (2001). *Can advergaming be the future of interactive advertising?* Working Paper. Retrieved from http://www.locz.com.b r/loczgames/advergames.pdf.

Chen, Q., Rodgers, S., & He, Y. (2008). A critical review of the e-satisfaction literature. *The American Behavioral Scientist, 52*(1), 38–59. doi:10.1177/0002764208321340

Cheung, R. C. T. (2006). Case study of successful internet advertising strategy in Hong Kong: A portal for teenagers. *Marketing Intelligence & Planning, 24*(4), 393–405. doi:10.1108/02634500610672125

Cho, C., Lee, G. J., & Tharp, M. (2000). Advertising responses to different forced exposure levels on the www. In *Proceedings of the 2000 Annual Conference of the American Academy of Advertising*. American Academy of Advertising.

Cho, C. H., Lee, J. G., & Tharp, M. (2001). Different forced-exposure levels to banner advertisements. *Journal of Advertising Research, 41*(4), 45–56.

Chuang, T. T., & Chong, P. P. (2004). Searching advertising placement in cyberspace. *Industrial Management & Data Systems, 104*(2), 144–148. doi:10.1108/02635570410522116

Chung-Chuan, Y. (1997). An exploratory study of the effectiveness of interactive advertisements on the internet. *Journal of Marketing Communications, 3*, 85–91.

Clarke, E. (1971). Multiparty pricing of public goods. *Public Choice, 11*, 17–33. doi:10.1007/BF01726210

Cleary, J. M. (1999). P & G's consumer centric approach to the web. *Direct Marketing, 62*(5), 47–50.

Comscore.com. (2009). *Leading ad networks company*. Retrieved from http://www.marketingcharts.com /interactive/top-25-ad-networks-in-april-platform-a-yahoo-lead-pack-9182/ comscore-top-25-ad-networks-unique-visitors-april-2009jpg/.

Coolsen, F. G. (1947). Pioneers in the development of advertising. *Journal of Marketing, 12*(1), 80–86. doi:10.2307/1246303

Cornin, M. J. (1996). *Global advantage on the internet*. New York, NY: Van Nostrand.

Coupey, E. (1999). Advertising in an interactive environment: A research agenda . In Schumann, D. W., & Thorson, E. (Eds.), *Advertising and the World Wide Web* (pp. 197–215). Mahwah, NJ: Lawrence Erlbaum.

Coyle, J. R., & Thorson, E. (2001). The effects of progressive levels of interactivity and vividness in web marketing sites. *Journal of Advertising, 30*(3), 65–77.

Crano, W. D. (1995). Attitude strength and vested interest . In Petty, R. E., & Krosnick, J. A. (Eds.), *Attitude Strength: Antecedents and Consequences* (pp. 131–157). Mahwah, NJ: Erlbaum.

Crcomputerrepair.com. (2011). Click fraud - Threatening the internet economy. Retrieved 9 September from http://www.crcomputerrepair.com /articles/ppc-advertising/46010.php.

Cunningham, M. J. (2000). *B2B: How to build a profitable e-commerce strategy*. Cambridge, MA: Peruses Book Group.

Cushing, P., & Douglas-Tate, M. (1985). The effect of people product relationships on advertising processing . In Alwitt, L. F., & Mitchell, A. A. (Eds.), *Psychological Processes And Advertising Effects: Theory, Research, and Applications* (pp. 241–259). Hillsdale, NJ: Lawrence Erlbaum Associates.

Dahlen, M. (2002). Learning the web: Internet user experience and response to web marketing in Sweden. *Journal of Interactive Advertising, 3*(1).

Dahlén, M. (2002). Thinking & feeling on the world wide web: The impact of product type and time on world wide web advertising effectiveness. *Journal of Marketing Communications, 8*, 115–125. doi:10.1080/13527260210142347

Dahlén, M., & Bergendahl, J. (2001). Informing & transforming on the web: An empirical study of response to banner ads for functional & expressive products. *International Journal of Advertising, 20*(2), 189–205.

Dahlén, M., Ekborn, Y., & Mörner, N. (2000). To click or not to click: An empirical study of response to banner ads for high & low involvement products. *Consumption . Markets and Culture, 4*(1), 57–76. doi:10.1080/10253 866.2000.9670349

Dahlén, M., Malcolm, M., & Nordenstam, S. (2004). An empirical study of perceptions of implicit meanings in world wide web advertisements versus print advertisements. *Journal of Marketing Communications, 10*, 35–47. doi:10.1080/1352726042000177391

Darly, W. K., & Smith, R. F. (1995). Gender differences in information-processing strategies: An empirical test of selectivity model in advertising response. *Journal of Advertising, 24*(1), 41–56.

Darroch, J., Miles, M. P., Andrew, J., & Cook, E. F. (2004). The 2004 AMA definition of marketing and its relationship to a market orientation: An extension of Cooke, Rayburn & Abercrombie. *Journal of Marketing Theory & Practice, 12*(4), 29–38.

Devlin, P. L. (1995). Political commercials in American presidential elections . In Kaid, L. L., & Holz-Bacha, C. (Eds.), *Political Advertising in Western Democracies: Parties & Candidates on Television* (pp. 186–205). Thousand Oaks, CA: Sage Publications, Inc.

Dibb, S., & Simkin, L. (1991). Targeting, segments & positioning. *International Journal of Retail & Distribution Management, 19*(3), 4–10. doi:10.1108/09590559110143800

Double Click. (2002). *Internet audience dynamics: How can you effectively use online as a reach medium?* Retrieved from http://www.Doubleclick.Net.

Double Click. (2003). *Rich media: What? Where? Why: A Double Click white paper*. Retrieved June from http://www.Doubleclick.Net.

Doubleclick.com. (2004). *Online advertising*. Retrieved from http://www.doubleclick.com /us/products/online_advertising/.

Dragan, R. (1998). Microsoft site service 3 commerce edition. *PC Magazine*. Retrieved from http://www.zdnet.com /filters/printerfriendly/ 0,6061,374713-3,00.html.

Drew, S. (2002). E-business research practice: Towards an agenda. *Electronic Journal of Business Research Methods*. Retrieved from http://www.ejbrm.com /,Accessed1.

Dréze, Z. (1997). Testing web site design and promotional content. *Journal of Advertising Research*, •••, 77–91.

Ducoffe, R. H. (1996). How value & advertising on the web. *Journal of Advertising Research, 36*(5), 21–35.

Duffy, D. (2004). Case study: Multi-channel marketing in the retail environment. *The Journal of Consumer Research, 21*(4), 356–363.

Duncan, T. (2002). *IMC: Using advertising and promotion to build brands.* New York, NY: McGraw-Hill.

Duncan, T., & Moriarty, S. E. (1998). A communication-based marketing model for managing relationships. *Journal of Marketing, 62*(2), 1–13. doi:10.2307/1252157

Durkin, M., & Lawlor, M. A. (2001). The implications of the internet on the advertising agency-client relationship. *The Service Industries Journal, 21*(2), 175–191. doi:10.1080/714005026

Dyer, G. (1982). *Advertising as communication.* London, UK: Routledge. doi:10.4324/9780203328132

Eagle, L., & Kitchen, P. J. (2000). IMC: Brand communications, and corporate cultures. *European Journal of Marketing, 34*(5), 667–686. doi:10.1108/03090560010321983

Eagly, A., Wood, W., & Chaiken, S. (1978). Causal inferences about communicators and their effect on opinion change. *Journal of Personality and Social Psychology, 36*, 424–435. doi:10.1037/0022-3514.36.4.424

Edelman, B., Ostrovsky, M., & Schwarz, M. (2006). Internet advertising and the generalized second price auction: Selling billions of dollars worth of keywords. In *Proceedings of the Second Workshop on Sponsored Search Auctions.* ACM Press.

Edwards, S. M., Li, H., & Lee, J. H. (2002). Forced exposure & psychological reactance: Antecedents & consequences of the perceived intrusiveness of pop-up ads. *Journal of Advertising, 31*(3), 83–96.

Ellis, S., & Johnson, L. W. (1993). Agency theory as a framework for advertising agency compensation decisions. *Journal of Advertising Research, 33*(5), 76–80.

Emarketer.com. (2003). *Has B2B e-commerce stagnated?* Retrieved April 2003 from http://www.Emarketer.Com.

Emarketer.com. (2005). *Email advertising report.* Retrieved from http://www.emarketer.com.

Emarketer.com. (2005). *SEMPO.* Retrieved from http://www.emarketer.com.

Evanschitzky, H., Hyer, G. R., Hesse, J., & Ahlert, D. (2004). E-satisfaction: A re-examination. *Journal of Retailing, 80*, 239–247. doi:10.1016/j.jretai.2004.08.002

Faber, Lee, & Nan. (2004). Advertising and the consumer information environment online. *The American Behavioral Scientist, 48*(4), 447–466. doi:10.1177/0002764204270281

Fam, K. S., & Waller, D. S. (1999). Factors in winning accounts: The view of agency account directors in New Zealand. *Journal of Advertising Research, 39*(9), 12–32.

Fastoso, F. (2007). International advertising strategy: The standardization question in manager studies. *International Marketing Review, 24*(5), 591–606. doi:10.1108/02651330710828004

Ferris, M. (2007). Insight on mobile advertising, promotion, and research. *Journal of Advertising Research.* Retrieved from http://www.docstoc.com/docs/31089160/Insights-on-Mobile-Advertising-Promotion-and-Research.

Fletcher, J. (2000, June 12). The great e-mortgage bake-off. *The Wall Street Journal.*

Gagnard, A., & Swartz, J. E. (1988). Top American managers view agencies and research. *Journal of Advertising Research, 28*(6), 35–40.

Galletta, D. F., & Lederer, A. L. (1989). Some cautions on the measurement of user information satisfaction. *Decision Sciences, 20*, 419–438. doi:10.1111/j.1540-5915.1989.tb01558.x

Gardner, M. P., Mitchell, A. A., & Russo, J. E. (1985). Low involvement strategies for processing advertisements. *Journal of Advertising, 14*(2), 4–12.

Gartner Inc. (2004). *Gartner G2 key business issues study: Web casting.* Retrieved from http://www.gartner.com.

Gibson, B. S. (1996). Visual quality and attentional capture: A challenge to the special role of abrupt onsets. *Journal of Experimental Psychology. Human Perception and Performance, 22*, 1496–1504. doi:10.1037/0096-1523.22.6.1496

Gibson, L. D. (1983). Not recall. *Journal of Advertising Research, 23*(1), 39–46.

Globithink. (2008). *Annual U.S. advertising expenditure report*. Retrieved from http://www.galbithink.org /adspending.htm.

Godin, S. (1999). *Permission marketing*. New York, NY: Simon & Schuster.

Goodman, J. (2005). Pay-per-percentage of impressions: An advertising method that is highly robust to fraud. In *Proceedings of the Workshop on Sponsored Search Auctions*. Vancouver, Canada: ACM Press.

Gorn, G. J. (1982). The effects of music in advertising on choice behavior: A classical conditioning approach. *Journal of Marketing, 46*, 94–101. doi:10.2307/1251163

Green. A. (2007). *The promise of online video, dynamic logic market norms*. White Paper. Retrieved from http://www.dynamiclogic.com.

Gretzel, U., Yuan, Y., & Fesenmaier, D. R. (2000). Preparing for the new economy: Advertising strategies and change in destination marketing. *Journal of Travel Research, 39*, 146–156. doi:10.1177/004728750003900204

Groves, T. (1973). Incentives in teams. *Econometrica: Journal of the Econometric Society, 41*, 617–631. doi:10.2307/1914085

Gummesson, E. (1994). Making relationship marketing operational. *International Journal of Service Industry Management, 5*(5), 5–21. doi:10.1108/09564239410074349

Gurau, C. (2008). Integrated online marketing communication: Implementation and management. *Journal of Communication Management, 12*(2), 169–184. doi:10.1108/13632540810881974

Hagel, J. (1999). Net gain: Expanding markets through virtual communities. *Journal of Interactive Marketing, 13*(1), 55–65. doi:10.1002/(SICI)1520-6653(199924)13:1<55::AID-DIR5>3.0.CO;2-C

Haig, M. (2003). *The B2B e-commerce handbook*. London, UK: Kogan Page Ltd.

Hairong, L., & Leckenby, D. L. (2004). *Internet advertising formats & effectiveness*. Retrieved from http://www.kaschassociates.com /49101web/LIB2004AdvertingFormatsEffectivness.pdf.

Haley, E., & Wilkinson, J. (1994). And now a word from our sponsor: An exploratory concept test of PSAs vs. advocacy ads. In *Proceedings of the 1994 conference of the American Academy of Advertising*, (pp. 79-87). American Academy of Advertising.

Hanafizadeh, P., & Behboudi, M. (2008). *Internet advertising: New opportunity for promotion*. Tehran, Iran: Termeh Publication.

Hanafizadeh, P., Moosakhani, M., & Bakhshi, J. (2009). Selecting the best strategic practices for business process redesign. *Business Process Management Journal, 15*(4), 609–627. doi:10.1108/14637150910975561

Hanson, W. (2000). *Principles of internet marketing*. Cincinnati, OH: South-Western College Publishing.

Harmon, R. R., & Coney, K. A. (1982). The persuasive effects of source credibility in buy and lease situations. *JMR, Journal of Marketing Research, 19*(2), 255–260. doi:10.2307/3151625

Harris, J., & Taylor, K. A. (2003). The case of greater agency involvement in strategic partnerships. *Journal of Advertising Research, 43*(4), 346–352.

Harvey, M. G., Lusch, R. F., & Cavarkapa, B. (1996). A marketing mix for the 21st century. *Journal of Marketing Theory & Practice, 4*(4), 1–15.

Haugtvedt, C. P., & Wegener, D. T. (1994). Message order effects in persuasion: An attitude strength perspective. *The Journal of Consumer Research, 21*, 205–218. doi:10.1086/209393

Heeter, C. (1989). Implications of new interactive technologies for conceptualizing communication . In Salvaggio, J., & Bryant, J. (Eds.), *Media Use in the Information Age* (pp. 217–235). Hillsdale, NJ: Erlbaum.

Heinz, M. (2004). It's the message, stupid. *Imedia Connection*. Retrieved from http://Www.Imediaconnection. Com /Content/3084.Asp.

Helgesen, T. (1994). Advertising awards and advertising agency performance criteria. *Journal of Advertising Research, 34*(4), 43–53.

Hennig-Thurau, T., Gwinner, P. K., Walsh, G., & Gremler, D. D. (2004). Electronic word-of-mouth via consumer-opinion platforms: What motivates consumers to articulate themselves on the internet? *Journal of Interactive Marketing, 18*(1), 38–52. doi:10.1002/dir.10073

Hiebing, G. R., & Cooper, W. S. (2003). *The successful marketing plan: A disciplined and comprehensive approach.* New York, NY: McGraw-Hill Professional.

Hochstotter, N., & Koch, M. (2009). Standard parameters for searching behavior in search engines and their empirical evaluation. *Journal of Information Science, 35*(1), 45–65. doi:10.1177/0165551508091311

Hoffman, D. L., & Novak, T. P. (1995). *Marketing in hypermedia computer-mediated environments: Conceptual foundations.* Working Paper. Nashville, TN: Vanderbilt University.

Hoffman, D. L., & Novak, T. P. (1996). Marketing in hypermedia computer-mediated environments: Conceptual foundation. *Journal of Marketing, 60*(3), 50–68. doi:10.2307/1251841

Hoffmann, D., & Novak, T. (1995). *Project 2000: Research program on marketing in computer-mediated interactive advertising bureau: IAB internet advertising revenue reported, 2007.* Retrieved from http://www.iab.net.

Holbrook, M. B., & Lehmann, D. R. (1980). Form versus content in predicting starch scores. *Journal of Advertising Research, 20*, 53–62.

Hovland, C. I., & Weiss, W. (1951). The influence of source credibility on communication effectiveness. *Public Opinion Quarterly, 15*, 635–650. doi:10.1086/266350

Hultman, K. (1998). *Making change irresistible: Overcoming resistance to change in your organization.* Palo Alto, CA: Davies-Black.

Hurley, K. B., & Varian, H. (1998). *Internet publishing and beyond.* Cambridge, MA: MIT Press. Retrieved from http://www.elabresearch.ucr.edu /blog/.../vita.novak. March%2010%202009.pdf.

IAB. (2006). *Internet advertising revenue report, October 2006.* Retrieved from http://www.iab.net.

IAB. (2007). *IAB's 28 reasons to use interactive advertising.* Retrieved from http://www.iab.net.

IAB. (2007). *Internet advertising revenue report, October 2007.* Retrieved from http://www.iab.net.

IAB. (2007). *Internet advertising revenue report: 2007 full-year, May.* Retrieved from http://www.Iab.Net.

IAB. (2007). *Pop up guidelines & table.* Retrieved September 16, 2011, from http://www.iab.net.

IAB. (2008). *Internet advertising revenue report, October 2008.* Retrieved from http://www.iab.net.

IAB. (2008). *Online lead generation: B2C and B2B best practices for U.S.-based advertisers and publishers.* Retrieved from http://www.Iab.net /Lead_Generation.

IAB. (2009). *Internet advertising revenue report, 2008 full-year results March 2009.* Retrieved from http://www.iab.net.

IAB. (2009). *Internet advertising revenue report, 2008 full-year results, March 2009.* Retrieved from http://www.Iab.Net.

IAB.com. (2000). *Internet ad revenue report.* Retrieved April 23, 2001 from http://Www.Iab.Net /News/ Pr_2001_04_23.Asp.

IAB.com. (2007). *Pop up guidelines & table.* Retrieved September 16, 2007 from http://www.Iab.Net.

IAB.com. (2008). *Internet advertising revenue report, 2007 full-year, May.* Retrieved from http://www.Iad.Net.

IAB.com. (2009). *Internet advertising revenue report, 2008 full-year results, March 2009.* Retrieved from http://www.Iad.Net.

IAB.net. (2011). *23% year-over-year increase demonstrates growing importance of digital marketing & advertising.* Retrieved 26 May 2011 from http://www.iab.ne t/about_the_iab/recent_press_releases/ press_release_archive/press_release/pr-052611.

Ibid labs. (2010). *Ibid Labs announces IBID release.* Retrieved from http://blog.ibidlabs.com /?page_id=48.

ICT.com. (2007). *Communication ministry online report on internet bandwidth*. Retrieved from http://Www.ICT.Com.

IDC. (2004). *Worldwide dynamic pricing B2B ecommerce sales volume 2003-2008 forecast*. Retrieved March 2005 from http://www.Idc.Com /Getdoc.Jsp?Containerid=30892.

Idc.com. (2004). *Worldwide email usage 2004-2008 forecast: Spam today, other content tomorrow*. Retrieved August 26, 2011, from http://www.idc.com.

Imedia.com. (2002). *Logo placement affects skyscraper success*. Retrieved November 11, 2010 from http://www.imediaconnection.com /news/958.asp.

InfoCaptor. N. J. (2008). *InfoCaptor's pharmacy financial analytics dashboard*. Retrieved from http://www.dashboardinsight.com%2Fdashboards%2Fproduct-demos%2Finfocaptor-pharmacy-dashboard.aspx.

Insidefacebook.com. (2011). *Facebook now reaches 687 million users – Traffic trends and data at inside Facebook gold*. Retrieved June 6, 2011, from http://www.insidefacebook.com /2011/06/10/facebook-now-reaches-687-million-users-traffic-trends-and-data-at-inside-facebook-gold-june-2011-edition/.

Intermarket Group L. P. (2004). *The internet commerce briefing, online advertising & digital marketing report*. Retrieved from http://Www.Intermarketgroup.Com.

International Data Corp. (2002). *Email marketing*. Retrieved from http://www.Idcresearch.Com.

Internetworldstats.com. (2011). *Internet usage statistics, the internet big picture, world internet users and population stats*. Retrieved July 18, 2011, from http://www.internetworldstats.com /stats.htm.

Jan, F., & Zizi, P. (2009). *Online privacy as legal safeguard: The relationship among consumer, and privacy policies*. Retrieved from http://nms.sagepub.com.

Jancic, Z., & Zabkar, V. (1998). Establishing marketing relationships in the advertising agency business: A transitional economy case. *Journal of Advertising Research*, *38*(6), 27–36.

Janiszewski, C., & Meyvis, T. (2001). Effects of brand logo complexity, repetition, and spacing on processing fluency and judgment. *The Journal of Consumer Research*, *28*(1), 18–32. doi:10.1086/321945

Jones, J. P., & Slater, J. S. (2003). *What's in a name: Advertising and the concept of brands*. Armonk, NY: M. E. Sharpe.

Jupiter Institute. (2005). *Digital video report*. Retrieved from http://www.Jupiter.Com.

Jupiter Research Institute. (2006). *Behavioral targeting to transform online advertising*. Retrieved from http://www.marketingvox.com /jupiter_behavioral_targeting_to_transform_online_advertising-021979/.

Kamakura, W. A., & Wedel, M. (1995). Life-style segmentation with tailored interviewing. *JMR, Journal of Marketing Research*, *32*(3), 308–317. doi:10.2307/3151983

Kannan, P. K., & Kopalle, P. K. (2001). Dynamic pricing on the internet: Importance and implication for consumer behavior. *International Journal of Electronic Commerce*, *5*(3), 63–83.

Kaplan, R. S., & Norton, D. P. (2001). *Strategy-focused organization: How balanced scorecard companies thrive in the new business environment*. Boston, MA: Harvard Business School Publishing Corporation.

Katona, Z., Zubcsek, P. P., & Miklos, S. (2010). *Network effects and personal influences: The diffusion of an online social network*. Unpublished Paper. Retrieved May 15, 2011, from http://www.cs.bme.hu/~zskatona/pdf/diff.pdf.

Katz, J., & Aspden, P. (1997). Motivations & barriers to internet usage: Results of a national public opinion survey. *Internet Research: Electronic Networking Applications & Policy*, *7*(3), 170–188. doi:10.1108/10662249710171814

Kavassalis, P., Spyropoulou, N., Drossos, D., Mitrokostas, E., Gikas, G., & Hatzistamatiou, A. (2003). Mobile permission marketing: Framing the market inquiry. *International Journal of Electronic Commerce*, *8*(1), 55–79.

Kaynak, E., & Kara, A. (1996). Consumer life-style and ethnocentrism: A comparative study in Kyrgyzstan and Azarbaijan. In U. Schoeneberg (Ed.), *49th Esomar Congress Proceedings*, (pp. 577-596). Amsterdam, The Netherlands: ESOMAR.

Keller, K. L. (1993). Conceptualizing, measuring, and managing customer-based brand equity. *Journal of Marketing, 57*, 1–22. doi:10.2307/1252054

Keller, K. L. (2001). Mastering the marketing communications mix: Micro and macro perspectives on integrated marketing communication programme. *Journal of Marketing Management, 17*, 819–847. doi:10.1362/026725701323366836

Kelman, H. C. (1958). Compliance, identification, and internalization: Three processes of attitude change. *The Journal of Conflict Resolution, 2*, 51–60. doi:10.1177/002200275800200106

Kessler, S. (2011). *The history of advertising on facebook.* Retrieved June, 29, 2011, from http://mashable.com /2011/06/28/facebook-advertising-infographic/.

Kevin, J. D. (2005, May 3). Internet ads click with firms: Some shift budgets. *Wall Street Journal*, p. B8. Retrieved from http://proquest.umi.com /pqdweb?did= 831167291&sid=9&Fmt=3&clientId=9269&RQT=309 &VName=PQD.

Kim, K. H., Park, J. Y., Ki, D. Y., & Moon, H. I. (2001). Internet user lifestyle: Its impact on effectiveness and attitude toward Internet advertising in Korea. In C. Ray (Ed.), *Proceedings of the 2001 Annual Conference of the American Academy of Advertising*, (pp. 19-23). Salt Lake City, UT: American Academy of Advertising.

King, L. T. Y. (2002). Internet advertising and selling strategies. *Malaysian Journal of Technology, 36*(D), 71-82.

Kitchen, P. J., Brignell, J., Li, T., & Jones, G. S. (2004). The emergence of IMC: A theoretical perspective. *Journal of Advertising Research, 44*(1), 19–30. doi:10.1017/S0021849904040048

Kitchen, P. J., & Pelsmacker, P. (2004). *Integrated marketing communication: A primer*. London, UK: Taylor & Francis.

Klein, T. A., & Nason, R. W. (2001). Marketing and development: Macro marketing perspectives . In Bloom, P. N., & Gundlach, G. T. (Eds.), *Handbook of Marketing and Society*. Thousand Oaks, CA: Sage.

Ko, H., Chang, H. C., & Roberts, M. S. (2005). Internet uses & gratifications structural equation model of interactive advertising. *Journal of Advertising, 34*(2), 57–70.

Ko, H., Cho, C. H., & Roberts, M. S. (2005). Internet uses and gratifications structural equation model of interactive advertising. *Journal of Advertising, 34*(2), 57–70.

Korgaonkar, P. K., & Wolin, D. L. (1999). A multivariate analysis of web usage. *Journal of Advertising Research, 39*(2), 53–68.

Korgaonkar, P. K., & Wolin, D. L. (2001). Web usage, advertising, and shopping: Relationship patterns. *Internet Research: Electronic Networking Applications and Policy, 12*(2), 191–204.

Korgaonkar, P. K., & Wolin, D. L. (2002). Web usage, advertising, and shopping: Relationship patterns. *Internet Research: Electronic Networking Applications and Policy, 12*(2), 191–204. doi:10.1108/10662240210422549

Kotler, P. (2001). *Marketing management* (10th ed.). Upper Saddle River, NJ: Prentice-Hall, Inc.

Kotler, P. (2001). *Marketing management millenium edition* (10th ed.). Upper Saddle River, NJ: Prentice Hall, Inc.

Kotler, P., & Armstrong, G. (2001). *Principles of marketing* (9th ed.). Upper Saddle River, NJ: Prentice Hall.

Kotler, P., Wong, V., Saunders, J., & Armstrong, G. (2005). *Principles of marketing* (4th ed.). London, UK: Prentice Hall Europe.

Kowalczykowski, M. (2002). Disconnected continent. *Hayward International Review, 24*(2), 40–43.

Lan, Z., & Nagurney, A. (2007). A network equilibrium framework for internet advertising: Models, qualitative analysis, and algorithms. *European Journal of Operational Research*. Retrieved from http://www.elsevier.com /locate/ejor,2007.

Larose, R., Dana, M., & Estian, S. M. (2001). Understanding internet usage: A social cognitive approach to uses and gratification. *Social Science Computer Review, 19*(4), 395–413. doi:10.1177/089443930101900401

Laudon, K. C., & Traver, C. G. (2007). *E-commerce: Business, technology, society*. Upper Saddle River, NJ: Prentice Hall.

Laurent, G., & Kapferer, J. (1985). Measuring consumer involvement profiles. *JMR, Journal of Marketing Research, 22*(1), 41–53. doi:10.2307/3151549

Lavidge, R., & Steiner, G. (1961, October). A model for predictive measurements of advertising effectiveness. *Journal of Marketing,* •••, 59–62. doi:10.2307/1248516

Lee, J. W., & Lee, J. K. (2006). Online advertising by the comparison challenge approach. *Electronic Commerce Research and Applications, 5,* 282–294. doi:10.1016/j.elerap.2006.05.002

Lee, Y. H. (2000). Manipulating ad message involvement through information expectancy: Effects on attitude evaluation and confidence. *Journal of Advertising, 29*(2), 29–43.

Levinson, J. C., & Rubin, C. (1995). *Guerilla marketing online.* New York, NY: Houghton Mifflin.

Li, H. (1999). *Conceptualization of internet advertising: Practical and theoretical issues.* Working Paper. East Lansing, MI: Michigan State University.

Li, H., & Leckenby, D. J. (2004). *Internet advertising formats and effectiveness.* Retrieved from http://www.Ciadvertising.Org /Studies/Reports/Measurement/Ad_Format_Print.Pdf.

Libai, B., Biyalogorsky, E., & Gerstner, E. (2003). Setting referral fees in affiliate marketing. *Journal of Service Research, 5*(4), 303–315. doi:10.1177/1094670503005004003

Li, H., & Bukovac, J. L. (1999). Cognitive impact of banner ad characteristics: An experimental study. *Journalism & Mass Communication Quarterly, 76*(2), 341–353. doi:10.1177/107769909907600211

Limaconsulting.com. (2007). *The 9 essentials to effective online marketing best practice guide.* Retrieved from http://www.LimaConsulting.com.

Lin, C. A. (1999). Online-service adaption likelihood. *Journal of Advertising Research, 39*(2), 79–89.

Loewenstein, G. (1994). The psychology of curiosity: A review and reinterpretation. *Psychological Bulletin, 116*(1), 75–98. doi:10.1037/0033-2909.116.1.75

Lutz, R. J. (1985). Affective and cognitive antecedents of attitude toward the ad: A conceptual framework. In Alwitt, L., & Mitchell, A. (Eds.), *Psychological Processes and Advertising Effects Theory, Research and Applications.* Hillsdale, NJ: Erlbaum.

Lutz, R. J., & Kakkar, P. K. (1933). In Murchison, C. C. (Ed.), *The psychological situation as a determinant* (2nd ed., pp. 94–127). Handbook of Child Psychology Worcester, MA: Clark University Press.

Maddox, K. (1998). E-commerce becoming reality. *Advertising Age.* Retrieved October 26, 2010, from http://www.adage.com.

Maddox, K. (2001). Outlook brightens for web advertising. *B to B, 86*(15), 10.

Magretta, J. (2002). Why business models matter. *Harvard Business Review, 80*(5), 86–92.

Mahadevan, B. (2003). Making sense of the emerging market structure in B2B e-commerce. *California Management Review.* Retrieved from http://www.iimb.ernet.in /~mahadev/cmrb2b.pdf.

Management-report.com. (2007). *Search engine advertising is essential for modern marketing.* Retrieved May 2007, from http://www.Management-reports.com.

Margrethe, D. T. (1996). *Advertising on the internet.* Masters Dissertation. Westminster, UK: University of Westminster.

Marketwisesolution.com. (2010). *B2B lead generation.* Retrieved February 8 from http://www.Marketwisesolutions.Com /B2b-Lead-Generation.Htm.

McDaniel, C., Lamb, C. W., & Hair, J. F. (2006). *Introduction to marketing* (8th ed.). Cincinnati, OH: South Western Publishers.

McInnis, D. J. (2005). Marketing renaissance: Opportunities and imperatives for improving marketing thought, practice, and infrastructure. *Journal of Marketing, 69,* 14–16.

McMillan, & Hwang, S. J. (2002). Measure of perceived interactivity: An exploration of the role direction of communication, user control, and time in shopping perceptions of interactivity. *Journal of Advertising, 31*(3), 29–42.

McQuarrie, E. F., & Mick, D. G. (1999). Visual rhetoric in advertising: Text-interpretive, experimental, and reader-response analyses. *The Journal of Consumer Research, 26,* 37–54. doi:10.1086/209549

Meeker, N. (1997). *The internet advertising report*. New York, NY: Morgan Stanly Corporation.

Mehta, A. (2000). Advertising attitudes and advertising effectiveness. *Journal of Advertising Research, 40*(3), 67–72.

Mehta, A., & Sivadas, E. (1995). Direct marketing on the internet: An empirical assessment of consumer attitudes. *Journal of Direct Marketing, 9*(3), 21–32. doi:10.1002/dir.4000090305

Menon, S., & Soman, D. (2001). Managing the power of curiosity for effectiveness web advertising strategies. *Journal of Interactive Marketing, 31*(3), 1–14.

Methvin, D. W. (1999, August). How to succeed in e-business. *Windows Magazine*, 98-108.

Millar, M. G., & Tesser, A. (1987). Attitudes and behavior: The cognitive-affective mismatch hypothesis. *Advances in Consumer Research. Association for Consumer Research (U. S.), 17*, 86–90.

Mills, P. K., & Margulies, N. (1980). Toward a core typology of service organizations. *Academy of Management Review, 5*(2), 255–265.

Moorey-Denham, S., & Green, A. (2007). *The effectiveness of online video advertising*. Retrieved from http://www.Dynamiclogic.Com.

Morris, J. D., & Moo, W. C. (2003). Internet measures of advertising effects: A global issue. *Journal of Current Issues and Research in Advertising, 25*(1), 25–43.

Morris, M., & Ogan, C. (1996). The internet as mass medium. *The Journal of Communication, 46*(1), 39–50. doi:10.1111/j.1460-2466.1996.tb01460.x

Mullen, M. R., Beller, E., Remsa, J., & Cooper, D. (2001). The effects of international trade on economic growth and meeting basic human needs. *Journal of Global Marketing, 15*(1), 31–55. doi:10.1300/J042v15n01_03

Murphy, I. P. (1996). On-line ads effective? Who knows for sure? *Marketing News, 30*(20), 38.

Na, W., Marshall, R., & Son, Y. (2003). How businesses buy advertising agency services: A way to segment advertising agencies' markets. *Journal of Advertising Research, 43*(1), 86–95.

Newman, J. E., Donald, E., & David, S. E. (2004). Banner advertisement & website congruity effects. *Industrial Management & Data Systems, 104*(3), 273–281. doi:10.1108/02635570410525816

Ngai, E. W. T. (2003). Selection of the best web site for online advertising using the AHP. *Information & Management, 40*, 233–242. doi:10.1016/S0378-7206(02)00004-6

Nilsson, C. P. (2006). *Attention to advertising*. PhD Dissertation. Umeå, Sweden: Umeå University.

Norris, M., & West. (2001). *E-business essentials* (2nd ed). Chichester, UK: John Wiley and Sons, Ltd.

Novak, G. J., Cameron, G. T., & Delorme, D. (1996). Beyond the world of packaged goods: Assessing the relevance of integrated marketing communications for retail and consumer service marketing. *Journal of Marketing Communications, 2*(1), 173–190.

Novak, T. P., & Hoffman, D. L. (2000). Advertising and pricing models for the web . In Hurley, B. K., & Varian, H. (Eds.), *Internet Publishing and Beyond: The Economics of Digital Information and Intellectual Property*. Cambridge, MA: MIT Press.

Nowland. (1962). *The effects of media context on advertising: A study conducted for life*. New York, NY: Nowland and Company.

Okazaki, S., & Rivas, A. J. (2002). A content analysis of multinationals' web communication strategies, cross-cultural research framework and pretesting. *Internet Research: Electronic Networking Applications and policy, 12*(5), 380-390.

Oliver, R. L. (1997). *Satisfaction: A behavioral perspective on the consumer*. New York, NY: McGraw-Hill.

Osterwalder, A., & Pigneur, Y. (2002). *An e-business model ontology for modeling e-business*. Paper presented at Ecole des HEC. Bled, Slovenia.

Palmer, J. W. (2002). Web site usability, design, and performance metrics. *Information Systems Research, 13*(2), 151–167. doi:10.1287/isre.13.2.151.88

Papacharissi, Z., & Rubin, M. A. (2000). Predictors of internet use. *Journal of Broadcasting & Electronic Media, 44*(2), 175–196. doi:10.1207/s15506878jobem4402_2

Papatla, P. (2001). Identifying locations for targeted advertising on the internet. *International Journal of Electronic Commerce, 5*(3), 23–44.

Papatla, P., & Bhatnagar, A. (2002). Choosing the right mix of on-line affiliates: How do you select the best? *Journal of Advertising, 31*(3), 69–81.

Parasuraman, A., Zeithaml, V. A., & Berry, L. L. (1988). SERVQUAL: A multiple-item scale for measuring customer perceptions of service quality. *Journal of Retailing, 64*, 12–40.

Pavlou, P. A., & Stewart, W. D. (2000). Measuring the effects and effectiveness of interactive advertising: A research agenda. *Journal of Interactive Advertising, 11*. Retrieved from http://Jiad.Org/Vol1/No1/Pavlou.

Pelsmacker, P., Geuens, M., & Anckaert, P. (2002). Media context and advertising effectiveness: The role of context appreciation and context/ad similarity. *Journal of Advertising, 31*(2), 49–61.

Percy, L. (1997). *Strategies for implementing integrated marketing communication*. Chicago, IL: NTC Business Books.

Perry, M. (2002). Fortune 500 manufacturer web sites: Innovative marketing strategies or cyber brochures. *Industrial Marketing Strategies, 31*, 133–144. doi:10.1016/S0019-8501(01)00187-0

Petty, R. E., Cacioppo, J. T., & Goldman, R. (1981). Personal involvement as a determinant of argument-based persuasion. *Journal of Personality and Social Psychology, 41*, 847–855. doi:10.1037/0022-3514.41.5.847

Petty, R. E., Cacioppo, J. T., & Schumann, D. (1983). Central & peripheral routes to advertising effectiveness: The moderating of involvement. *The Journal of Consumer Research, 10*(2), 135–146. doi:10.1086/208954

Petty, R. E., Gleicher, F., & Jarvis, W. B. G. (1993). Persuasion theory and AIDS prevention . In Pryor, J. B., & Reeder, G. D. (Eds.), *The Social Psychology of HIV Infection* (pp. 155–182). Hillsdale, NJ: Erlbaum.

Petty, R. E., & Wegener, D. T. (1998). Attitude change: Multiple roles for persuasion variables . In Gilbert, D. T. (Ed.), *The Handbook of Social Psychology*. Oxford, UK: Oxford University Press.

Politz, A. (1962). *A measure of advertising effectiveness: The influence of audience selectivity and editorial environment*. New York, NY: Alfred Politz Research, Inc.

Porter, M.E. (2001). Strategy and the internet. *Harvard Business Review, 79*(3), 62–78.

Prabhaker, R. P. (2000). Who owns the online consumer? *Journal of Consumer Marketing, 17*(2), 158–171. doi:10.1108/07363760010317213

Prendergast, G., Shi, Y., & West, D. (2001). Organizational buying and advertising agency-client relationships in China. *Journal of Advertising, 30*(2), 61–71.

Previte, J. (1998). *Internet advertising: An assessment of consumer attitudes to advertising on the internet*. Paper Presented at the 1998 Communication Research Forum. Canberra, Australia.

Priester, J. R., & Petty, R. E. (1995). Source attributions and persuasion: Perceived honesty as a determinant of message scrutiny. *Personality and Social Psychology Bulletin, 21*, 637–654. doi:10.1177/0146167295216010

Przemysław, K., & Adamski, M. (2007). Adrosa—Adaptive personalization of web advertising. *Information Sciences, 177*, 2269–2295. doi:10.1016/j.ins.2007.01.002

Ranganathan, C., & Ganapathy, S. (2002). Key dimensions of business-to-consumer web sites. *Information & Management, 39*, 457–465. doi:10.1016/S0378-7206(01)00112-4

Ranjay, G., & Garino, J. (2000, June). Bricks to clicks. *Silicon India*, 75-78.

Rappa, M. (2005). Managing the digital enterprise. *North Carolina State University*. Retrieved from http://digital-enterprise.org /index.html.

Rashtchy, S., Kessler, A. M., Bieber, P. J., Schindler, N. H., & Tzeng, J. C. (2007). *The user revolution, the new advertising ecosystem and the rise of the internet as a mass medium, investment research, internet media*. Retrieved from http://www.scribd.com.

Rhodes, N., & Wood, W. (1992). Self-esteem and intelligence affect influenceability: The mediating role of message reception. *Psychological Bulletin, 111*, 156–171. doi:10.1037/0033-2909.111.1.156

Rice, B., & Bennett, R. (1998). The relationship between brand usage and advertising tracking measurements: International findings. *Journal of Advertising Research, 38*(3), 58–66.

Richards, J., & Curran, C. M. (2002). Oracles on advertising: Searching for a definition. *Journal of Advertising, 31*(2), 63–77.

Richins, M. L., & Root-Shaffer, T. (1988). The role of involvement and opinion leadership in consumer word-of-mouth: An implicit model made explicit. *Advances in Consumer Research. Association for Consumer Research (U. S.), 15*, 32–36.

Ries, A., & Ries, L. (2000). *The 11 immutable laws of internet branding.* New York, NY: Harper Business.

Ringold, D. J., Calfee, J. E., Cohen, J. B., & Pollay, R. W. (1989). The informational content of cigarette advertising: 1926–1986: Counting advertising assertions to assess regulatory policy: When it doesn't add up: Filters, flavors . . . flim-flam, too! *Journal of Public Policy & Marketing, 8*, 1–39.

Rodgers, S. (2003). The effects of sponsor relevance on consumer reactions to internet sponsorships. *Journal of Advertising, 32*(4), 68–76.

Rodgers, S., & Thorson, E. (2000). The interactive advertising model: How users perceive & process online ads. *Journal of Interactive Advertising, 1*(1), 26–50.

Rodrigue, S. C. (2006). *The impact of masking of persuasive message effectiveness.* PhD Dissertation. Baton Rouge, LA: LSU.

Rogers, E. M. (1995). *Diffusion of innovations* (4th ed.). New York, NY: Free Press.

Rossiter, J. R., & Bellman. (1999). A proposed model for explaining and measuring web ad effectiveness. *Journal of Current Issues and Research in Advertising, 21*(1), 13–31.

Rossiter, J. R., & Percy, L. (1997). *Advertising communications & promotion management* (2nd ed.). New York, NY: McGraw-Hill.

Ruggiero, T. E. (2000). Uses and gratification theory in the 21st century. *Mass Communication & Society, 3*(1), 3–37. doi:10.1207/S15327825MCS0301_02

Russell, R. J., Feuer, K. R., Meeker, M., & Mahaney, M. (2001). *Correction: Does internet advertising work? Yes, but.* New York, NY: Morgan Stanley Dean Witter.

Salmon, C. (1986). Perspectives on involvement in consumer & communication research . In Dervin, B., & Voigt, M. (Eds.), *Progress in Communication Sciences* (pp. 243–268). Norwood, NJ: Ablex.

Sands, M. (2003). Integrating the web and e-mail into a push-pull strategy. *Qualitative Market Research: An International Journal, 6*(1), 27–37. doi:10.1108/13522750310457357

Schiffman, L. G., Sherman, E., & Long, M. M. (2003). Toward a better understanding of the interplay of personal values and the Internet. *Psychology and Marketing, 20*(2), 169–186. doi:10.1002/mar.10066

Schlosser, A. E., Shavitt, S., & Kanfer, A. (1999). Survey of internet users' attitudes toward internet advertising. *Journal of Interactive Marketing, 13*(3), 34–71. doi:10.1002/(SICI)1520-6653(199922)13:3<34::AID-DIR3>3.0.CO;2-R

Schramm, W. (1955). How communication works . In Schramm, W. (Ed.), *The Process & Effects of Mass Communications* (pp. 3–26). Urbana, IL: University of Illinois Press.

Schwartz, E. I. (1998). *Webonomics: Nine essential principles for growing your business on the world wide web.* New York, NY: Broadway.

Schwarz, N. (1990). Feelings as information: Informational and motivational functions of affective states . In Higgins, E. T., & Sorrentino, R. M. (Eds.), *Handbook of Motivation and Cognition: Foundations of Social Behavior* (pp. 527–561). New York, NY: Guilford.

Scribd. (2000). *Project report on advertising agency.* White Paper. Retrieved from http://www.scribd.com / doc/3671764/Advertising-agencies-project.

Sempo.org. (2005). *Revenue of search engine marketing.* Retrieved from www.sempo.org /.../research/sempo_research/...2005/SEMPO-12-05-05new.

Severin, W. J., & Tankard, J. W. (1997). *Communication theory: Origins, methods, and use in mass media* (4th ed.). White Plains, NY: Longman.

Shavitt, S., Swan, S., Lowery, T. M., & Wänke, M. (1994). The interaction of endorser attractiveness and involvement in persuasion depends on the goal that guides message processing. *Journal of Consumer Psychology, 3*, 137–162. doi:10.1016/S1057-7408(08)80002-2

Shaw, M., Subramaniam, C., & Gardner, D. (1999). Product marketing on the internet. In *Handbook of Electronic Commerce*. Berlin, Germany: Springer-Verlag.

Sheehan, K. B. (1999). An investigation of gender differences in online privacy concerns & results behaviors. *Journal of Interactive Marketing, 13*(4), 24–38. doi:10.1002/(SICI)1520-6653(199923)13:4<24::AID-DIR3>3.0.CO;2-O

Shimp, T. A. (2000). *Advertising promotion: Supplemental aspects of integrated marketing communications* (5th ed.). Fort Worth, TX: The Dryden Press.

Shipley, D., & Jobber, D. (2001). Integrative pricing via the pricing wheel. *Industrial Marketing Management, 30*, 301–314. doi:10.1016/S0019-8501(99)00098-X

Shop.org & Forrester Research. (2004). *The state of retailing online 7.0*. Retrieved from http://www.shop.org /research/SRO7/SRO7main.asp.

Smith, P. R., Berry, C., & Pulford, A. (1997). *Strategic marketing communications: New ways to build and integrate communication*. London, UK: Kogan Page.

Socialmediab2b.com. (2010). *Increase B2B lead generation using social media*. Retrieved February 13 from http://Socialmediab2b.Com /2009/07/B2b-Lead-Generation-Social-Media/.

Squire, L. R. (1986). Mechanisms of memory. *Science, 232*, 1612–1619. doi:10.1126/science.3086978

Steiniger, S., Neun, M., & Edwardes, A. (2006). *Foundations of location based service*. Retrieved August 5, 2007, from http://www.geo.unizh.ch /publications/cartouche/lbs_lecturenotes_steinigeretal2006.pdf.

Sterne, J. (1997). *What makes people click: Advertising on the web*. Indianapolis, IN: Que Corporation.

Sterne, J. (1997). *What makes people click: Advertising on the web*. Indianapolis, IN: Que Corporation.

Sternthal, B., Dholaika, R., & Leavitt, C. (1978). The persuasive effect of source credibility: A test of cognitive response analysis. *The Journal of Consumer Research, 4*(4), 252–260. doi:10.1086/208704

Subramanian, C., Shaw, M. J., & Gardner, D. M. (1999). Product marketing on the internet. In M. Shaw, R. Blanning, T. Strader, & A. Whinstone (Eds.), *Handbook on Electronic Commerce*. New York, NY: Spring-Verlag.

Sundar, S. S., & Kalyanaraman, S. (2004). Arousal, memory, & impression-formation effects of animation speed in web advertising. *Journal of Advertising, 33*(1), 7–17.

Szymanski, D. M., & Hise, R. T. (2000). E-satisfaction: An initial examination. *Journal of Retailing, 76*, 309–322. doi:10.1016/S0022-4359(00)00035-X

Taylor, C. P., & Neuborne, E. (2002). Getting personal. *Adweek, 39*(44), IQ1.

Teltzrow, M., & Kobsa, A. (2004). *Impacts of user privacy preferences on personalized systems: A comparative study*. Retrieved from http://www.ics.uci.edu /~kobsa/papers/2003-CHI-kobsa.pdf.

Thomsen, M. D. (1996). *Advertising on the internet*. Masters Dissertation. Wesminster, UK: The University Of Westminster.

Thorson, E., & Leavitt, C. (1986). *Probabilistic functionalism & the search for taxonomy of commercials*. Unpublished Paper.

Thorson, E. (1996). Advertising . In Salwen, M. B., & Stacks, D. W. (Eds.), *An Integrated Approach to Communication Theory and Research* (pp. 211–230). Mahwah, NJ: Lawrence Erlbaum.

Thorson, E., Chi, A., & Leavitt, C. (1992). Attention, memory, attitude and conation: A test of the advertising hierarchy. *Advances in Consumer Research. Association for Consumer Research (U. S.), 19*(1), 366–379.

Timesonline. (2010). *The top ten viral ad campaigns*. Retrieved January 15, 2010, from http://www.Business.timesonline.uk.

Timmers, P. (1998). Business models for e-commerce. *Electronic Markets, 8*(2), 3–7. doi:10.1080/10196789800000016

Toncar, M., & Munch, J. (2001). Consumer responses to tropes in advertising. *Journal of Advertising, 30*(1), 55–65.

Triki, A., Redjeb, N., & Kamoun, I. (2007). Exploring the determinants of success/failure of the advertising agency-firm relationship. *Qualitative Market Research: An International Journal, 10*(1), 10–27. doi:10.1108/13522750710720378

Turban, E. (2006). *Electronic commerce: A managerial perspective.* Upper Saddle River, NJ: Prentice Hall.

Turban, E., King, D., Viehland, D., & Lee, J. (2006). *Electronic commerce: A managerial perspective.* Upper Saddle River, NJ: Prentice Hall.

Turban, E., King, D., Viehland, D., & Lee, J. K. (2006). *Electronic commerce: A managerial perspective.* Upper Saddle River, NJ: Prentice Hall.

United Nations Development Program. (2000). *Driving information and communications technology for development.* Retrieved from http://www.undp.org.

Vakratsas, D., & Ambler, T. (1999). How advertising works: What do we really know? *Journal of Marketing, 63*(1), 26–43. doi:10.2307/1251999

Van den Bulte, C., & Joshi, Y. V. (2007). New product diffusion with influentials and imitators. *Marketing Science, 26*, 400–421. doi:10.1287/mksc.1060.0224

Varadarajan, P. R., & Yadav. (2002). Marketing strategy and the internet: An organizing framework. *Academy of Marketing Science, 30*(4), 87–99. doi:10.1177/009207002236907

Vaughn, R. (1986). How advertising works: A planning model. *Journal of Advertising Research, 26*(1), 57–66.

Vickrey, W. (1961). Counter speculation, auctions and competitive sealed tenders. *The Journal of Finance, 16*, 8–37. doi:10.2307/2977633

Villanueva, J., & Hanssens, D. M. (2007). *Customer equity: Measurement, management and research opportunities: Foundations and trends in marketing.* Boston, MA: Now.

Waller, D. S. (2004). Developing an account-management lifecycle for advertising agency-client relationships. *Marketing Intelligence & Planning, 22*(1), 95–112. doi:10.1108/02634500410516940

Wang, Y., & Tang, T. (2004). A validation of the customer information satisfaction instrument for digital market context. *International Journal of Electronic Business, 2*, 567–582. doi:10.1504/IJEB.2004.006126

Wang, Y., Tang, T., & Tang, J. E. (2001). An instrument for measuring customer satisfaction toward web sites that market digital products and services. *Journal of Electronic Commerce Research, 2*, 89–102.

Warrington, P., & Shim, S. (2000). An empirical investigation of the relationship between product involvement & brand commitment. *Journal of Psychology & Marketing, 17*(9), 761–782. doi:10.1002/1520-6793(200009)17:9<761::AID-MAR2>3.0.CO;2-9

Wasserman, T. (2011). *Facebook ads perform half as well as regular banner ads.* Retrieved January 31, 2011, from http://mashable.com /2011/01/31/facebook-half-click-throughs/.

Web Analytic Association. (2006). *Key web analytics.* Retrieved from http://www.webanalyticsassociation.org.

Weisman, R. (2006, February 12). Virtual ads pose real threat to traditional media. *Boston Globe.*

Weiss, M. J. (2001). Online America. *American Demographics, 23*(3), 53–60.

Widing, R. E., & Talarzyk, W. (1993). Electronic information systems for consumers: An evaluation of computer interaction – Assisted formats in multiple decision environments. *JMR, Journal of Marketing Research, 30*(2), 125–141. doi:10.2307/3172823

Wienbr, S., & Kinzelberg, C. (2008). New targeting technology strategy for internet advertising boom. *Thomson Venture Capital Journal.* Retrieved from http://www.Scalevp.Com /Downloads/News/Vcj_Scalevp.Pdf.

Wills, J., Samli, A. C., & Jacobs, L. (1991). Developing global products & marketing strategies: A construct & a research agenda. *Journal of the Academy of Marketing Science, 19*(1), 1–10. doi:10.1007/BF02723418

Wood, M. C. (2004). Marketing and e-commerce as tools of development in the Asia-Pacific region: A dual path. *International Marketing Review, 21*(3), 301–316. doi:10.1108/02651330410539639

Xavier, D. (2003). Francois-Xavier Hussherr, internet advertising: Is anybody watching? *Journal of Interactive Marketing, 17*(4), 8–32. doi:10.1002/dir.10063

Xie, F. T., Naveen, D., Ritu, L., & Osmonbekov, T. (2004). Emotional appeal and incentive offering in banner advertisements. *Journal Of Interactive Advertising, 4*(2). Retrieved from http://Jiad.Org/Vol4/No2/Xie

Yang, K. C. C. (2004). A comparison of attitudes towards Internet advertising among lifestyle segments in Taiwan. *Journal of Marketing Communications, 10*, 195–212. doi:10.1080/1352726042000181657

Yarom, I., Goldman, C. V., & Rosenschein, J. S. (2003). The role of middle-agents in electronic commerce. *IEEE Intelligent Systems, 18*(6), 15–21. doi:10.1109/MIS.2003.1249165

Zaichkowsky, J. L. (1985). Measuring the involvement construct. *The Journal of Consumer Research, 12*(3), 341–352. doi:10.1086/208520

Zeff, R., & Aronson, B. (1999). *Advertising on the internet* (2nd ed.). New York, NY: John Wiley.

Zeithaml, V. A., Parasuraman, A., & Malhotra, A. (2000). *E-service quality: Definition, dimensions and conceptual model*. Working Paper. Cambridge, MA: Marketing Science Institute.

Zeithaml, V. A., Parasuraman, A., & Malhotra, A. (2002). Service quality delivery through web sites: A critical review of extant knowledge. *Journal of the Academy of Marketing Science, 30*, 362–375. doi:10.1177/009207002236911

Zenithoptimedia. (2009). *Internet advertising expenditure report*. Press Release. Retrieved from http://zenithoptimedia.com.

Zenithoptimedia.Com. (2009). *Advertising expenditure press release*. Retrieved April 14, 2009, from http://www.Zenithoptimedia.Com.

Zooknic Internet Intelligence. (2006). *History of gTLD domain name growth*. Retrieved December 4, 2006, from http://zooknic.com /Domains/counts.html.

Zwass, V. (2003). Electronic commerce and organization innovations: Aspects and opportunities. *International Journal of Electronic Commerce, 7*(3), 35–47.

About the Authors

Payam Hanafizadeh is an Assistant Professor of Industrial Management at Allameh Tabataba'i University (formerly called Tehran Business School) in Tehran, Iran, and a member of the Design Optimization under Uncertainty Group at the University of Waterloo, Canada. He was a visiting research fellow at the University of Canberra, Australia, in 2010, and a visiting scholar at the University of Waterloo, Canada, in 2004. He received his MSc and PhD in Industrial Engineering at Tehran Polytechnic University and pursues his research in information systems, particularly e-commerce, e-business models, and e-readiness assessment and decision making under uncertainty. Dr. Hanafizadeh is the co-author of *Electronic Commerce, Definitions and Barriers* (2ⁿᵈ edition) which is used a reference text book at Payame-Noor University (formerly named Open University) throughout the country. He has authored several other successful books such as *Holding Companies: Definitions, Concepts, and Structures*, *Multi-Dimensional Construct Research Method in Persian*, and he has written over 50 articles for leading journals such as: the *Information Society, Systemic Practice and Action Research, Management Decision, Journal of Global Information Management, Telecommunications Policy, Mathematical and Computer Modeling, Expert Systems with Applications, International Journal of Information Management, Energy Policy, Journal of Information Technology Research, Higher Education Policy, Business Process Management Journal,* to name only a few. Meanwhile, he has been serving on the Editorial Review Board for the *International Journal of Information Technologies and Systems Approach*, the *International Journal of Enterprise Information Systems, the Journal of Information Technology Research*, the *Journal of Electronic Commerce in Organizations*, and the *International Journal of Decision Support System Technology*. Dr. Hanafizadeh was named as the best researcher of Tehran Province in 2006. He was also invited to lecture at several top management schools in the country as well as joint international MBA programs with LinkÖpings University, Sweden, in Tehran, Iran. Dr. Hanafizadeh has also served as a consultant to several major public and private organizations including the Ministry of Information, Telecommunication and Technology, the Ministry of Interior, National Petrochemical Company, pharmaceutical companies, automotive companies, and many more.

Mehdi Behboudi is a Lecturer of Marketing at Department of Business Management, School of Management and Accountancy, Qazvin Branch, Islamic Azad University, Qazvin, Iran. Mehdi Behboudi is also a Lecturer and Head of Business Management Department at Ghazali's Higher Education Institute. He has a background in teaching marketing principles, marketing research, marketing seminar, international marketing, and international business for undergraduate and graduate students. He also is Manager of the Online Advertising and Internet Marketing Department at Management and Productivity Research Center, MPRC. He has authored several successful books such as *International Marketing* and *Successful Entrepreneurs* in Persian, and his articles have been appeared in international journals, including: *International Journal of Online Marketing, International Journal of Business and Management, International Business Research, International Journal of Marketing Studies, Interdisciplinary Journal of Research in Business, Journal of Basic and Applied Scientific Research, African Journal of Business Management, Indian Journal of Science and Technology,* and *Australian Journal of Business and Management Research.* In this regard, he is serving as member of editorial review board for *International Journal of Marketing Studies.* Meanwhile, Mehdi Behboudi was named as the best researcher of Qazvin Province in 2010. As an advertising expert, Mehdi Behboudi is Chief Marketing Executive, CME, at Hadef Subsidiary in Iran. He is known as an online advertising and Internet marketing Author, Speaker, and Consultant. He has delivered many speeches for different companies in marketing and advertising context. He has a knowledgeable experience in branding, online advertising strategies, inverse advertising, online reputation management, search engine advertising, and viral advertising strategies.

Index

CPSIA information can be obtained at www.ICGtesting.com
Printed in the USA
BVOW022342150812

298027BV00011B/17/P